TO All

W...

Patricia Lebeut

P.S. never forget you!

THE
BUFFALO
NICKEL
REDEMPTION

PATRICIA LEBERT

ISBN: 978-1-956793-12-3

Dedicated to Mary Ann, as if not for her I would never have started writing to begin with.

This book was her last request. Eight years later I've finally finished traveling down memory lane under the shade of the family tree, and all because my sister made me do it.

For Patsy, Bobby, Carole, Sharon, Rosie, Linda, Nancy, and Lulu, who grew up together in Michigan in the 1940s and '50s.

Also, for Michelle, Holly, Michael, and Ryan, who are the stars that light my path.

A special thank you to Cousin Monica for the many prayers I needed to accomplish this work.

Lord bless this endeavor that it be for your glory for only you know the soul of all works in progress.

Stella 1936

EVERYBODY HAS A STORY

When you grow up with ten people in a small house, you learn to walk in the middle of the road, and sleep in the same bed with three or four blanket hogs who all had beans and cornbread for supper. Inevitably you start wondering how you got to a city named Y and Dot living with looney tunes. You figure your folks must have started it so you go to the fountain of knowledge and ask them how they met. Being the character that he was, Leonard said Stella crossed a bridge on a buffalo looking for him. Somewhere in this flippant answer was a measure of truth. Everyone has their perspective. This is mine.

As luck would have it, I grew up the eldest of our gang. Now here I am 70 years later, stuck in front of a computer thinking what's wrong with this picture. It's October in Florida and the humidity is finally letting up. I wanted to be out gallivanting in retirement, instead I'm locked inside. Only sheer force of will keeps me here, wondering where to start a journey that feels like a million miles. The smell of a neighbor's cooking comes wafting through the open window and I remember chicken frying in a big, black, cast iron, pan. Suddenly I'm a little kid again looking up at the stove. Memories begin to tumble from my little girl mind... My name is Patsy. The building where we live has brown asbestos shingles, our entrance is in the back alley. We always hurry in so the rats running around the garbage thingy don't see us. There's a stairway on the side of the wall going up to our apartment. The door opens into the kitchen with the white iron sink where mommy bathes me on the sideboard. When more babies come to live with us, they get bathed in it too with Ivory soap, it's the one that floats.

Memories split across my mind's eye, a fragile glimpse into dark places of many yesteryears. Though I can't fully attest to their sequence, my earliest memories are between the age of three to five years old.

IT'S NIGHTTIME.

There's yelling. A scream. "Help!" Banging on the door. "Open up or we're coming in!" Blurry people moving around fast. Water trickles down a red window.

IT'S MORNING.

Auntie Bella and Auntie Marie are here, they keep whispering. I want to know where mommy is, but they won't tell. They talk different and I don't understand French. Daddy comes back but mommy is still gone so he cries. My aunties whisper some more. "I don't feel sorry for him a bit." "Me neither Sis, not one little bit."

THE PONY

It walked on the sidewalk and took a picture with me and Bobby. I didn't like being up there, but big girls don't cry. Bobby cried, cuz he's not big like me.

AUNTIE MARIE

My auntie took me downtown. Men in tall white hats were cooking in her boyfriend's restaurant. Pots and pans hung in the air by themselves It's magic! He said we could have anything we want so I got ice cream. I can't wait to tell mommy all about it.

BABY CAROLE.

They said we have a new baby sister but she's not coming home. So where is she then? Everybody keeps talking about her, but I don't see her. They said they don't know when she's coming home, so what's she waiting for? Me and Bobby go whenever mommy says. How come the new baby doesn't do that? She's finally here! Baby Carole's finally here but what are we supposed to do with her? We can't pick her up; they said she's too tiny. What's so fun about a baby sister? My doll is bigger than her. She doesn't do anything cept eat formla stuff in a bottle. It's spose to make her big but it's not working. She had a birthday and still looks like a baby to me. Mommy says she can play when she starts to crawl. Wonder when's that's gonna happen?

Fire! Fire! Someone is yelling and pounding on the door. "Everybody out now!" We hurry through black smoke and go across the alley to a neighbor. Everyone is dressed funny. Then a rubber man comes to the door in a funny red hat. "Everybody can go home, the fire is out. Your neighbor started it frying chicken." "My mommy fries' chicken, and she doesn't make a fire happen!" "Be quiet Patsy, yer alweez a talkin. U talk too much," ...my daddy says but I don't think so.

BABY SHARON.

"How come we got 'another' baby Daddy? We already have one." "Carl Ann's not th baby eny mo Patsy. Sharn's th baby now." My daddy talks funny, but I understand, even when he staggers around. "But why did we get another one Daddy?" "Cuz Carl Ann needed a playmate. U got Bobby fer yer buddy." "But if Carole isn't a baby anymore Daddy why is baby Sharon bigger than her?" "Cuz Carl Ann weren't but a teeny lil thang frum th get go Patsy. She weren't no biggern a sack a taters, she weight lessen three pounds an lived in th inkerator fer a reel long spell.""Baby Carole was in the fridge rater!" "It weren't no fridge rater Patsy, it wuz a teeny lil bed fer teeny babies. U wuz jess three yars ole when she's borned, u ain't gun member eny that.""Auntie says baby Carole is a miracle Daddy. What's that mean?"

THE NIGHTMARES.

Dark shadows in the doorway, a white light overhead, water trickles down a red window, whispers... "poor Stella could die." I wake up screaming. "Mommy! Mommy!" "I'm here Patsy, Mommy's right here, I'll never leave you alone again."

LADY WITH SUNSHINE HAIR

She asks; "How do you like having two baby sisters now Patsy?"

"Carole isn't a baby anymore and I can hug them whenever I want, long as I don't wake them up. Sharon has real long eyelashes, so mommy combs them, that's funny. Sometimes I can hold them and give them formula stuff in a bottle."

"I have some formula in a bottle too Patsy, it makes my hair yellow."

"Gosh how do you get all that hair in a bottle Miss Christine? Uh oh, I smell chicken burning. You better go home before you burn the house again." Boy, mommy sure got mad at me. I don't know why.

Another time Carole and Sharon were crying so me and Bobby started crying too. Then Daddy was yelling his head off too. "We gotta move outa here fore one theez youngun's takes anuther shit, Stella Bee. That landlord sed e ain't fixin no moe plumin problums. We gotta git us a house. We dun run our sef off, havin all theez babies."

Pretty soon we were leaving so I ran to tell. "Goodbye Miss Christine. We're moving far away to Y and Dot. I'm sorry about your burnt chickens." The pretty lady with sunshine hair hugged me. "Goodbye little Patsy. I'm going to miss you."

WYANDOTTE 1949

There was a song back then that went like this; 'Green door, what's that secret you're keeping?' Daddy said some vet runs got the white bungalow with a green door for us. Mommy said it was very nice of those veterans to do that. Someday I'm going to find them and say thank you very much. We have a real house now. I'm so happy! The upstairs had one long bedroom, for kids only, no big people allowed. The four of us kids slept together in one big bed. When Bobby started school, he got his own bed. Until then they were all blanket hogs, every single one of them. All the houses on our block were cookie cutter, with few exceptions. They had hardwood floors throughout, except kitchen and bath. Every Saturday my mother and I scrubbed the kitchen floor together on our knees. Me counting the red and black squares, three across, three down, trying to keep up with her. The kitchen table set was retro style, with a white metal top and chrome legs, the chairs had red vinyl seats. After years of kids leaning on it the table collapsed and daddy said it was ready for the junk wagon. The Rag Man came down our street in a big wood wagon. Clip clop, clip clop, horse hooves sounded on the pavement. The lone horse trotted slowly pulling its load, with a man at the reins calling; "Rags, metal, wood, to buy, sell, or trade. Rags, metal, wood, to buy, sell, or trade." My mother stood on the porch and waved him down. The mountain stopped. The old man climbed from the wagon, gave her a few coins, and took our only table away. "Next time you hear the rag man's horse coming down the street let me know Patsy, so I can get rid of more junk. Wish he'd get some better things so we could make a trade." My mother's wish was always followed by long sighs.

THE LAST BUFFALO NICKEL

For a long time, I wondered how I got here. I don't mean how did I get to Y and Dot. I mean how did I get on this planet with all these people? So I went to the fountain of knowledge and asked my folks how they met. "Yer alweez askin queschuns ain'tcha Patsy? Well Ah'l tell ya how Ah met yer muther. Ah had me a hankering fer sum poke chops n herd tell sum place n Dee -Troit wuz bess, so Ah went to London Chop House n thar she was. Th purdy lil thang jess cot ma fancy thas what she dun. Them poke chops was so dad gum good Ah went back thar an Ah be dog gone if she dint say she wants to go out wif me. Thas how Ah met yer muther Patsy, yes sirree."

"Stop calling me a 'thing' Leonard!" My mother's voice rose sharply from the kitchen. "Why can't you ever tell a story right? You kept coming back to pester me till I went out with you."

"Aww go own Stella Bee; say u liked me sum."

"Maybe I did, you crazy man, but I must have been goofy in the head."

"Aww go own u nickel immigrant, u couldn't wait till Ah showed up agin."

"What's that nickel word mean Dad?"

"Yer mother crossed a bridge on a buffalo lookin fer me."

"What!? Mom rode on a buffalo!?"

"Yes sirree, she come frum Canada n got in ma country with er last buffalo nickel! An Ah been takin care-a her evar sance." My mother just stood there glaring at him. "Stop given me yer ole eagle eye Stell."

"You were born in the hills Leonard, that's why you never bother to shut the barn door."

"What does that mean Mom?"

"Never mind Patsy, I was talking to your dad. You don't need to know that."

"Where were you born Dad?"

"In the mountains a Kentucky an A'hma goin back thar sum day."

"So why did you leave Canada and come here Mom?" "Because my sisters were here, and I missed them." "Which sisters Mom?" "Your Aunt Marie and Aunt Bella." "Why did they come here Mom?" "For goodness' sake Patsy, so many questions. Who knows why they came here they just did."

"Boy, Canada and Kentucky are a long way apart. You came all that way and met each other. So how did I get here?"

"You came from Canada too."

"What? But Mom told me before that I was born in Detroit, Dad!"

"Stop telling her things to confuse her. You were born in Detroit, Patsy, ignore goofy talk."

"But why did Dad say that Mom?"

"Never believe what a drunk man says Patsy. Never."

Footnote: The buffalo nickels of my childhood were struck by the US mint in 1912, with an Indian head on the front, a buffalo on the back, depending on how you look at it. Though plentiful in the '50s circulation faded after minting stopped in 1938.

THE WINNER IS

A big fight was going on about sending the kid to school. Dad yelled he was a Free Will Baptist, and the Catholic Church had no place in school. Mom yelled he owed it to her, and the fight was over. But every year when tuition was due there was another free for all. Dad yelling the public school was good enough. Mom yelling her kids would get a good education if it killed her. Saint Joseph and my mother won, five years in a row.

LEARNING LESSONS

Since I have no recollection whatsoever of going to kindergarten, assumingly I did not. My first- grade teacher was Sister Bartholomew. She had whiskers on her chin, but I liked her anyway, she had nice teeth. I walked 14 blocks to school playing a game of count the blocks, 13, 12, 11, only ten more to go. Lunchtime we ate at our desks, following the quiet rule, or you don't go out for recess. This kid followed the rules. No way was I gonna be stuck inside with Sister Bart. My brown sack lunch had another p b and j on wheat each day, which was often somewhat rancid tasting by lunchtime. Sister B doled out a pint of C and D to me and the little girl with red curls. Milk at our house was rationed for babies. Other kids' lunches made my stomach growl. That kid has ham and cheese, a thermos of milk, apple and Twinkies! Wish I had his lunch. He must have heard my hungry mind. "You want my apple?" Thanks! I'd rather had milk and Twinkies but was learning. It's better not to always say what you're thinking.

A LUCKY KID

Raffles and fundraisers were often held at school. This time the prize was a tall chocolate fudge cake. Boy, I'm going to win that. Every coin found on the street went in the raffle box, earning another ticket. Time came for the drawing, and something told me; you're the winner, and Sister called my name. I carried my prize home in a tall white box, smelling it all the way. As soon as I walked in the door, I was a hero. What a great time we had with that cake. My mother doled it out one sliver at a time, making it last all week.

I often thought of myself as lucky. Something inside told me so. Sometimes I'd dream of finding loose change on the street, and the next day there it was. I'd stop at the drug store soda fountain on the way home from school, and slurp a milk shake till my stomach was full.

Another raffle at school. This time the prize was a 'Barbie like' doll. She had no bust hence she was not Barbie. Her white shoes were also flat, she was obviously born before Barbie. Nevertheless, her dress was made of Kleenex, tied together in layers with tiny bows of blue yarn. She was the prettiest doll I'd ever seen. To me she was Cinderella in a white satin ball gown and blue silk ribbons. I wanted that little doll more than anything. There had to be more dropped coins on 14 blocks of sidewalks, so off I went on roller skates to search. Every found coin was donated to the cause. The Cinderella doll was waiting. Raffle day arrived and I held my breath as Sister reached into the glass bowl. She pulled out the small slip of paper and read my name! I arrived home beaming with joy, Cinderella in hand. "My goodness Patsy, you won again. You're such a lucky kid." My mother confirmed. "You'll have to keep that doll up high somewhere so your little sisters can't reach it, or that Kleenex dress will fall apart the minute they get their hands on it. I can already see that little doll is going to cause big trouble around here." Right again Mom. Cinderella was destined for doom. She wanted to stand on top the dresser my sisters and I shared. I should've listened to mom instead of fairytale lady. It never occurred to me that my little sisters would drag a chair and climb up to get her. Another lesson learned. Never make a dress out of Kleenex, no matter who's going to wear it.

THE OVERPASS

There was a big overpass crossing Eureka Road, back then they were called viaducts. Every day I walked under this dimly lit stretch of concrete. Hurrying to pass through what seemed in my little mind, a dark cave shutting out the sun. One afternoon I was halfway through when a horrific loud rumbling noise started. The cement walls of the structure began to vibrate scaring me out of my wits. Convinced it was falling I ran as fast as I could go to get through it. The next day, same time, same place it started again. The loud rumbling, the walls vibrating, so I ran faster. The third day I approached monster walk in stark fear. There was no other way to go. Please God, don't let it start shaking again and fall on me. I ran faster than ever, praying to reach the other end before it fell. At midway the rumbling started again. The walls trembled even harder than before. The sound was deafening. It was going to fall on me if I didn't run even faster! I pushed on with all my might and burst into the sunshine, still running to get away from the noise. Then I stopped and looked back to watch it fall.   And what to my wondering eyes did appear... a long train was rolling by on top that viaduct! Oh my gosh, how did a train get way up there? I asked my little self out loud. After that I was never afraid to walk alone again.

MY BUDDY

Then my buddy started school, the 14 blocks was our world now. We knew all the short cuts. Walking past Roosevelt high school was enlightening. "Those teenagers are playing kissy face again," Bobby announced every time. "They get away with it cause there ain't no nuns at this school Patsy." The next year little Carole was tagging along. A year later Sharon joined us. In winter, the snow was up to our knees. Bobby and I had to pull them out of snowdrifts, their legs were so short they got stuck in it. Time and again we were walking backward to pull them forward. We couldn't just leave them stuck in the snow, could we? But those two sure could poke along and make us late for church. Mass was required attendance every morning before school started. If we arrived after, we were considered late. If a tardy mark appeared on our report cards, we were terrified of the terrible leather strap. The first day our sister's started school, we were warned; "U two r gonna git skinned alive if yer sister's git n eny trouble n tht school er eny whar else, ya hear me?" "Yes dad, we hear you!" Boy that was scary stuff. I would never tell on them. That would be plain stupid. All I had to do was get everybody to church on time, and we'd all be in the clear. Another lesson learned.

All in all, I went to mass every morning five times a week, plus Sundays, for five years. That's got to multiply out to a nice round number and count for something. Kneeling in church for an hour is no small feat for a kid with a busy mind. A whole rosary can skip through in minutes flat. Then it's on to roller skating, if I ever got out of there. Every morning 30 or more kids knelt in pews with classmates. One nun behind each class. A portrait of little angels in their finest hour. Me wondering how nuns could be so good all the time. I figured if I promised to be a nun someday, God would make me a good kid. Until Sister Agnes said, "God can read your mind." Boy I'm in trouble if he can do that. The next morning pondering what she said, I looked around and she was staring right at me! Another lesson learned. When you feel like someone is watching you; they are.

In the old days, corporal punishment was acceptable in school. My ponytail got pulled so hard my eyes watered and scalp screeched. You bet your bippy the next time I stayed in line. Another lesson learned. We also got whacked on the knuckles with a ruler for writing above the lines. Boy, that smartens you up fast. Nowadays I sometimes scribble like a doctor, all over the place. Just because I can. Other than those instances the nuns were swell. Those little penguin ladies in head to toe black and white robes, taught me enough in five years to last a lifetime. Selflessly determined they crammed our heads with ABC's, reading, writing, and arithmetic all morning. No breaks. Just work. After lunch and recess, English, history, and spelling filled the afternoon. Lucky me, spelling came naturally but math was a different story. Adding, subtracting, multiplying and dividing, got me through life with a few fractions. Thank goodness I didn't aspire to be an architect. Those nuns really knew their stuff. Knew we were thirsty little sponges ready to soak it all up. All kidding aside, the greatest lesson they taught me was to love God.

Another lesson we quickly learned was...never go home and complain of being reprimanded in school, or you were in trouble all over again. Anybody in authority was always right. If you weren't doing something wrong to begin with, you wouldn't be in trouble. That's the way it was, because that's what they said. What they said was the law, and you better believe it if you know what's good for you.

BUICK AUTOMOBILES

"Come see what the good ole boys at GM dun went n give me kiddies. Ah shore do love my new Buick. Come look at er Stella Bee." "Gosh this is a swell car Dad. I love red but pink is my favorite." "They ain't given out no pink cars Patsy."

"Stop telling her things like that Leonard! Nobody gives you anything Patsy. Your dad had to work hard for that car. You'll have to work hard for everything you get too." The next year dad came home with a shiny black Buick. "Come see ma new car kiddies. The good ole boys made a trade n din't ask fer a buffalo nickel." My mother just shook her head. "I liked the red car better and I see you didn't say anything to me before trading a year-old car. Now I see I have to talk to these kids again before they get the wrong ideas in their heads from listening to more goofy talk."

MISSING GRANDPARENTS

It bothered me that my mother's parents died when she was very young. She wouldn't talk about it, so I kept asking until she did. "Ok Patsy, I'll tell you now. I didn't want to tell you before because you were too young. I was nine years old when my father died. It was such a hard time for us. I missed him so much. There was always so much work to do on the farm and the older kids were already gone. They had their own farms to work. My mother got so sick from doing all that heavy work, her legs swelled so bad she couldn't walk. Her legs got so big she couldn't get out of the bed. I missed a lot of school to stay home and help her. All those years I took care of my poor mother until she died." "How old were you when Grama died Mom?" "I was 18 Patsy." "How old was Grama when she died?" "She was only 56 Patsy. My mother taught me how to cook from her bed. She would tell how to do it and I would just do it. I brought her meals to the bed and bathed her in her bed too." "How can you bath someone in a bed Mom?"

"It's called a sponge bath Patsy. If you want to hear the story, stop interrupting when I'm trying to tell it. My mother taught me to keep going no matter what. After our father died, I had to take care of the baby and my younger brother so our mother could do the farm work. Little Joe got so mischievous, he thought he didn't have to mind me because I was just a kid like him. But he sure changed his tune when our older brother got hold of him. He had to go live at Fred's and didn't want to. Our oldest sister Edna took baby

Therese. I didn't want them to go but Fred and Edna said it was for the best. They knew I couldn't handle all that being a young kid. But Joe always had to do things his way. The first chance he got he went and joined the Army. He was such a kid we didn't know how he got in there in the first place. When we heard he was missing in the war we prayed for him day and night. That poor sweet kid, what he must have gone through being captured by Hitler's soldiers. Don't look so sad Patsy. The war is over now. It's been over for a while. Your Uncle Joe is at home in Canada. You'll meet him one of these days. I'm only telling you these things to warn you. Life is never easy. There will be good times and bad times. You have to take the good and the bad together. You'll have to work hard for everything you get. Nothing will ever come to you on a silver platter. That's not the way it goes. Nothing good ever comes easy. You'll mark my words someday."

It would be many years later before I learned how my grandfather died. On August 10, 1929, he was rushed to the hospital with appendicitis. They gave him 'ether' to put him to sleep for surgery, without knowing that he had asthma. The ether killed him. He was 48 years young.

ELIZABETH PARK

Occasionally we piled into the Buick and went to Elizabeth Park for a picnic. At times dad's sister Drexie joined us with her kids, Margaret, Eva, and baby girl Terri. This aunt called me Patsy Honey and made me feel loved. The little kid inside remembers that park, swinging on the swings with Bobby, walking with Aunt Drexie, stopping to watch the pony rides, and Mom's special potato salad and fried chicken at mealtime. Today meals are referred to as breakfast, lunch and dinner. Back then meals were called breakfast, dinner and supper. Supper you say. What's that? Well supper was dinner, and dinner was lunch. Ok, ok, just shut up and eat kids if you know what's good for you. Supper at our house was the same time every day. Everybody sat down together. If you didn't like what was on the table, you didn't eat. More often than not, supper was a bowl of pinto beans and cornbread. It was a surprise if was chicken and dumplings or beef stew. It was a real celebration if we had windmill cookies or potato chips. Wow, the good fairy must have been here.

A BLESSED MOTHER

That dreaded school uniform, itchy navy wool skirt, and plain white blouse. The time came when I noticed other girls were wearing, lace trimmed white blouses, silky fabric skirts, black patent leather shoes, lace trimmed socks, and a different uniform each day. An observation that said we were always on the outside looking in. The four of us had one top and one bottom garment, worn day in and day out, wash and wear as needed. Our scruffy shoes had holes in the bottom, leaving cold feet for hours. Yet we went walking to a private school, carrying pb and j. Our blessed mother was doing what she believed was right. Her kids were in that good school, and she would give up everything to keep them there by God. They weren't going to miss any school either. "They're all going to go to that good school. They're smart kids. They're going to grow up and do well. All of them. You just watch and see Leonard." Our mother was a good seamstress, despite never owning a sewing machine. Every perfect stitch she did by hand. Every night after kids were in bed, she repaired many pieces of clothing. Darning socks, sewing on buttons, fixing rips, hemming, all done by hand. If something was too short, she let out the hem, when it no longer fit, it was passed down to the next kid. Occasionally, a big box arrived from Canada with hand me downs, and we were thrilled to get them. I recall being in a strange little store one day with my mother. It was cramped and crowded with everything from soup to nuts, including clothes. My first time in a thrift shop, I was fascinated. We were there to find a 'new' uniform, and sure enough my mother found both pieces for a nickel. The skirt was too long so the nickel squeezer hemmed it up, to be taken down when I grew. I was happy. It was new to me. I'd never seen it before. Plus, it didn't itch.

THE SOUP LINE

"That school's gonna put me in th soup line. Doan know why theez kids cain't go to public skool like otha kids. Ah ain't no rich man. Ah cain't make nuff ta feed em all. We goin haf to cut back own groceries again this week Stella."

"Stop it, Leonard! You're scaring the kids. We might have to give up your new car to afford their education. I don't want them to end up squeezing every nickel like we have to do." Kitchen chairs started flying across the room in a rage, never saw chairs get so mad. "Who air heard a woman tell a man what to do. This is a man's world! Ah make th rules roun here! Ah wear th pants n ths house n what ah say goes! Ah ain't givin up ma car! Lees u got a house fer theez kids. Ma bruther's n me come up n a tar shack side of a hill, n had more fun than theez kids evar will."

"Oh, be quiet Leonard. I'll talk when I want to talk. You and your brothers were sneaking out at night drinking moonshine when you were kids, and you call that having fun. That wasn't fun, it was a sin. Our kids are doing good there and they'll do even better when they grow up. You wait and see."

LIZZY LIZARD TONGUE

The whole school took tap dancing lessons once a week in the gymnasium. Elizabeth danced next to me in line. One day she invited me to her house for playtime. I was excited about making a friend. Her mother picked me up at home and we drove to the other side of town, until she finally stopped at a huge gray house on the Detroit River. Oh my gosh this must be what rich is! Elizabeth is a rich kid. The pretty little girl with velvet black hair was an only child. She had so many dolls and doll furniture it astounded me. I didn't even know doll furniture existed. Her closet was packed with clothes and shoes. It baffled me why she had so much stuff. Being a nosy little kid, of course I had to ask. "They're for going out." Lizzy answered all snooty like, but I didn't get it. I'd never met snooty before. "Going out? You mean you wear all this nice stuff to play in the park?" "I don't play in parks," she snapped. "My mother takes me to parties and things like that." Well, I had no idea what 'things like that' was. Or why her mother kept watching me the whole time we played. But soon we were leaving the beautiful castle house.

One day at school sister left the classroom and Lizzy started handing out invitations to her birthday party. She walked toward me with the last envelope in hand, and I smiled expectantly. "You're not getting one," she snapped, and raised her voice so loud the whole world heard. "My mother says you're poor, and you live in an ugly little house!" I sank into my desk trying to disappear as everyone laughed. Except for one girl who watched silently with sad eyes. Our family was at the park again when I saw her, the little girl with red curls. She waved and I waved back. Then she ran over and asked if I wanted to play jump rope with her and another girl. We had a swell time, but she never invited me to her house, and I never invited her to mine. That was fine with me. Snooty Lizzy went to the head of the line in tap dancing, I blocked her out of my mind. She disappeared like she wasn't in the room.

DAD'S FAMILY

There were five siblings in dad's family. When he was drinking, he often rambled on about them, repeating himself. I could never figure out what was true and what wasn't. "Them two girls dun all rite, followed us boys ere frum Kintucky. Caught em a husband. They dun all rite. Ma bruther's n me wuz hobos. Went hoppin trains findin work. Workin fer nickels n dimes. Some times only a meal. Yah buddy. It wuz bad times. That war kilt many a good ole boy. They come from everwhars. Black n white fightin long side each otha. Good ole boys. Loved em all. They wuz ma bruthas. Yes sirree." Then he would cry, and I was afraid to go to sleep. I'd stay awake listening, expecting another mood swing. Knowing when it came, all hell would break loose. Many times, he talked to himself all night. "Yeah buddy, Ah lef n went hoppin trains. Workin n theez factrees now. Ah dun all rite too."

A SHORT-TERM GRAND PAW

Lissen up kiddies. Yer grand paw's comin ta stick with us a spell. He don't get no peace livin with yer grand maw, she stays own th warpath day n nite. Ain't changed nary a bit since she lef thm hills, she's worse n ever. Yer good-hearted Aunt Drexie went n moved em in with her an havin a hell of a time. We gotta cut er a break, she sho needs one."   Grand Paw sat in his rocking chair in the corner. Chatterbox wanted to talk to the old man with a nice face, but he wouldn't talk. It was almost like he wasn't there. One day Mom gave him a shave and a haircut at the kitchen table. He smiled and mumbled, "thank ye kinely." Then apparently, slipped out the keyhole since no one saw him leave. Nobody knew anything. Until someone said someone saw him boarding a Greyhound bus asking the driver; "Kin ye kinely carry me own to ma ole Kintucky home?"

A MEAN OLE GRAND MAW

"Lissen up kiddies, it's yer grand maws turn liven ere. Jes be nice n we'll see whar she blows." Wonder what he means by that? Then grand maw walked in the door glaring at me. "Stay away from her Patsy," my mother warned. "Be really nice when she's around, because we never know what she might do. She's old and mean and can't seem to help herself." I was duly warned but didn't listen. Kids at school talked about the fun they had with their grandparents. This old lady was my last chance to have one, so I would make her laugh and win her over. "Look out Grand Maw I'm gonna getcha." "Hey Grand Maw, what came first, the chicken or the egg?" "Hey Grand Maw, why did the cow jump over the moon?" No matter how I tried to make her laugh, she scowled, until finally I left her be.

UNCLE CHARLIE

Every weekend dad's two brothers rolled in, ready for a party. Their funny colloquiums made us laugh, and after a few drinks, their vernacular became more exaggerated. They delighted in telling stories of past mischiefs, and grand maw expanded on their reputation. "Ma boys kin fine evar party n town, eny time eny whar." Dad and his brother winked at each other in devil may care attitude and Grand Maw didn't miss it. "Ah spect theez boys n truble fore Mundey. They b gone razin hell who knows whar. Best sen Charles long er they b runnin hog wild n nare come back see theez younguns."

"Hush Mommy, we b takin care of em. Looka here young'uns. Lissen up. One thez days we gun take ya'all down home n see the blue grass mountains. We lef thar cuz they run out a possum. We caught evar one of em, sho nuff. Tied em own a clothesline by thar tails, n tied a chicken n th middle watchin hell break loose. Yer gran maw cooked em up, n we ate em."

We ran out of the room hands over our ears, escaping further possum stories. Uncle Charlie was the only one who could coax us back. "Come own back younguns, they's jess funning ya. We dint eat em. Yer granmaw chased us thru th mountains, strap n hand, switch n otha, hollerin she's gun beat tar outa us, n skin our hides. We run off a spell but she got us later own. U boys stop scaring theez young'uns now ya hear me? Ah ain't gun letcha do it no moe. Come own younguns, don't pay em no mind. Uncle Charlie ain't gunna let em tell ya no mo possum stories."

Uncle Charlie had a dimple in his chin and one in each cheek. When he smiled his whole face lit up, brown eyes twinkling, and dimples dancing. Each time he visited, he told us another story of where he'd been and what he'd seen. As a conductor on a train, we thought he had the most exciting job in the world. Bobby and I listened intently to his adventures. "U kids sho do tickle me." He'd laugh merrily. When it was time for him to leave, we were sad and didn't want him to go, but Uncle Charlie had a way to brighten us up.

"Ah gotta git back own th train n git ta workin. Ah be seein ya'all agin. Got a lil somethin fer u youngins til nex time. Take theez buffalo nickels n git yersef sum ice cream, an go own down the movie house n see a cowboy show. Don't be tellin them lil one's n hurt thar feelins. They ain't big nuff ta go so fer a stretch. Soon's they git ta growin sum Ah'll git em all handfuls a nickels."

Soon as possible me and Bobby ran to the corner drugstore to share a chocolate malt. Then took the city bus to Wyandotte theatre to see a Lone Ranger and Tonto movie, or Roy Rogers and Dale Evans. Afterwards we went in the five and dime with the last nickel to get a box of Boston Baked Beans candy, and Juju Bees candy for our little sisters. They counted each piece excitedly amongst them, until all had equal amounts. We never told them where we got it. Candy hero's never spill the beans.

Whenever a train went by and blew its whistle, we'd chime in. "There's Uncle Charlie!" Then Grand Maw would comment from her rocking chair. "Ma boy Charles ain no hell raiser like thm otha two. E nair got marrid cuz e ain't good lookin like them. Sides he be runnin all time ta kitch a train. Too bad cuz e loves kids, jess cain't get off a train long nuff to make one." All the grownups laughed but I wondered why Uncle Charlie couldn't get a kid as easy as we did. They popped up at our house almost every year like cute little groundhogs.

After a while Uncle Charlie didn't come to visit anymore. Me and Bobby figured he couldn't get off the train, until we listened in to grownup talk. "Your brother says he's not going out with family men anymore because it's not right Leonard. Why don't you stop this running around and stay at home like your good brother said, instead of going to bars with the wild one."

"Charles jess doan know howda ave 'im sum fun Stella Bee." Boy that really fired up my mother's feisty temper, but nothing could stop the hell raisers. They were going no matter what she said. Then Grand Maw had something to say too. "Thars ma otha boy comin ere agin. Truble walkin. E thanks e's Casanova. Cordin to him e's the best lookin brutha n th wimen love em. Them boys gun carry on till dooms day. Gun b hell ta pay. Ya watch n see if Ah hain't rite." As soon as my mother stepped out of the room the 'boys' winked and punched each other in the arm. "Let's run off!" And off they went like little kids chasing an ice cream truck. Then

Grand Maw piped up again. "Too bad ole Charles ain't roun no mo. E'd keep them boys frum truble."

Bobby and I really missed our uncle after that. I never saw him again. Maybe my brother ran into him at some later date. Or maybe Uncle Charlie took a midnight train to Georgia and found a simpler place. But wherever he went one thing is certain. His whole face will light up, brown eyes twinkling and dimples dancing every time he gives another kid a handful of nickels.

Eventually dad came home, and mom was yelling to make him pay. Until grand maw went off her rocker and put in her two cents. "Linnerd ain't dun haf bad what tht otha boy dun. E went steppin n deep dudu this time. His wife's gone th corner ta fix Blondie's wagon. Stop waggin yer tongue Stella. Ahm tired a hearin ya, so shet the hell up." Bobby and I wondered about a lady with a broken wagon, then rumor said our uncle's wife was moving back home whether he went or not. She had enough. My mother put her foot down too, and said grand maw had to live someplace else. She had enough of an old lady who didn't like her kids. Furthermore, she wasn't putting up with an old bag who was meaner than any man. Dad agreed, and said grand maw was meaner than a junk yard dog.

AUNT DREXIE

Sometime later my aunt asked me to come to her house for the weekend. After arriving I asked what she wanted me to do, assuming she needed a little help around the house. "You're my guest here Patsy Honey. There'll be no working or dish washing for you in my house. You and me are just gonna set an talk an enjoy our time together." The next day I watched her setting the dining room table while we went on talking. Sudden intuition told me to move so I stepped slightly to the side at the same moment that my aunt started screaming. "Stop Mommy Stop!"

From my peripheral vision I saw the wood chair coming down on me but too late. Pain shot through my neck, shoulders and back, leaving me stunned speechless. "Patsy! Are you ok child?!" My aunt continued to scream at her mother. "Good God Almighty! What have you done to this child, you crazy old woman? What's wrong with your head? Have you done lost all your senses? You could of hurt her for life or even killed her!" Grand maw yelled back defiantly; "Be shed a her, ain't no kin o mine, nary Linnerds!"

"You're plumb loco Mommy! Git on out of here before I call the police on you! And don't you think I won't. Don't care where you go, just get gone from my house. Seen you do some things, but this beats all. Git gone from here before I push you out myself!"

"Patsy- are you still in one piece Honey Child? Let me look you over. Lordy be, but you're going to have some bad pain and bruising from that crazy ole woman. I'm so sorry Honey Child, never would have brought you here if I thought she'd do such awful thing." My aunt cried and she and my little cousins gathered around to cry with me. "Don't pay no mind to nary a word she said Honey Child. That ole woman's my mother but she doesn't know a lick about beans. You go on and forget about her. My girls and me love when you visit, but I know you won't want to come back here long as a crazy ole woman's' round and can't blame you for that. Once I get her where she can't hurt a body, I hope you'll come stay with us again Patsy Honey."

The incident was never spoken of again. I sent that old lady to my 'forget it zone.' She wanted to kill me and shouted something I was too naïve to understand. Who cares? Forget her.

SUMMERTIME

It was playing in the rain in your bathing suit on hot summer days, happy rain falling on your head. Running barefoot in the grass. Catching fireflies in jars. Running through neighbor's sprinklers. Riding in Bobby's red wagon in a parade. Bobby liked to collect worms in a glass jar and pop up and stick them in our face, which made all the girls scream. Always finding ways to taunt, he made sling shots out of twigs and shot us with green peas. He thought he was big stuff when he earned enough to buy a detective Joe Friday badge and a Dragnet cap gun. Every spring, my brother and I went around the neighborhood selling flower and garden seeds. Until he decided he wasn't going to be outsold by a girl. He put on his Cub Scout uniform, got on his bicycle and off he went. "Ha ha ha Patsy, I outsold you." We played simple games like kick the can, hide and seek, jump rope, hopscotch, drawing on the sidewalk with chalk. There was one pair of roller skates to share between all of us. The metal skates had a key to adjust the width and length. Then you attached the skates to your hard soled shoes, tied the straps around your ankles, and were ready to roll. If you fell you picked yourself up, skinned knees and all, and kept going. Otherwise, someone pulled the skates off your feet while you cried, and you'd have to wait days for another turn. Comic books were circulated throughout the neighborhood. We sat on the sidewalk reading Superman, and Flash Gordon, and Casper the friendly ghost, or Veronica, Reggie and Betty's love triangle. Mom bought a set of children's classic story books from a door-to-door salesman, and reading became my favorite thing. The love of fairy tales and forever after was born.

THE MILK SHOOT

On the north side of the house was a small metal door about a foot square, where bottles of milk were left inside. The milkman arrived in a white truck; the word 'milk' emblazoned on both sides. Dressed in a white uniform and cap, he resembled Milky the clown. In inclement weather the milk bottles were retrieved from inside the house. The milk shoot was 'the thing' back then. When all the milk was gone, mom always had to remind us about the empty bottles. "I suppose those bottles are going to have to walk back to the milk shoot themselves, because no one wants to take them. You kids should know they can't get there alone. Someone needs to take them if you want to drink nice cold milk again. You know we don't have a cow in the backyard. Those poor bottles are just going to sit there and wait for you like a little dog." She tried everything to convince us and still no one wanted to go to that dark milk shoot leading into the broom closet. But whenever we were really bored the milk shoot would suddenly come into play. Crawling through the dark space would seem like a great idea. It wasn't an easy task; some bravery was required. Once you started to crawl through you had to keep going, and scary stuff was bound to happen. Everything came to life in the dark. Spooky things thrashed around. A bony witch with straggly wet hair reached out. Cobwebs got in your face. Dead people's bones fell on you. Bugs and spiders were sure to come out next. Then all kinds of weirdness crashed through the closet door, tumbling down the basement stairs screeching in the dark. And mom came running. "For heaven's sake you kids have to quit scaring me like that! Now get in here and pick up your mess and put my broom closet back the way I had it!" It was fun scaring mom.

DETROIT ZOO AND BELLE ISLE

As a very young child I remember going to the Detroit Zoo, and riding around Belle Isle. One day we stopped in front of a huge glass building. Inside the glass house I saw palm trees and cactus from Florida and Arizona. How far is Florida?" How far is Arizona? Someday I'll get on Uncle Charlie's train and see palm trees that touch the sky. How do they grow in this glass house Mom?" "It's called a conservatory Patsy. It was built special so they can grow in here." "Someday I going to have a tree like this in my yard with a white picket fence." "You're such a funny kid Patsy. Maybe you'll have all that if you work hard."

Packing for outings at the park took forever. Sweaters in case the weather changes. Blankets, baby bottles, baby food, diapers. The red check tablecloth. Facecloths because you can't play with a dirty face. Toilet paper in case the park runs out. Soap to wash your hands before you eat. Extra underwear for the little kids. The picnic basket. The big thermos of real lemonade. When half the house was packed, girls piled into the back seat. Bobby rode in front on the bench seat between mom and dad. The current baby sat on mom's lap, and we were raring to go. "Let's go Dad!" Off we went in the hot summer without air conditioning. Crank the windows down, sister's hair flying in your face as well as your own. Modern cars of yesteryear didn't have seatbelts. Who needed them, packed in there like marshmallows. There's no way we could fall out. Minutes later little girls started bickering. "Scooch over." "No! You move over. You got more room than I do." "Get off me." "Ouch you're pulling my hair." "Move over seat hog." "Eww, your breath smells." "Are we almost there?" "Uh oh, I gotta go pee."

"You should've peed at home, now you have to hold it till we get there." The Park was only fifteen minutes away but after five patience was worn thin. "U girls better settle down back thar if ya know what's good fer ya. Ah best not haf ta stop this car u hear me?" "Yes Dad, we hear you."

WINTERTIME

Michigan winters were bearish winds, let the cold winds blow, let em blow, let em blow. Snowdrifts four to five feet, icicles hanging from roofs, slipping and sliding, all part of winter. On the back of the house was a very small door about a foot square. "What's that little door for Daddy? It's too small for people."

"It's fer th monster n th basement Patsy." Winter came in with a roar. "Ah gotta git more food fer th monster. It ain't gonna go till Ah feed it."

"Stop filling her head with nonsense Leonard, you're scaring her." A big truck came and dropped stuff through the little door. It rolled into the basement making loud thuds and smutty black stuff filled the air making everyone cough."We gotta have this stuff, kids, the monster ain't gunna eat nuthin else." Dad claimed and went downstairs to feed it. Curiosity made me peek down the stairwell to see the monster who wouldn't leave until it was fed. Watching from a safe place as a shovel full of chunky food went into its big red mouth. It snapped, crackled and popped and red sparks flew from its cavernous face. "Look out Daddy the monster's going to get you!" "Come on down n hep feed it Patsy." "No Sirree not me!" I ran back to safety. "Mommy the monster's going crazy!"

"There's no monster Patsy," my brother laughed. "Daddy's trying to scare you and it worked." "How do you know mister smarty pants?" "I just know Patsy. It's a big iron furnace and that's all it is." Time passed and another conversation was going on about the made-up monster. "Sho glad we got rid a th monster that wuz eatin us out a house n home Stella Bee." "Me too Leonard, gas is best."

ON THE FARM

When one of my mother's family was coming to visit, they wrote a letter and she started preparing. She must have learned to work like a horse on the farm because she never stopped working until someone visited. One summer Aunt Edwidge came for a few days. While she was there, they decided I would go back to Canada with her for two whole weeks. I was on my way to another country. It was the most exciting thing that had ever happened to me. It seemed like forever to get there. We drove forever seeing nothing but cornfields, and dust clouds following the car down dirt roads. "Hey that's a kid driving that tractor!"

"All hands stay busy when you live on the farm Patsy." I started daydreaming of driving a tractor. Then just as magnetic eye closing cornfields lulled me to sleep, auntie announced. "There's our farm Patsy." A big white farmhouse rose from the cornfields surrounding it on all sides. Hmmm, I wonder what came first, the house or the cornfield? It's like the chicken and the egg thing. We stopped in front of a huge barn with doors open wide. A group of fat chickens came running to greet us clucking excitedly. That night everything was blacker than pitch. The next morning a very loud 'cock a doodle do,' startled me from sleep. "What was that?!" Cousins Doreen, Yvonne, Roger, Angela and Annette just laughed. "This is a farm Patsy; we wake up like that every morning." Outside the sun reflected on golden fields so bright, I had to squeeze my eyes shut. All around were yellow fields and blue skies. How beautiful it all was. Feeding funny chickens wasn't a chore. They ran around clucking at each other, neither listening to the other, making me homesick for my silly sisters. When all the chores were done, we climbed makeshift steps on the barn wall to swing on a rope falling into piles of hay. Being on the farm was a whole different world. The sound of the wind blowing through the fields. The smell of clean air. Peace and serenity. I loved it. Until bath time, which was a big scrub basin in an enclosure on the back porch with holes in the walls. Auntie said not to worry there weren't any peepers around. They lived so far in the country they hardly ever saw a car, much less a person. When far off neighbors headed to town, they rang them up through the operator. Did they want a ride to town? Other than that, we wouldn't see or hear from anybody, except for chickens talking. Sunday morning my cousins and I got dressed for church. As I followed them, I wondered where we were walking to since there wasn't another building in sight, much less a church. When we reached the dirt road my cousins stuck out their thumbs. "Holy Cow we're hitchhiking! If my dad finds this out, he'll skin me alive!" When my aunt heard about my outburst, she pursed her mouth in the little pout that was only hers, and with twinkling blue eyes spoke in French...pu Patsy, ma Cherie amour."

Sunday is a day of rest, but when you live on the farm rest happens after chores are done, and all the animals are fed. Afterwards we were going to visit Uncle Willie and Aunt Bern's farm. Another adventure down country roads, in the middle of nowhere, somewhere pass someplace, only further. After a while all the wheat and cornfields looked the same. I closed my eyes a second. "Wake up Patsy we're here! You were sleeping sound as a rock. Good thing we didn't let you drive, eh?"

 "Maybe Uncle Willie will let me drive the tractor!" "Only boys can drive a tractor Patsy. Maybe he'll let you help milk the cows. You know your uncle grows soybeans on this farm, eh?" Soybeans, schmoy beans, never heard of em. I wanna drive a tractor, if boys can do it, so can I.

Uncle Willie came from the barn to greet us then took us back to his favorite place. "Holy cow this is a barn mansion, these cows are so lucky!" My uncle laughed and blue eyes twinkled. He showed me the milking machines that went from the cow into stainless steel containers. All very impressive to a city kid who'd never even seen a cow up close. "It's so clean you could live in here Uncle Willie." "Don't let your aunt hear you say that Patsy."

Since that vacation as a very young child, the farm that was Aunt Edwidge and Uncle Fred's is no longer in the family. Uncle Willie and Aunt Bern's farm has made many changes over the years. For one thing, cousin Richard and his wife Pauline own it now... minus the cows.

THE WAR HERO

The first time I met Uncle Joe and Aunt Leah, I thought they were movie stars, because they arrived wearing black sunglasses. Aunt Leah was color coordinated from head to toe. Earrings, shoes, purse, lipstick, all matched her dress. And surely my uncle was Red Buttons in disguise. He had to be. He looked just like him. Mister Buttons was playing a trick on us, pretending to be our uncle. Any minute he was going to start performing his funny routine. "Ho ho, he he, ha ha, strange things are happening." But the hours passed, and he didn't act funny, not even once. When the time came for them to leave, I watched them go, greatly disappointed not to get a live performance from Mister Red Buttons. Years later I learned of the burden my uncle carried throughout his life. I wish to take this opportunity to pay tribute to the man I once mistook for comedian Red Buttons. Uncle Joe went in the Army when he was barely 17. He became a Prisoner of War sometime in the early 1940's. During captivity, his family didn't know for years whether he was dead or alive. Only that he was listed missing in action. When the war ended Joe came walking into his hometown of Stoney Pointe Ontario, surprising many people. The young boy who'd gone into the Army came home a haunted man. He suffered from post-traumatic stress disorder the remainder of his life. Rest In Peace now dear Uncle Joe.

Recently my cousin Nancy, his daughter, sent copies of the following publications: The Globe and Mail Publication dated February 23, 1944. Official list issued by the Department of

National Defense. Casualties - Missing in Action...which lists her father's name along with many others. Cousin Nancy also sent the Official list of Liberated Canadians, dated May 26, 1945.

Thank you, Canada, sister country; and thank you to all our veterans.

AUNT BELLA

As a kid Canada seemed like one big farm on the other side of the world, and you had to cross a very long bridge to get to that country. Or you could get there through a tunnel. Since my mother didn't like the tunnel idea, neither did I. A day off for a farmer's family is rare, as animals and crops had to be tended, therefore visits were special. Aunt Bella and Uncle Leo's farm was in Lapeer Michigan, so we saw our cousins, Pauline, Raymond, Monica and Mary Lou more than other cousins. We called this aunt 'the prune lady' because she always brought prunes. "Eat your prunes mon Ange," she'd insist. Ye gads doesn't she know kids don't like prunes? Aunt Bella's bright blue eyes showed great interest whenever we spoke, yet she missed our disgust for wrinkly old prunes. For my mother she was wise counselor. Oftentimes I'd hear them whispering. Afterwards mom would sigh with relief after unloading on her sister. "Bella gives me courage to go on. A good listener is worth their weight in gold." My mother would say and I thought auntie was rich because she weighed about a hundred pounds.

MYSTERY TRIPS

"Ah got a new job fer ya Patsy. stop warshin dishes n lissen to me. Frum now own when ah'm gone yer n charge. Ah gotta git gone fore yer muther comes questionin. Go watch thm kids till she gits up frum th basement an don't let er know Ahm gone, ya hear me?" "Yes Dad, I heard." Just as he drove away, my mother came rushing up the basement stairs with armloads of laundry. "Was that your dad's car I heard leaving Patsy?" "Yes Mom. He said I'm in charge and not to tell you he's gone." "That dirty rat tricked me again. Where's he going by himself this time?" "I don't know Mom."

28

No one knew but each time was the same. We wouldn't hear from him until he walked in, a week or two later with a carton or two of cigarettes. "Went n got me sum smokes." He'd say nonchalantly and all hell would break loose. "Who do you think you're talking to Leonard? Where've you been all this time? Answer me!" Communication in our house was always a problem. The years I lived there we never had a phone. If there was an emergency, we ran to a neighbor house to use theirs. Bad news came by telegram. Good news came by mail. "Dear Sis, coming to visit for a couple days next week. Can't wait to see you. Love Bella."

Usually, my mother was very happy when one of her sisters visited but this time, they sat in the kitchen whispering while my mother cried. Of course, I had to listen in to see if she was ok. "I don't know where he goes Bella, he disappears and reappears like nothing happened. The neighbor lady told me she saw him with the same woman at the bar. Before you leave let's go ask her to find out where that woman lives, then you can drive me to her house. I need to tell her that he's a married man with all these kids. You know no decent woman would be seen in public with a married man. He has to be lying to her too!" They looked around and caught me listening. "Go away big ears." My mother snapped. "I tell you Bella that kid should've grown up on the farm. She's got the ears and nose of a farmer and doesn't miss a thing." Soon my auntie was leaving. "Goodbye Patsy, don't forget to eat your prunes." Oh, yuk not those things again. "Yes Auntie, I'll remember."

"Did you and Aunt Bella find out where that woman lives Mom?" "No! And I wish you'd stop asking questions that are none of your business Patsy!" "Geez Mom, it is my business because I'm the oldest." "Just because I count on you Patsy, doesn't mean you should be listening to grown up things. Go to bed now and don't you worry. God will fix him for this."

But God never did. Weeks passed and he was still gone. I was hoping he didn't come back, so it would always be nice in our house. One evening I was busy in the kitchen and heard the front door slam and figured he was back. Mom was either going to be happy or mad, there was no in between. All remained quiet so I went to check. Mom was stepping carefully in the dark over a puddle on the floor in the hallway. "I sent Bobby to the neighbor to call the doctor Patsy. When he gets back, tell him to go upstairs and keep your sisters up there so they don't see this."

"What is that Mom? Why is the light off? Why is the doctor coming?" "Don't start with all your questions Patsy, there isn't time for that. Hurry and grab a towel and wipe this up before the doctor gets here." She switched on the light, and a pool of murky liquid was spreading across the floor. "Where did that come from Mom?"

"Never mind Patsy just clean it up and don't worry. It's going to be ok." A few minutes later Bobby came rushing back in. "What's wrong with Mom, Patsy?" "I don't know Bobby; she said you have to go upstairs and keep Carole and Sharon up there."

Soon the doctor came rushing in with a neighbor. The doctor went in mom's room and talked to her, then the two men carried kitchen chairs to her room. They lifted the foot of the bed and set it up on the chairs. The doctor said raising the bed would stop her blood from coming out. Oh my God! What does he mean? What's wrong with my mother!?

"When will your husband be home Mrs.?" "I don't know doctor but Patsy's here if I need anything." The men left, leaving questions I was too afraid to ask. "You can sleep with me tonight, Patsy," my mother said. "Is my blood going to stop if I sleep upside down Mom?" "You're such a funny kid sometimes Patsy." My mother said smiling and I knew everything was ok, so I climbed onto the upside-down bed and went to sleep next to her.

BABY ROSEMARY

Sometime later dad returned home and took mom to the hospital. A few days afterwards she came home smiling radiantly with another pink bundle in her arms. "You can hold her a few minutes Patsy. Look how beautiful she is. I'm so happy she's healthy. As soon as I saw her, I thought of my mother. She'd be so happy about this little girl with red hair. I named her Rosemary after my mother. Your grandmother was such a strong woman, she worked like a man on the farm after my father died. I see my mother in this baby, she looks just like her. Your grandmother had long red hair to her waist"

"I always wanted to know my grandmother. I'm glad you named our baby after her, but why do you think she looks like your mother? The baby only has a little red fuzz on her head."

"For goodness' sake Patsy, her hair is going to grow the same way Carole and Sharon's hair did when they were babies." "Gosh I know that Mom, but the baby looks like a doll, not a grandmother. Now I have three dolls, Carole and Sharon and Rosemary. Can I feed her pleeeeeze?"

"Your sisters are not dolls, Patsy but I know you're always careful with them. You can help me feed her later when we can do it together." Our new baby was so funny when she started to eat baby pablum. She ate like a bunny twitching her nose, testing it before deciding if she liked it. If she didn't, she spit it back. Pretty soon she was toddling around the house, blue green eyes flashing under the auburn red hair she got from our grandmother.

"U think u kin handle theez kids by yer sef Patsy? Me n yer muther got bizness ta do n we can't take younguns thar." "Sure, I can do it Dad." "You foolish man, we can't leave a new baby with Patsy!" "Gess we best take lil Rosemary with us then. We cain't have Patsy droppin er on er head." Bobby and I thought that was really funny. "U best be hepin yer sister watch theez girls Bobby. Ya hear me?" "Yes Dad, I hear you."

Hours later they returned, looking anxious but surprised that me and Bobby were quietly enjoying our favorite snack, a bowl of cold milk and bread sprinkled with sugar. Short cut recipe for French toast. "How'd evarthin go taday Patsy?"

"It went fine Dad; I just did what mom does."

"Ahm mitey sprised how ya dun ere today, frum now own u kin watch em evar Saterdey."

"Bobby helped me dad. He watched Carole and I watched Sharon, he's a good helper."

"Ya doan say? Ah mite haf ta git that boy a bysickle n let 'im git out an start earnin 'is keep."

So, my little brother got a bicycle and rode around the neighborhood selling flower seeds. He came home with pockets full of nickels and from then on, we went door to door together. Him on his bike, me on the other side of the street on roller skates.

MISS DELLA

Our neighbor Miss Della was a smaller version of Dolly Parton, a sweet southern lady with so much charm she could charm bees out of their own honey. Never failing to make my mother smile she called her 'hooooney' ...dragging honey all over the place. Miss Della lived three doors north and often walked down to visit. In one hand carrying a pan of fresh baked pastry, a cup of coffee in the other, good smells surrounding her.

"Seems I cain't getchur momma to visit Patsy, how bout chu? When you finish helping, come own down n mash own my doorbell an say howdy."

My mother wouldn't take a break, she worked nonstop and never smiled anymore. "Why don't you go over to Della's and sit with her awhile Mom? She's such a nice lady."

"I'm too busy to sit Patsy. You go visit her, she's lonesome and needs company. Maybe she'll stop bugging me if you stop and see her now and then." Miss Della's house smelled like fresh lemons. The wood floors were waxed to a high shine and everything was in its place. She didn't have any kids, just nice furniture. "Got me a new record player n sum hillbilly music Patsy, what cha say...u wanna hear sum?" One song after another she played her favorite country music. I'd stop by her house just to say, "Howdy Miss Della," and she'd invite me in to hear another record. Then shoo me off with fresh baked cinnamon rolls for my mother. Miss Della's favorite singer was Patsy Cline. Lyrics filled the air, and she sang along to the song. "Come own Patsy sing with me!" she coaxed until my frog and I sang. "Sing louder honey!" she coaxed until I sang louder. "Crazy. I'm crazy for feeling so lonely. I'm crazy for feeling so blue."

"Yer doin good hoooony. Someday you'll find that sweet voice of yourn and you'll be singing the likes of Miss Patsy Cline. She ain't got nuthin on you sugar. Jess keep on singin hooooney." To an impressionable kid, Miss Della was special. She wore red lipstick and flowery dresses, and always smelled like lemons and cinnamon. "Didn't you stop at Della's after school today, Patsy?" "Yes, I did Mom, but she didn't bake anything today."

"That's too bad, I was hoping you'd bring something home. Maybe I'll find time later to make those little cinnamon bites you kid's like so much. Did you have a nice time with Miss Della?" "Yes mom, we sang again. She says someday I'll sing like Patsy Cline." "That's nice Patsy. Take your sisters out now for some fresh air so they'll sleep good later."

THANKSGIVING

It was almost turkey day and kids in school were talking about going to grandma and grandpas for Thanksgiving. It made me sad because we had four chances to get a grandma or grandpa and didn't even get one. Mom's parents were dead. Dads were back in Kentucky. Thanksgiving morning, I woke to quiet. Not a sound could be heard coming from the kitchen. Why wasn't mom calling me to help cut up stuff for her special turkey stuffing? I padded down the stairs following my nose. Looked in the oven, no turkey. That's ok, a stuffed chicken is good too. Looked in the refrigerator but there was nothing. Not even a bony old left over. I waited all day for that chicken to show up. It was going to make a late appearance. It had to. Today was Thanksgiving. The hours ticked by and still there were no good smells coming from the kitchen. Where's that damn chicken? I'm getting mad now. I'm hungry. Finally, we were called to supper. My stomach fell to my toes at the sight of a lonely bowl of beans in each person's place. I took one look at those sad looking beans and decided I wasn't eating them. Not today. And maybe not ever again. My stomach was growling but it didn't matter. No beans! I knew I better have a good reason for not eating what was on the table, or I was in trouble. We had to be grateful for what we got, because children in other parts of the world were starving. That was sad, but I didn't see how other parts of the world related to my eating or not. The kids at my school are having turkey, mashed potatoes, and cranberry sauce, with their grandma and grandpa today. It's bad enough we don't have a grandma or grandpa, now we gotta eat beans. This is a bad day! I'm not eatin no beans. If kids in other worlds can starve, so can I. Boy my sisters are being awfully quiet about this, but their eyes are saying yuk, dumb ole beans again. Geez look at Bobby. He's chowing down. He gobbled his up already and is eyeing mine. Well, he can have them all. "I'm not hungry Dad, can Bobby have my beans?"

"S matter Patsy, think yer too good ta eat beans wif th rest of us?"

"Gosh no dad, I'm not good, I have a stomachache. Can I please leave the table?"

"Go own then, but git back here n do yer job cleenin up when we're dun."

DREAMS OF BEING AN ACTRESS

Bobby and I took our earnings from selling garden seeds again and went to the movies. This time we agreed to see the pretty ladies on the billboard. Jane Russell and Marilyn Monroe were wearing hot pink dresses and singing 'diamonds are a girl's best friend.' All the way home I told Bobby about my dream. I was going to be an actress and a singer and have diamonds coming out my ears. It was all I could think about and talk about. I was going to be an actress! Eagerly I joined the choir at school. Saturday was a good time to practice while mom and dad were grocery shopping, and the kids were taking naps. Bobby fell asleep on the couch, so I stopped singing. "Why did you stop singing Patsy?" "Because I didn't want to wake you up Bobby." "That's ok Patsy, sing some more. It was real nice, it put me to sleep." After that I went around the house singing all the time dreaming the dream. Until dad had something to say about it. "U bess git thm crazy notions outcher head. Ya cain't sing an ya ain't gunna be no actriss. U ain't gitten up own no stage makin no fool a me. Stop yer damn singin!" I quit the choir.

A ONE KID SHOW

In third grade we were given an assignment in art class. Divide into groups, elect a captain, and choose a theatrical project. As captain I suggested we put on a play. The next day I brought one of the children's classic storybooks from home. One story had always fascinated me. The others liked it so we decided to use it for the play. Everyone parts were chosen, and I copied each script doing it all in longhand, which became several nights of homework. We practiced our parts, and it went without saying they should memorize their lines. The day of the play arrived with much anticipation. Overall excitement ran throughout the school. Other groups went on stage making their theatrical debut, then it was our turn. Everything started out good. It was a great feeling being lost in bigger than me. But somewhere along the lines the worst thing that could happen, happened. One kid forgot his lines. We stood and waiting forever, but nothing came from him. Something had to be done. I turned my back to the audience and whispered his lines to him, but the red-faced kid refused to speak. To make things worse, stage fright was a catchy disease. It spread to another kid. And there we were, withering under the bright lights of Broadway while the audience waited. Then we waited some more. What am I going to do now? I'm the only one   up here who knows everybody's lines. I started whispering his lines to him too. Surely sooner or later they'd catch on, but they looked so scared I thought they'd peed their costume. They're not ever going to speak. Now what'll I do? The show must go on. Sister Mary's face filled with stern disappointment. Oh no, she's mad. I must do something about this! Improvisation was born. There I was. A one kid show. A hundred years later the play came to, 'The End.'

"How did your play go at school today, Patsy? my mother inquired when I got home. "It was sooooo awful, two kids forgot their lines and everybody got confused and I got stuck saying them all. It was the worst thing ever. Now I'll never get to be an actress!" At first my mother tried not to laugh but it got the best of her. She laughed until I nearly cried. "What's so funny Mom? I'm going to get an E and flunk art class! Nobody's ever flunked art! Besides that, dad's really going to be mad because he told me not to get on a stage."

"I'm sorry for laughing Patsy. I wasn't laughing at you." "Geez Mom- who were you laughing at then? No one else is here." "Don't worry Patsy, it'll be ok. I'll talk to your dad." Then she started laughing all over again. Boy, I'll never understand my mother. She laughs when she's not supposed to, and cries when she's supposed to laugh. When report cards came out, I was afraid to open it. But there it was, an A plus with three stars after it! How did that happen? Well, I'm not asking. Maybe I'm not an actress and maybe I'm not a singer. But someday I'll have a good job and travel everywhere.

MOM VISITS DELLA

"Della made me promise to go there today, Patsy. Maybe those ladies will stop pestering me to visit them if I go this time. I don't know where they find the time to talk, talk, talk. I can't get anything done when she comes here. I won't be gone long. Help your dad to watch the kids."

I was happy mom was finally taking a break with the nice neighbor ladies. Every time I passed their house, they asked about her. They always seem so concerned. Wonder if they know about us. Wonder if they heard the yelling and windows rattling. Yeah, those ladies know about us.

After mom was gone a while, dad told me to go check on her. I skipped down to Della's hoping she had cinnamon rolls and rang her doorbell. The laughter inside was so loud no one heard so I went to the side door and went in. then waited in the kitchen for someone to see me. Boy is that my mother laughing so loud, I never heard her laugh like that. She's wearing red lipstick too. Gosh my mother is beautiful!

"Tell another joke ladies, and let's make Stella laugh some more." One lady called as I waited quietly, watching my mother being happy and felt happy because she was. "Ladies! Your attention please! We have a child in the room now, so watch what you say." All the joking came to an abrupt stop, as well as my mother's laughter. It was so disappointing. "Oh, hello Patsy, I didn't see you come in honey. Why are you here, are the kids all right?" "Dad said I should come and check on you Mom." "Tell your dad he doesn't have to worry about me one bit, I'm having a good time over here!" She replied gaily and all the ladies roared with laughter.

What's so funny about that, I wondered turning to leave and noticed the big pile of baby gifts in the corner. Wonder why Miss Della has all that baby stuff. She doesn't have a baby. Is she going to get one? As I walked back home a knowing hit me. Oh no! It's us! We're the ones getting another baby! I cried right there on the sidewalk in broad daylight. Where were we going to put another one?

Later the ladies walked mom home with all the presents from her surprise baby shower. "Where are we going to put another baby Mom?" "I should've known you'd start with your questions as soon as you found out Patsy. Just wait and you'll see." "Geez o Mom, this makes six kids. Is this going to be the last?" "Stop Patsy. You're too young to be wondering about things like that." What kind of answer is that? Why doesn't my mother explain stuff?

MEN'S JOBS AND WOMEN'S JOBS

Cleaning was always going on in our house, it never stopped. It started as soon as my mother woke up, until the kids went to bed. Then she darned socks. On laundry days we used a big potbellied washer in the basement filled with boiling hot water and Tide. The clothes sloshed around a half hour until every germ was dead, then mom fished them out with a wood dowel. She pushed them through the wringer to remove soapsuds and they tumbled into the cement sink where she rinsed them by hand. Then back they went through the wringer to squeeze out the water. When all that happy stuff was done, she shook each piece with gusto to take out some of the wrinkles. Weather permitting, we hung them on the clothesline in the backyard. My mother was a fresh air fiend and preferred drying them outside. Bobby's job was to watch the little ones while we did the laundry. If it started to rain, there was a mad dash bringing the clothes inside. Then down the basement we'd go to hang them on a different clothesline. Women's work was never done. There was men's work, and there was women's work. Men didn't belong in the kitchen. That was a woman's job. The men did lawn mowing and leaf raking, shoveling snow, hauling furniture, car fixing, or anything to do with a toolbox. My mother never learned to drive. She stayed home and raised babies. That was her job. Mom made me feel important in the care of my sisters, encouraging my efforts. Working alongside her was our time. The times when I felt loved. "Put some lipstick on Mom."

"Why would I do that you silly kid, I'm working now." "You look happy when you wear red lipstick." "Don't be silly Patsy, let's hurry and finish this, then you can take the kids out for fresh air, so they'll sleep good again tonight. Thank goodness I have you. You're my other pair of hands."

My mother taught us there was a right way and a wrong way to do a job. Do it right the first time and you don't have to do it again. She was the original Mrs. Clean, insisting we wash the floors on hands and knees to clean the corners and baseboards. When her stomach got big, I was stuck doing it alone. Boy, she needs this exercise more than I do. "Ah hear ya grumblin n thar Patsy, stop b for ah git ma belt. You'll git sum help when Carole n Sharon git old nuff. Keep quiet n do yer werk if ya know what's good fer ya." "Yes Dad." As soon as each sister reached the kitchen counters, they were old enough. "U girls kin git n thar n hep out now, yer big nuff now an doan b sayin ya doan know how, it ain't no scuse. Larn fass or Ah'l git ma belt out." The belt was always a motivator, scaring he be gee bees out of everybody. Mom became the softie. "I'm glad I have you girls to work with me. Someday you'll be cooking in your own kitchens for your husbands." I bet you'll never see me cooking beans and cornbread in my house.

BABY LINDA

"Leevin u in charge again Patsy, me n yer muther goin visitin the hospital." Guess I was supposed to know by osmosis they were going to get a baby. I figured they were going to visit someone. Just because my mother's stomach grew didn't mean I connected the dots. How would I know a baby was in there? I figured she got fatter that's all. Then dad came home without mom and said they had a surprise for me. I figured it was shoes or something like that. But a few days later he brought mom back home. In her arms was another pink bundle. Surprise!

The new baby's birthday was Memorial Day and baby Linda was cuter than a June bug. We peeked inside the pink blanket, and she laughed! That's right. This adorable baby with twinkling blue eyes and curly black hair laughed at us. "Isn't it the sweetest thing you ever heard? Bebe is laughing again. Bebe Ange Cherie," auntie murmured at our bundle of joy. "Maybe this one looks like Patsy eh Sis?""Aww, does she really? Let me hold her Auntie. It's my turn now."

Oh my gosh they still haven't figured out where we're going to put her. There aren't enough beds in this house. I knew this was gonna happen, I knew it. At the very last minute they've decided to go buy a bunk bed. "A Bunk Bed! Why do we need a bunk bed? She's only a baby!" "Never mind Patsy. Wait and you'll see when we get back." Later the bunk beds came through the front door and worrywart started. "How are we gonna keep the baby on a bunk bed Mom?"

"Just wait Patsy and you'll see." Patience was not one of my virtues. I followed the procession of bunk beds up the stairs glumly, my busy little mind ready to explode. This is so stupid. Putting a baby up here. I'll have to stay awake all night watching so she doesn't roll off the bed. "Holy cow Mom, we won't even be able to talk up here or we'll wake the baby up."

"Don't be a silly goose Patsy. The baby's going to sleep downstairs in Rosemary's crib." "So, where's little Rosie going to sleep then Mom?" "She's coming up here with all of you." "Geez o Petes Mom, that makes five blanket hogs in one dumb ole bed." "Stop Patsy! Why do you think we got the bunk beds?" "So, who gets to sleep on the bunk beds then Mom?" "You and Bobby because you're both getting bigger and need your own beds. Carole and Sharon and Rosemary will sleep in the big bed." "But what about blankets......

"Stop yer yammerin Patsy!" Dad barked. "Whatcha doin up ere enyways? Nobody tolt ya ta come ere. Yer spose ta b watchin them kids. Git back downstairs n sen Bobby up here on the dubble with ma toolbox. Ah need 'is hep settin this thang up.

As soon as baby Linda could walk, she was dancing, then she was climbing trees. Years later she could be found alone in her room drawing cartoons, for which she had a natural given ability.

ANOTHER FLEETING DREAM

"Young Authors Wanted. Top dollars paid." The ad in the magazine popped off the page. "Searching for young writers. Send your stories to Dreams Come True Publishing Company and become a published writer. Make big money."

Oh my gosh, this is it! This will save us. I'll give the money to mom, and she can leave dad, and nobody will ever get beat up again. Within days I finished writing a story and walked to the post office and mailed it. Every day I rushed home from school to check the mailbox before anyone else. Surely a response was coming soon. One day there it was an envelope with my name on it, the publishers name in the top left corner.

"Dear Miss, thank you for submitting your recent story in our search for new author's. We regret ...at this time...did not meet... send other stories .... dada, dada, dada... and so on, and so on." Poof. Another dream bites the dust. They want me to send more stories. How am I supposed to do that? There isn't time to do anything except take care of babies. We're stuck here forever. Bobby's getting beat up all the time. Will my little sisters be next? Why doesn't mom do something about dads drinking and beating us up? I want to run away but who will protect them?

One day mom was complaining to me about him. "Why don't you just leave him Mom?" "And just where do you think I'm going to go with all these kids Miss Smarty?" "We'll find a place Mom. I'll help you." "It's not that easy Patsy. It's easy to say but doing it is another story."

As far back as I can remember, I was never comfortable around dad. Instinct told me to watch out. I knew what was coming whenever my mother said something he didn't like. Why didn't she know that? Why couldn't she see what I saw? She would speak up and he'd start hitting her. The next thing I knew I'd be in the middle, waving my arms frantically, trying to stop it. "Damn crazy lil bear. Gunna gitcher block knocked off one theez times. Caint ya see what goes on in here Patsy? Yer muther starts all theez fights."

"It doesn't matter who starts it! It's not right to hit!" I yelled back and amazingly the fight stopped. After that they started coming to ask my advice. "Your dad said this Patsy what should I tell him?" "Yer muther sed tht Patsy why don'tcha talk ta er? Ah'll b damned but she lissens ta u. She sho doan lissen ta me."

Please God, make someday come faster so I can get away from here. I wish, I wish, I wish, for a prince like the one who found Cinderella. Please make him kind, and handsome, and funny, and smart but please don't make him be nothing like dad.

ANOTHER MYSTERY TRIP

He was slapping aftershave on in the mirror, talking to himself; "Yer a handsome devil." Uh oh, he's up to something and mom's not going to like this. He slipped quietly into his room. Minutes later he was out, dressed in a suit, white shirt and tie. I knew it. Wait till mom sees this. Sure enough, she appeared from out of nowhere. "Why are you dressed like that Leonard? Where's your factory uniform?" He ignored her and strutted toward the door. She ran ahead to stop him. "Where are you going Leonard? Please don't leave." She scuffled with him at the door. Each time he opened it, she pushed it shut with all her hundred ten pounds. "No Leonard don't go," she pleaded. He wasn't smiling anymore. His eyes had grown mean, yet she kept trying to stop a man dead set on leaving. My mother was going to get hurt again! "Let him go Mom! I screamed and they stopped scuffling, surprised to see me there. "Lissen ta yer daughter n stop acting th fool," he shouted and swept her aside like a rag doll. The door slammed shut behind him, the sound reverberating in my head. My mother slumped against it and slipped quietly to the floor. Defeated. "Stand up Mom! Stand up! Why do you let him treat you like this?" I yelled at her, but my mother just stared at me, her eyes dark with sadness. Forever passed before she answered. "You don't understand Patsy." "Yes, I do, Mom, you have to leave him!" I yelled louder this time, so she would hear me. "I can't leave Patsy" she answered softly.

There it was again. Her patient defeat. It drove me crazy. "Nobody will ever treat me like this!" I screamed at the top of my lungs and started running. Running from being disciplined. Running from the shame of yelling at my poor defenseless mother. Running from the guilt of breaking the fourth commandment; 'Honor thy father and thy mother.' God was going to punish me for that. I was a bad kid. I committed a mortal sin because I knew it was wrong. I ran faster so God couldn't catch me. I ran until I reached the quiet little field. Alone at last to think.

My life will is never going to be like my mother's. I will not live the way she does. She says actions speak louder than words. Dad's actions don't show love. She begs him to stay but he leaves. That means he doesn't love her. Why does she want someone who doesn't love her? I'll never stay with someone who doesn't love me. I'll never ask a man for anything. If he doesn't offer it first, I won't take anything from him. I'll take care of myself!

It was my defining moment. The decision that would rule my entire life.

PILLSBURY DOUGH BOYS

Two babies were rolling around on the bed laughing, baby powder flying everywhere. "Stop wasting all that powder Patsy, it doesn't come free you know." "They look like the Pillsbury Dough Boy with all that powder on them, Mom. They're so sweet and funny. I love babies. Look how cute they are. I love how they smell, don't you?" "You're such a good kid Patsy. I don't know what I'd do without you." "Gee thanks Mom."

 Maybe she gave me more credit than I deserved. The fact is when dirty diaper time rolled around, I did my best to get out of dodge. Sometimes if I was lucky, a tell- tale warning would come over a beet red little face, and that was all I needed to see. I was off to the basement or outdoors for air. My mother could be heard grumbling through an open window. "Where'd that kid go the minute I need her? Patseeee...I need you for a minute honey."

Oh brother, now she calls me honey. "Ok Mom, be there in another minute." Maybe I'll be lucky, and it'll all be done. Boy something needs to be done about those dirty diapers. We have to dunk that junk in the toilet and boil those things in the washing machine. How gross is that? Why can't we just throw them in the garbage? Well, everybody knows what happened after I put that thought out into the universe. Somebody grabbed it and made disposable diapers. Oh brother, I could've been filthy rich.

PROMOTED TO BOSS

Weekends were becoming the same, Saturdays meant they were going grocery shopping. "U keep thez kids n line Patsy, sum buddy's gotta do it. Yer th oldest so yer th boss. An yer guuna be doin it frum now own. Bobby yer next n line so make em do rite. U kids hear me?" "Yes Dad, we hear you." "Yer both gunna git skinned alive if theez girls git in trouble, U hear me?" "Yes Dad, you told us that before and we didn't forget it." Bobby and I didn't want any part of that. We would do a good job that's for sure. And since I was going to have to boss all these girls around every weekend, I figured I better start practicing and getting good at it. But one day dad stopped me short. "Yer gittin mitey damn bossy roun 'ere. Who ya thank ya are?" "Geez Dad you told me to be the boss and keep them in line because I'm the oldest." "Did ah say that? Well ah b damn but ah think yer rite. U wuz lisnen weren't cha? All ritey then, u keep own bein th boss buy a best member who th 'real' boss is here. U hear me?" "Yes Dad, I hear you." "Who's the boss n this house Patsy?" "You are Dad." "Thas rite. Ah'm the boss. Yer muther ain't no boss. U keep em in line cause ah sed so."

Boy I'm a boss now. Guess that means me and mom are partners.

TOO MANY BABIES

"Oh no! Not another baby Mom. Isn't six enough? Now it'll be seven. Where are we going to put one this time? Geez o Pete, there's no room in here already."

"Stop Patsy, I can count you know. I might try and fit another crib next to Linda's. That way the babies will be together in the same room. It won't be so hard this time. You'll see."

"Geez Mom is this the last one this time? All I do is take care of babies. I can't even go out and roller skate anymore. I want to be alone sometime but there's always a little kid hanging on me."

"Don't talk that way Patsy! It sounds so mean when you talk like that. I know you love your little sisters; you're always hugging and kissing them."

"I love them forever and ever but why do we keep getting more? They're too much work for you and me Mom. We can't keep up with them anymore. And dad said there's not enough to take care of them now."

"I told you not to listen when your dad says crazy things."

"How do I know if it's crazy or not Mom? He says there's not enough to feed them!"

"There'll always be enough Patsy. Jesus fed thousands with two fish and five loaves of bread."

"But we're not Jesus, and babies can't eat fish and bread, they don't have teeth."

"What am I going to do with you Patsy? Why can't you be like the other kids and laugh. You've got to stop worrying or you'll get wrinkles before your time like I did. God will always provide a way. Have faith Patsy. Pray and you'll see. It's all going to be ok."

BABY NANCY

Like before dad came back from the hospital alone and like before this ten-year-old still didn't know about the birds and bees. Why did it take my mother so long to pick out a baby at the hospital? "Where's Mom, Dad?"

"She be comin along. We dun picked out cutest lil tike ah air did see, two days afta ma birfday, funny lil valentine girl. Don't it beat all."

Mom arrived home with baby Nancy wrapped in the famous pink blanket. Her personality popped out from under that silly pink thing, she wanted out of there to play with the other kids. A shock of red hair and bright blue eyes snapped above a sprinkling of freckles skipping across her cute nose. In no time at all, little Nancy was climbing out of that crib not bothering to toddle around like the rest of the girls. The little tomboy just climbed over everything in the house, laughing with the impish charm she held over all. Soon she and Linda were running outside, climbing trees together.

THE FIELD OF FLOWERS

"Got terrrrble news fer this household, jest terrrrble. The ole boys dun let us off today n it ain't no layoff. The factree's closin down tighter'n a drum."

"My God Leonard! What will we do if you don't get another job right away? We barely make it from paycheck to paycheck as it is."

"Ah ben out checkin awreddy. Went ever whars n nobody's hirin. Gotta git thm kids out a that spensive skool first thang n mornin. Cain't give tht skool a nuther nickel. Gotta turn ma car back ta th factree. Wone b long fer th bank's gonna pull ths house frum us. We gotta rent a house. Now who th hells gonna rent ta seven kids? Why'd we go off n have all theez babies? Now what ama gunna do ta put food on this table?"

"Something good is bound to happen Leonard, you'll see," My mother said, tears in her eyes. The look of despondency on their faces was frightening. "Longest damn day evar wuz, Ah need me a drink!" He exclaimed, dashing out the door.

"What's going to happen to us Mom?" "Pray Patsy. Just pray and don't worry. Go talk to God."

Without another word I walked out of the house heading for my quiet field. The sound of a far-off train whistle blew. Not even Uncle Charlie and his buffalo nickels could help us this time. The day was gray and bleak, without a trace of sun. As I approached the field, all was quiet but for the sound of dried underbrush snapping beneath my feet. I shuffled along feeling the weight of the world on my shoulders, head down, tears in my eyes. Blinking through my tears I started seeing patches of green on the underbrush. Then a few tiny pink flowers appeared along the path and with each step I took there were more. The path grew wider, and the sun began to rise over my head. It grew brighter and brighter until suddenly I was standing in a field of flowers. Glorious flowers of every variety and color were growing side by side. I twirled around in a circle, and they were all around me as far as my eyes could see! "Oh my God they're everywhere! How did they get out here?" I asked out loud and started to laugh. "How did all these flowers grow in this field? Who's taking care of them? Nobody lives out here! There's no houses anywhere!" I continued to ask but all was still. There was no sound whatsoever. Only absolute peace over a splendor of flowers, sun and sky touching the horizon. I stayed amidst the wondrous sight in waist high flowers an unknown amount of time. Then slowly began to walk amongst them, until it seemed as though I'd walked out of the circle. Sudden knowing came over me. 'Mom is very sad and wants me home right now!' I ran all the way as fast as I could go.

"Oh, thank God there you are! Thank God you're ok! I was so afraid something happened to you! Where were you Patsy? Why did you go so long? Don't ever do that again! You have to tell me where you're going so, I know where you are!"

"Ok Mom, next time I will. You told me to go talk to God, so I went to the little field and it's full of flowers today! All different kinds of flowers growing together! You need to see them! Please go with me now and s...."

"Stop Patsy, I need to fix supper now. I was so worried about you I forgot to start it, and the kids are acting fussy because they're hungry. I need to hurry to get it ready. Take Bobby with you tomorrow to see the flowers." "But Mom you have to s.." "No but's Patsy just peel the potatoes and set the table. You can go tomorrow with Bobby." The next day Bobby and I walked out to the field, but there were no flowers in sight. I persuaded him to walk back a second time, but all around was nothing but a dry barren field. There were no flowers to be found anywhere. Not a single solitary one. "Maybe they're further out Bobby but I thought they were right here in this field."

"There's no use walking around out there any more Patsy, there's no flowers anywhere." "Honest to God, they were here Bobby, a

47

whole field of them, and all different kinds too!" "Well, they're not here today Patsy and I'm not going to keep walking back and forth. You've never lied to me so if you say you saw them, then you saw them. I believe you. I don't know how that could happen, but I believe you anyway." "Thank you, Bobby."

I never forgot how I felt when my brother believed what he couldn't see. Extraordinary things were going to happen in our lives that others may find hard to believe. Out of the ordinary happenings aren't easy to comprehend, or even to explain. Yet I no longer question them, I just know they happened. Though the reasoning is beyond me, it doesn't matter. I still believe. Someday I hope to return to the field of flowers.

LAST DAYS AT ST JOSEPH'S

Sometime afterwards day dad came home in an old brown Chrysler, with a back seat big enough for a whole flock of kids. "It doesn't look bad at all Leonard," mom smile but dad just shook his head sadly. "Too bad th factree hadda close. Sho wuz good workin thar, Ah'm gunna miss em." "Was your job fun Dad?" "Ah liked workin fer thm ole boys at GM they wuz good to th workin man Patsy."

The next morning the whole family piled into the new/old car, and we all went to school. "It sho was nice what that princple sed when Ah tried pullin r kids out a skool. Sed she wants ta keep em rest th year so's not to mess up thar good grades. An she doan spect us ta pay a nuther nickel cuz ah lost ma job. Sed God would spec St. Joe ta do that. Nary herd a nicer thang n all ma days. Then she went n sed she's prouda all of em an that jess beat evar thang Stella Bee!"

"Yes, that was very nice to hear Leonard. You see now? I always told you to thank God our kids were doing so good in that school." "That's what ya keep sayin Stell, but now we gotta ask 'im ta git sum buddy lined up ta rent a house ta all theez kids. ""That's not the way you ask God for his help Leonard." "Well u go own n ask him, seein u know how to do it, cuz we sho need help."

A CHANGE OF MIND

Right around this time the fifth-grade class was getting ready to make the sacrament of Confirmation. Someone other than a parent, had to stand as my sponsor so I asked another neighbor who had befriended my mother. Dorothy and her brother lived a few houses away from us, taking care of their old mother as was the custom in their country of Romania. The custom when making your Confirmation is to add a saint's name to your given name. When my mother asked what name I picked, she seemed shocked at my choice. "Why did you pick 'that' name?" "Dorothy told me about Saint Bernadette, and that's her confirmation name, so I took it too."

Later mom and I walked to the little thrift store to find a dress for me for this event. The pretty pink dress was lovely but itchy and uncomfortable. Mom said I looked pretty so I was happy with itchy. Holy Confirmation didn't stick to me like that dress. Sometime afterwards I came home from school greatly distressed.

"The priest came into our classroom today, Mom. He said we can eat meat on Friday again. I've been thinking about t all day. For five years they said it was a mortal sin to eat meat on Friday. Now it's not a sin. I never had a bite of meat on Friday's because I didn't want to go to hell. I thought it was God's rule, but they made it up. I'm not going to be a Catholic anymore because they make their own rules." My poor mother looked like she was going to faint, but she sure recovered fast. "You shut that mouth of yours right now! You don't understand the rules. You'll go to church with me every Sunday if I need to drag you there! And you'll be quiet about it too, or I'll wash your mouth out with soap again!" I went along quietly, wondering why they could change the rules, but I couldn't change my mind.

THE WORRYWART

Oh my gosh summer's over and all I did was sell garden seeds with Bobby. We lost summer! How did that happen? Mom's stomach

49

is getting big again and she can't help scrub the floors. School starts soon and we don't know where we're going. We don't even know where we're going to live. This is terrible. we're all going to flunk out of school! Worrywart just kept fretting and fretting, until the issue was finally addressed."We got no time lef in ths house. The banks puttin us out awreddy. We gunna be livin n the yard, wakin up n cain't brush r teeth. All our thangs out on th lawn fer th nabors ta see."

"Shut up you fool you're scaring her. She listens to everything you say. Can't you see that?"

Dad raised his jumbo-sized beer wrapped in a brown paper sack and toasted merrily. "To the great outdoors! Whasa matter Patsy, doncha wanna live outside?" "No Dad winters coming.:" "Whasa matter u scareda lil cold?" "It's going to be freezing outsidee Dad, there'll be snow and ice on everything." "Nah we ain't gunna live outside Patsy. We're gunna b outa here for that bank kin put u kids out'n th snow. Wer pickin a 'ouse ta day n yer new skool starts nex week. Ah reckon wer gunna take th house wif th big yard fer u kids ta run roun in. But yer muther ain't too happy with tht ole house. She doan like it." Now I was worrying another bone. Oh no, we're going someplace even mom doesn't like. "Stop it Leonard. Why do you keep telling her things when you know she thinks about every little thing you say? Stop telling her things she doesn't need to know."

TAYLOR

Leaving Y and Dot was the end of childhood as I knew it. The move to Taylor happened on a broiling hot day. Everyone who could walk carried things to the truck. When it was piled high with furniture, we were ready to go. We drove behind in our new/old car. Don't know who drove the truck but it didn't drive itself. So, picture this. A tired bunch of dirty faced, smelly people on the edge of crabby, slaphappy. "Keep a watch own that mountain up yonder, Ah doan want nuthin ta fall off kiddies. We cain't afford ta lose nuthin else. Ya got dirt on yer face Stella Bee, ya look like hell."

That's when all the fun started. "Take a look at yourself old man. You don't look so good either." They looked at each other then turned to check us out. "Well Ah'll be dad gum if this family doan look like a pack a wild heathen!" He wisecracked and us kids were delighted with the new word. "You're a wild heathen!" "You're in this family so you're a wild Heathen too." "Sooo, you're dirtier than me." "Sooo, you're bigger than me so you're a bigger wild Heathen." "Sooo... you're dirty all over cause you're smaller; you little wild Heathen."

"Too bad we hadda leave that new furness, we jest paid off Stella Bee. That greedy bank's gitten it after they went n pooshed us out so fass. We shooda brung it wif us." "Don't be foolish Leonard, what would we do with an extra furnace?" A bunch of overtired, hungry kids started laughing themselves silly about bringing a furnace along. "Ah shood a thot a sumthin so's that bank dint git thar grubby paws own it." We found that even funnier, so dad rubbed his chin thinking hard to come up with funnier. "Ah got a humdinger idee, too bad dint think it up sooner. Ah could a painted it red, n put it out yonder fer kids ta play own. Evar kid n th naborhood wood come runnin ta play on it!" That was it. We collapsed in a fit of laughter, laughing all the way to the new/old house. As we pulled in the driveway mom tried her best to quiet us. "You have to stop laughing so loud kids, the new neighbors are going to think we're crazy!"

"The hell with the nabors Stella Bee, aint it the truth? Go own kids, laugh yer ass off."

"You dirty mouth thing! Teaching the kids to laugh at that. You shameless man." That little exchange sent us over the top, nothing could stop our laughter now. "Stop saying things to make them laugh more Leonard and help me get them in the house. They need to eat so they can stop laughing. The neighbors already know there's definitely something wrong with our crazy bunch." She was so serious we couldn't stand it. Now we were hysterical with laughter as we tumbled out of the car next to a small white house greeting modestly. The huge yard held several weeping willow trees, surrounded by hedges. My first sobering thought was; who's going to mow all of this grass?'

PUBLIC SCHOOL

The new school was an adventure that we weren't prepared for. We stood out like sore thumbs in our old uniforms, while other kids were styling, acting cool. I didn't quite know what to make of it. By the time we got home I'd made a decision. "Everyone needs to quit calling me Patsy. Call me Pat from now on." "I'll call you Pat if you call me Bob. No more Bobby stuff for me either." "Ok Bob, it's a deal."

After five years of strict regimen and stern disciplinarians, the new school was culture shock. All around was new freedom of expression. It was shocking to hear kids cursing out loud. That was something I only did in my head. Right or wrong I found it funny because they got away with it. The crazy humor I learned at home was akin to our new school. In our house being a little crazy meant survival. If you didn't have it, you better get some. Crazy was essential when dealing with an angry drunk person. If you were crazy enough to make him laugh, you might not get hurt. When he was sober his sense of humor was wickedly funny. Or so I thought. But my mother got spitting mad at both of us. Somehow, I was supposed to know better. Go figure. If I laughed at one of his off-color jokes, she made me scrub the kitchen floor again.

So, there we were in a new school with mean kids. I missed the small school I knew like the back of my hand. Where we'd played at recess on a small playground between the Rectory and the Convent. Where I knew my brother and sister's classrooms were a few feet from mine. Where there was a security blanket of nuns watching with eyes in the back of their heads. We were on our own now. Painfully aware of being gawked at in our old uniforms from St Joseph's. One afternoon Carole and Sharon came to me on the huge playground, tears rolling out of big blue eyes, splashing onto their white blouses. Some kids had been yelling mean things at them about how they were dressed. That's it! They can yell at me, and I'll give them the finger but they're not gonna yell at my little sisters. "Show me which kids yelled at you, I'll shut them up!" But Sharon stopped Carole from telling me. She knew when big sister got mad, no telling what she'd say. They were usually easy going, unlike motor mouth big sister. I thought about it and realized if I went after those kids, my sisters would be embarrassed. So, I went to mom instead. "We can't get any new clothes now Pat, maybe later. Tell those mean kids I'll go see their mothers if they bother your sisters again."

The curriculum was further behind in my new play school environment. Suddenly I knew all the answers and thought I was an overnight genius. Before long it caught up and passed me while I was daydreaming. Report cards came out, my grades dropped from As to Cs. "U bess git thm grades back up, or yer next whippin'll be one n inch frum yer life." I went to school with welts on my legs and arms. Everybody stared, but nobody said a word.

BIG BULLY

One morning dad warned us to stick together at the bus stop. The warning came timely. One big kid and his bobble-head friends had been pestering everyone. Now they were eyeing the insignia on Bob's shirt proclaiming St. Joseph. The Bully circled us several times giving us creepy looks like he was King Tut or somebody. "Hey Bob-bee! Why you wearing that ugly shirt every day Bob-bee? What does it say?" "My name's Bob. And it's none of your business what I wear. Or what is says on my shirt." "Come here and say that you little punk."

"Aw why'd you have to answer him, Bob? Don't go there or you'll be in trouble with dad again." Lucky for us, the bus showed up just in time. "Get on the bus girls, quick. Come on Bob! Stop looking back at him." "I'm waiting to see what he's gonna do Pat." "GET ON THE BUS NOW!" "Boy you really got a mouth on you Pat." "Just shut up and get on the damn bus!"

The next day Big Bully and his friends started closing in needling us. "Just ignore them Bob, talk to us and don't listen. Stick together, the bus will be here soon." "What's the matter Bob-beeeee? Your ugly sister afraid to fight?"

The day came when we were last off the bus, and they were waiting. We descended the steps and Bully and his friends started toward us. Let's get that little punk." Unbeknownst to them our dog Tricks was waiting too. "Sic em Tricks! Get em! Bite em Tricks, bite em!" Our big, little dog stood his ground, hair on end, baring sharp pointed teeth, "Grrrrr, Grrrrrrrrr!" Bully and friends eyed the dog and backed off. What they didn't know was Tricks never bit anyone in his life. He liked to play tricks that's all. That's how he got his name. He didn't want to fight any more than we did. "Good Boy Tricks, good boy." We walked home quietly but I could see that Bob was thinking, thinking, thinking. "I figured out what I gotta do Pat. I have to beat the biggest kid up, and the others will leave us alone after that."

Now I was very worried. There was a lot to worry about here. Bob was nearly half the size of Big Bully. Though he had more guts than a kid twice his size, he was still no match for him. But Bob wasn't concerned about that. Dad was already beating the crap out of him, so he wasn't afraid of any kid. But he was going to get both of us hurt, because if Bully laid a finger on my brother I'd have to jump in and poke his eyes out. If he could see after that, he'd flatten us like pancakes. I stayed awake all night envisioning what could happen, knowing my brother had a tough mindset and wasn't going to back off.

"Hey, we're early this morning Bob, let's walk slower to listen to the birds." My brother loved birds, but he didn't want anything to do with them that morning. "I'm on to you Pat. We don't need to be walking slower for the birds. I'm ready for that kid." "Well, I'm not ready! I don't know what to do. What if I start crying?" "You don't have to be ready. Just stay out of it Pat and don't get in my way." "You have to let that kid start the fight Bob or you're gonna get clobbered by dad too." "I don't care about that Pat, that kids gonna get my best shot from the get-go."

Looking ahead I could see Big Bully coming toward us. Uh oh, he's almost here. Think faster. How am I going to stop this? I pushed ahead of my brother. From my peripheral vision I could see his face geared up for the fight. He pushed harder trying to take the lead, but I pressed on with elbows out not letting him get past. Knowing he wasn't going to wait for Bully to get the jump on him, he was just going to haul off and slug him with all his might. Then it happened. Big Bully stopped right in front of me! I had seconds to do something before my brother got our guts splattered all over the street. I screamed the worst bully I'd ever heard. "Yer gonna git skinned alive if you don't leave us alone!" Big Bully's eyes widened in surprise. "Huh?" He muttered, then scurried away. "Why did you do that Pat? You messed me up. I'm goin after him!" Bob hissed angrily. "Oh no you're NOT! You stay here, or I'll tell dad that you started the whole thing!" My brother got so mad he turned bright red, then just as sudden he calmed down. "Nah I don't believe that Pat. You wouldn't turn on me like that, I know you. But I'm telling you right now. You better never get in front of me again. You don't know nothin about fighting so stay out of my way. That kid's gonna come back and I'll be ready for him. He's not gonna leave us alone till I fight him. I can beat him I know I can. Stop trying to talk me out of it or I'm not gonna talk to you ever again."

"Aww geez Bob, don't be mad. I didn't want you to get hurt that's all. I only got one brother. Hey, I got another idea. Let's sic little Rosie and Linda on him!"

"Stop trying to make me laugh Pat, it won't work. I'm not gonna change my mind. That kid's not gonna laugh at grasshoppers. He's a mean punk and only picks on kids smaller than him."

"Maybe he'll just leave us alone now after what I said, Bob."

"Naw, I don't believe that either Pat. But that kid thinks you're a witch, and maybe I do too!"

I started cackling loud as possible for Big Bully to hear and he looked the other way. Good I scared him, cackle, cackle, cackle, cackle. The next morning Bully's friend started toward us but he grabbed him by the arm and mumbled in his ear. What he didn't know was this little witch, heard every word he said. "Stay away from them, the big sisters a witch and skins people alive."

This time I cackled with glee. Boy I should thank dad for teaching us those words. But later that night I stayed awake worrying. Oh no, Bob's right! Big Bully's gonna come back as soon as he finds out I'm not really a witch. My brother sure is smart for a fourth grader. Somebody does need to kick Bully's butt. But not us. Bob's not big enough to do it, then the Bully's gonna come after our little sisters. Oh no! I better get Mom in on this!

"Mom I have to tell you something verrrrry verrrry important! I know we can't get new school clothes now, but we need to get a shirt for Bob. He can't wear that shirt one more day. Some big kids at the bus stop keep trying to pick a fight with him, because it says St. Joseph on it."

"My God! What kind of kids would be like that?!"

"Bad kids Mom, and Bob's gonna get clobbered Monday morning. He says he's gonna fight the biggest kid because he thinks they'll leave us alone after that. But I don't think so!"

"It's a good thing you came to me Pat. I'm going to talk to your dad about this right now."

Uh oh. What'd I do? I sure hope this turns out good or Bob's never gonna talk to me again. Later that night Mom took me aside; "Go ask the girl next door to baby sit tomorrow morning for your little sisters. The four of you are coming with us shopping."

Holy mackerel! I could hardly sleep that night from excitement. We were going shopping! The next morning, me, Bob, Carole, and Sharon, were waiting in the car long before mom and dad came out of the house.

"Ah heard tell a lil shop calt; 'A Kids Bo Teek.' Gunna fix ya all up wif clothes fer evarbuddy." We looked at each other like we got in the wrong car. We must be dreaming awake. Let's pinch each other and see. Oh my gosh we're awake. At the little store dad gave us instructions. "Go in thar n pick yer sef sum nice lookin shirts n pants yung man. U girls hep yer muther pic yers, an Ah doan wanna hear no fussin outa eny ya." Much later we ran out of that Kids Boutique, excited as a bunch of monkeys on the Fourth of July. Carrying bags and bags of clothes and shoes, even some rompers for the little kids at home. "Ah'm a happy man. Ah got a wife kin spread ma dough aroun. Lookit all theez nice thangs yer muther went a pickin. Mighty prouda u Stella Bee. U foun thangs n thar fer a nickel. Nare saw a woman culd squeeze th shit outa a buffalo nickel like u. Ya got all thez nice thangs fer a few dollars. Trunk's full n ain't nuff room n here fer me ta drive, we gunna haf ta walk home." My mother laughed out loud from all that praise. "Ahm tickled to death Stella Bee. Let's git a peachy pie ta take home fer everbuddy. We got money lef over."

"We better get going if we're getting a pizza Leonard. I still have to wash and hang all these clothes to dry so the kids can wear them to school on Monday."

"U kids best b thankin yer muther fer th good job she dun. An u dang well better git all A's n that school frum now own. That's yer job. U hear me?"

"Yes Dad, we hear you. Thank you, Mom, thank you Dad, this is the best day ever!"

They had found the best place in town to shop for kids, and I'd learned about thrifty shopping. Years later I would have a recurring dream of picking out stacks and stacks of clothes with a bunch of little kids as happy as monkeys.

Monday morning Bob was given new instructions. "Lissen up here yung man. Enybuddy takes ta botherin eny ya, u go on n beat th tar outa em. Enybuddy sez eny thang to ya- U tell em Ah tolt ya so. Tell em ta see yer ole man. U hear me?" "Yes Dad, I hear you."

Bob was far ahead of us that morning walking tall. I stayed behind, knowing he was ready for bear. Everyone at the bus stop eyed our new/old duds, then looked away. No longer interested. Except Big Bully. He made a snide remark and my big/ little brother walked right up to him. Bob stood there staring up into his eyes without saying a word. The bully kid looked down at him a few seconds, then flinched and walked away. Somehow that punk had shrunk.

The next morning while waiting for the bus, I happened to notice a brown car parked far down the street, with smoke billowing out on the driver's side. The lone figure of a man in a Fedora hat was behind the wheel. For several days afterwards it was there again, but soon as the bus came it drove away. "Hey Bob, you know what? I saw a brown car parked down our street a few times. Someone inside it was smoking like a chimney, I wonder if that was Dad." "Nah Pat, why would Dad sit on the street in his car? There's no reason for it."

"Hey Dad, I saw a car parked down the block a few times in the morning, was that you?"

"Stop mindin what u think Ah'm doin an mind what yer doin n that school n thas all. U hear?" "Yes Dad, I hear you."

"Jess keep yer eyes peeled on them kids n let me know eny buddy takes ta bothern eny ya." "Ok Dad, I will."

"That big ole boy take ta messin with yer brother eny mo?"

"No Dad, the big kid backed away from him when Bob stared him down with the old eagle eye."

"Well ah be damn, Ah dun went n made a man of 'im. Go own now Patsy n nair come questinin me agin if ya wanna stay out a trouble." After that the smoker in the hat, in the brown car, was never seen parked down the street again.

LUCKY STABLES

The house in Taylor was in the Township on a dirt road. Home styles varied greatly, there wasn't a cookie cutter among them. The city sewage system hadn't yet been installed. In fact, the house next door still had an outhouse. Day and night someone could be seen running to the pot. A half mile down the dirt road, at the very end, was an old barn. The sign said, 'Lucky Stables.' My brother and I were curious about this place. One early evening after another bean supper stomachache, we went for a walk. On reaching the mysterious barn two horses were coming out pulling a huge wagonload of hay. A group of people came out of the barn and climbed onto the wagon, jumping in the hay. The happy hayride rode past as we watched, until the sound of hooves could no longer be heard. Clip clop, clip clop, clip c....

"We saw some horses pulling a wagon full of hay and people at Lucky Stables! It sure looked like fun!"

"Whatchu doin walkin way down thar? Nuthin fer u ta see at tht place. Stay way frum thar!"

But Bob and I were curious George. The next time we happened by the barn door was open, so we walked closer. Music was playing so we went closer. A bright colorful jukebox was flashing. "Wow I never saw one of those before!" "Me neither Pat." All warning was forgotten. The jukebox was calling. "I'm goin in." "I'm goin if you're goin." We stood on the sideline watching as someone dropped a coin in the jukebox, then a couple started to dance. The music stopped and the jukebox beckoned again. We dropped our only nickel in and were trying to figure out how it worked when a loud male voice thundered. "Hey! What are you kids doing in here? Get out of here right now!" Frightened through and through we ran out, and complained all the way home how that jukebox got our nickel and we never even got a song.

THE FACTS OF LIFE

One day a boy at school yelled at me. "Hey you! You should learn the facts of life." Geez what does that mean? So back I went to the fountain of knowledge asking questions again. "Mom, a kid at school yelled at me and said I should learn the facts of life. What did he mean?" "Nice girls don't need to know that Pat." "But I don't even know the kid Mom, so why did he say that?" "Just ignore the bugger Pat, and he'll go away."

Why is everything always a secret in our house, nobody tells me nothing. Guess I'll just have to ask my little friend. "Hi Pollywog. I need to ask you something, but you can't tell anybody, ok?" "I won't." "You promise?" "I promise."

"Well, some kid yelled at me and said I should learn the facts of life. I asked my mother what it meant but she said nice girls don't need to know that."

"My mother told me Patty. I'll tell you but you can't tell anybody. Promise?"

"Cross my heart and hope to die, I promise I won't ever tell anybody. Nobody will ever know."

So Pollywog told me about secret stuff that goes on in the dark. "Eww yuk! They did 'that' every time they got another baby? Why do they keep doing that? We got enough babies already!"

The fact is none of us were ever told the facts of life. Not at home anyway. It's a wonder we survived the cardboard jungle. Maybe they figured if we didn't know we wouldn't do it. Go figure. I knew nothing about how babies grow in someone's stomach. Including how it got in there, and how it managed to crawl out. I once thought it might come out my mother's belly button. Kids who live on farms see cows make little cows, then they drop it in the hay out of somewhere. My older cousins told me that when I stayed with them on the farm that summer, but I had no idea what they were talking about. Cows making cows that dropped in the hay from somewhere. What's that about? I didn't want to be stupid, so I didn't say anything, I just listened. I was a city kid. We lived in the dark ages at our house. There was never any talk about s-e-x. It must mean something bad if they had to spell it. We didn't have a phone or a TV. One time dad got one in a thrift store, but it didn't work very well. When it did. my little sisters fell in love with Milky the Clown, we all had to watch that goofy clown. Then it was

Howdy Doody time with Buffalo Bob and Clarabelle the clown. After clown time was over, Bobby had to see Hopalong Cassidy and his horse Topper. Commercials told us; Wheaties is the breakfast of champions. Other commercials said Cheerios were better. He's got go power; there he goes! He's feeling his Cheerios. After that it was time for cartoons with Popeye the Sailor Man and his girlfriend Olive Oil. They were always the same old story. Popeye downed a can of spinach and knocked Brutus into the next world for lusting after his girlfriend Olive Oil. No kid would ever learn how babies get here watching TV shows like those. So, I watched my mother's stomach for clues. If another baby was on the way, I figured we should get ready for it. After all, I had to help take care of the little rug rat. It was only fair to let me know. That wasn't too much to ask, was it?

"Are we having another baby Mom?" "No! And stop being so nosy Miss Nosy. Mind your own business." Well, geez o Pete. I figured it was my business. Guess no one's going to tell me, so I'll just tune in to the latest news on Leonard's Inebriated Broadcast System. As sure as rain the forecast was imminent after a quart or two of booze. "Ya gotta watch yer sef theez days or a baby'll take all yer money. We gotta quit bringin babies n here. Nuther one comin n Ah cain't take care a what Ah got. Ain't got nuff fer baby food. How'm Ah gonna feed it?"

OH NO! Another baby is coming, and we can't feed it! I burst out crying. Why did I listen to the news? Now I feel worse. Where's another baby going to sleep this time? There's not enough room to walk in here already. Oh well, I guess they'll just have to get more bunk beds. There's always air space when you run out of floor space.

BABY LUCILLE

They were off to the hospital again. One year old Nancy hanging on my hip waiting for mom to come home. Sometime later dad came back. He sat down at the kitchen table and proceeded to scare me half out of my wits. "Gotta us a surprise this time Patsy, two lil

61

babies. Yer muther dun named em Lucille n Lucette. Lucky thar alive. Ah gotta git back the hospittle, yer muther hadda hard time, n might not make it." What does he mean my mother had a hard time? How can she not make it? And what could be wrong with two brand new babies? I don't believe anything he says, especially not this! "I'm going to the hospital with you Dad, I have to see Mom and the babies!"

"Jest settle down thar Patsy, they ain't letten no kid go whar yer muther is. Sides Ah need ya here watchin theez kids. U n Bobby take over, Ahl be back tomorrey." Then he was gone. I prayed out loud so God would hear. "Please help us God. Please don't let anything happen to my mother. I can't do this without her. I need her help. Please don't leave us alone with him. I couldn't stand it. Please bring my mother home with the babies."

A few days passed and Mom came home with one baby, wrapped in the famous pink blanket. Baby Lucille had dimples in her cheeks, green eyes and a shock of golden-brown hair. Mom predicted she would be tall someday. My mother always seemed to know these things in advance. As for me, I thought little Lulu was an angel. She had a quiet demeanor and a shy sweet smile. When she finally cried for something, her cry was so quiet it was a great relief to me.

Days later, a private funeral service was held at Saint Alfred's Church for baby Lucette. The priest stood next to the small mahogany coffin across from Dad as he held Mom up to steady her. Confused overwhelming emotions washed over me. Happy, because my mother and baby sister Lucille had come home and were doing fine. Sad, because my other baby sister died. Guilt, because I'd said I needed my mother. Wondering, if God was mad at me for saying that.

When little Lucy started to walk, I could feel her following me. I'd look around and see the adorable little munchkin with a shy smile looking up at me. Whenever our little sisters got in a squabble, Bob and I were overly protective of our baby sister with the quiet reserved manner.

FOR THE LOVE OF LACE

"Ah need me a decent job! Cain't make what Ah used ta make no moe. Lost ma family's home n ma purdy car. Took thm kids outa that good skool. Nare gun b able ta sen thm other kids to a skool like that. Shood ben happy when Ah had it all. Sho ain't lookin like thangs'll pick up agin."

"Stop it, Leonard! Stop feeling sorry for yourself. We can't just give up. Maybe if you stop drinking and go to church with us things will get better again."

"God ain't gun lissen ta a poor man like me wifout a nickel fer church. E dun give up own me."

"Keep feeling sorry for yourself then Leonard, that'll help. It could get worse you know."

My mother always seemed to predict things. It did get worse. Patsy understood that we couldn't afford a lot of things. Pat grew hungry for better. She resolved that someday she wouldn't have to live the way her mother did. Her mother's shame of having to accept welfare instilled the belief that it was wrong. After the boxes of food items marked U.S. Government were empty, her mother hid them deep in the trash. Heaven forbid the garbage man saw them. Or even worse the neighbors. Now those neighbors were watching to see what we ate. Neighbors aside I was grateful for those huge blocks of cheese and dried noodles. Mom's magic spoon turned them into scrumptious macaroni and cheese meals, for which I was doubly grateful to not have another bean stomachache. And triple grateful when the house wasn't cold in winter. Laundry drying in the cold basement got stiff as a board in winter, so my mother brought it upstairs and scattered it around to dry. Embarrassing me to no end when someone happened to stop in. My mother also had a thing for plastic curtains. She bought them at the five and dime store. "They look like real lace don't they Patsy? The neighbors are going to think they're lace." She claimed after she hung them. "The hell with the neighbors!" Dad yelled pulling at the flimsy plastic to see out and they tore in jagged pieces. From then on, they hung there just like that. Those curtains were up, and Mom was keeping them, no matter how bad they looked. My mother wanted lace. She got plastic. Patsy wanted real lace. Pat didn't want any curtains at all, if they weren't the real thing.

LITTLE BROTHER BIG HERO

By this time Bob was catching the blame for every squabble us girls got into. So go figure, seven sisters. The poor kid was always in trouble. It pains me to think of it. He should be awarded the sister's medal of honor. The six younger ones paired up as buddies, and I didn't have time for my buddy anymore. I was babysitting the neighbor kids or hanging out with my new friend Kaye, on the other side of the fence. Bob on the other hand seemed to have all kinds of time to tease the girls after his chores were done. He got the hell beat out of him for no reason other than being a pest. When mom jumped in protesting, dad jumped all over her. "Stop coddlin the boy. Git outa ere fore u git it too. Makin a man of 'im. Ma bruthers n me got many a beatin, made us strong." One day sis Carole was waiting at the back door when I got home from babysitting. "Just letting you know, Bob got another beating for no reason, so keep out of the way." The next thing I knew I was standing in the tormentor's face demanding; "Why is my brother getting beat up all the time?" "Ahl teach u to defy me u little b----." I went to school with welts again.

Days later I was washing dishes when he started yelling at my brother in the next room. My tuning system went to high alert. 'Click.' At the sound of the dreaded belt buckle I was running to stop what was coming. "Stop! Leave my brother alone!" I yelled charging into the middle and the belt slashed over us again and again until I couldn't breathe. I fell to the floor seeing spots, hearing little sisters scurrying to secret hiding places. That night, sis Carole, Sharon and I were sitting up in the bed we shared crying, when our brother came into the room. "Don't ever do that again Pat." He growled angrily. "What do you mean Bob? I can't just stand there and let it happen."

"You have to Pat, or he just gets madder." "I can't do that Bob, I have to try and help you."

"Listen to what I'm saying Pat, you're not listening. You can get hurt bad doing what you did. You're just a girl. Don't ever do that again. I'll be ok. Don't worry about me." My brother was so mad he had tears in his eyes. How could he be mad at me when I was trying to help? If it would save him, I'd have to do the same thing again. My buddy who was there ever since I could remember, the only person who never got mad at me, was mad because I tried to help him. "Don't be mad at me Bob." I begged near tears at the thought. "I'm not mad at you Pat. I'm just mad."

"Oh, I see now, I get it. You know what Bob? I've been thinking and I'm going to find a way to get us out of here."

"OK Pat, when you're ready we'll go together."

"Take us with you! Don't leave us here!" Carole and Sharon cried.

Oh no, we can't leave them or the little ones either. Now what? Turned out we were all moving to Garden City. Wonder where that is?

THE CHICKEN BUSINESS

By this time, knocking on doors had become a habit for Bob and me. Our experience of shoveling snow, mowing lawns, and babysitting were worth more now in Garden City so we gave ourselves a raise. Then Bob got another job, shining shoes in front of the party store nearby. My brother was always trying to outdo me. When I got a second babysitting job, he got a second paper route, delivering the Detroit News as well as the Detroit Free Press, one in the morning, one at night. When my reputation grew in the neighborhood as the ace babysitter, my time was in big demand, so my rate went up again. Bob had to top that and he came up with a bigger moneymaker. "Look at this ad I found Pat. I'm gonna make more than you with this idea. I'm buying a hundred chickens for two dollars. They're delivering them free. I'm going in the chicken business!"

65

"A hundred chickens! Where are you going to put a hundred chickens Bob? That's crazy! They're gonna mess all over the yard. Mom's not gonna like that idea."

"She already told me yes Pat. They're not big chickens. They're baby chicks. Ha ha fooled ya! I'm gonna sell them for Easter. This time you watch and see what I can do."

Cardboard boxes arrived at our front door, peeps and chirps coming from the peepholes. Bob sat on the floor carefully removing carton tops. Suddenly a hundred little peeps were singing their happy little lungs out. It was love at first sight for seven sisters. What a huge sensation they created in the living room. Everyone oohing and awing over fluffy little peeps, picking them up to kiss each one. "I'm getting mixed up. Which one's didn't get kissed yet?" "Where'd we leave off?" "Hey that one already got two kisses." "How do you know?" "I got an idea, let's name them." "Good idea that way we won't miss one." "Aww, let's keep them Bob, don't sell them." Too bad we didn't have a movie video to capture that priceless scene.

Then Bob discovered two little peeps arrived dead and we all started crying. He wrapped them in a towel and ran out of the house and laid them under a tree. "I'll have to bury them later. I gotta get the other ones in new homes before something happens to them too."

He stacked the cartons of chicks in his Red Flyer wagon, added fresh water and chicken mash, and hurried off with the wagon tied to the back of his bicycle. Already well known in the neighborhood, the young entrepreneur with a red wagon load of fluffy yellow peeps was simply irresistible. Bob was back in a couple hours, exhilarated after giving it his best shot.

"Look Pat I'm rolling in dough. I made ninety-eight bucks from two dollars. And you thought it was a crazy idea. I sold them for a dollar each. What do you have to say now Big Shooter?" "Boy I'm proud of you Bob. It would take me a very long time to make that much babysitting." "Thanks Pat. Guess what? There's gonna be a lot of pet chickens running around here soon."

Boy oh boy was he ever right. Those little peeps grew up and ran up and down our city street clucking like they owned the whole neighborhood.

The chicken story has an aftermath. Years later it so happened I was in small town and decided to take a drive down memory lane. And guess what? A handsome rooster with shiny black feathers was strutting down our old street. I stopped to watch him strut through his neighborhood like cock of the walk. There he stood, straight and tall, crowing a fierce; "cock a doodle do!" Confirming his territory, he belted out another fierce, "Cock a Doodle Do!" Then shook his tail feathers proudly and walked on down the block with head held high. I sat in my car watching this tough old bird laughing myself silly. It took several more minutes before I could control myself enough to drive away. Still laughing about my brother's undeniable connection to that bad ass old rooster. And that's the story of how 'city chickens' got started.

THE FORGOTTEN CHRISTMAS

It seemed Christmas was forgotten since nothing was being done to prepare. Christmas was in a few days, and they hadn't started bringing things in to hide in the attic. Though there was never a lot, there had always been something for each person. This year there wasn't even a tree. "When are going to start bringing stuff in so I wrap it Mom? And where's the tree? What are we waiting for?"

"Good grief, you and your questions. Christmas is going to be different this year."

"What does that mean Mom?" "Just wait Pat and you'll see."

"Geez o Pete, I've been waiting and we're running out of time Mom, I want to get things ready." "It won't take much time Pat. Just wait. You'll see." Gadzooks my mother and that old cliché. She makes me nuts with her wait and see stuff.

The day wore on and it grew dark then dad said casually; "U kids stay in here with yer muther. Ah got work ta do out yonder n don't need ya n ma way." Sometime later a blast of freezing cold wind blew the front door open. Right behind it dad was pushing a huge pine tree into the room. "Outa ma way kiddies!"

"Where did the tree come from!" Mom exclaimed, a question all over her face. "Nair u mind Stella Bee, jess git em busy deck rating it." Suddenly we were all excitedly decorating the biggest Christmas tree ever, but big ears still overheard. "What's the landlord going to say when he sees a tree missing in the yard Leonard?" "Nair u mind Stell, 'e probly b thankin me. Too damn menny trees out thar eny ways."

Christmas Eve arrived, kids snug in their beds, visions of sugar plums dancing in heads. "Can I start wrapping presents now?"

"Ain't havin no Christmas thiz year Patsy." Dad answered quietly.

"What Do You Mean No Christmas!!?" I exclaimed robustly.

"Lower yer voice fore ya wake thm kids. Havin Christmas nex month, mebbe."

"Next month? We can't do that! The kids think Santa is bringing them nice gifts because I told them he is! Why don't you guys ever tell me anything? I would've done something about this."

"Jess what wood u a dun miss smarty?"

"I would've used my babysitting money and got them 'something' but I spent it on school clothes because I didn't know. Now it's gone and there's a blizzard outside and I can't even go to the party store and get them some chocolate."

"Don't cry Pat. It'll be ok. We just have to tell them we'll have Christmas later."

"It's not ok Mom. How can we tell little kids who believe in Santa, he didn't bring them anything? I can't stand it. Oh why. did I tell them he was bringing them a nice present? Now what am I going to tell them?"

"They'll just have to understand Pat. Sometimes things are hard in life."

Sometimes she says. Sometimes. Geez o Pete, its ALL the time. God where are you? Can you hear me? Can you please make Christmas for my little sisters? And my brother too. He deserves something nice. If you can just bring them a present, you don't have to bring me nothing.

As mom and I went about doing our nightly chores, I repeated the prayer silently over and over. When we were finished, I dawdled, hoping for an answer to my bargain with God. It grew late and I was equally tired, ready to fall asleep on my feet. "Go to bed Pat. Why are staying up so late? You look like you're ready to drop. Nothing is going to change. There's nothing more you can do tonight, go to bed."

"I was saying a good night prayer Mom. I'll go soon, ok?" Then there came a light knock at the door, seconds later it grew insistent. "Who in the world can that be at this hour of the night? My God I hope nothing bad happened at Christmas. It's always something bad when someone comes late. What else can go wrong in this house? Answer the door Leonard, I'm not going to answer it!" He opened the door and joy upon joy! Three angels dressed in red were singing as a blizzard of snow swirled all around them. "We wish you a Merry Christmas...we wish you a merry Christmas." They proceeded to carry in baskets of gifts and sat them down next to the landlord's tree, then lo and behold went back to their car and brought more. The last basket held a huge turkey and all the trimmings for a Christmas dinner fit for a king. It was some kind of wonderful, angels in red who sang and drove a car and brought presents. Guess angels can do just about everything. "Have a merry Christmas." They chorused, starting to leave. "Ah'm humbly grateful ta ya'all." Dad said with tears in his eyes. "Thank ye frum th bottom a ma heart fer makin this nice Christmas fer ma family." It was the nicest thing I ever heard him say. The angels smiled as they stepped out into swirling snow, and with a wave of red mittened hands they were gone with the wind. "Who were those people, Stella? U say somethin ta th nabers bout us bein flat broke?"

"My God, I never even see the neighbors Leonard. Why would I go and tell them what goes on in our house? I'm ashamed to talk about what we don't have. Why ask me? Who'd you talk to?"

"Ah ain't talkt ta nary a soul Stell. Did u talk ta eny buddy Patsy?"

"I talked to God tonight, Dad."

"Well, I'll b dern tootin!" He exclaimed, eyes popping in surprise. "It sho looks look like he done went n answered ya. Nare seen nuthin like it n all ma born days!"

The next morning, I watched the kids happily opening presents, and knew how wonderful it felt receiving the best gift of all. We never learned how those angels found us that late Christmas Eve in a blizzard of a snowstorm. Maybe angels in red come from the Salvation Army. What do I know? All I know for sure is that God heard a kid praying that night, and he answered her.

ON BECOMING A TEENAGER

There's a lot going on in Garden City today, my best friend and I said walking down Ford Road watching the hot rods cruise. Brightly painted souped- up jalopies with flames of neon colors on the sides. Man, o man, what a blast, those cool cars were the biggest thing happening in this burgeoning metropolis we considered to be four miles long and four miles wide. Cruising was it baby girls. Barb and I were eighth graders in junior high school, a tall blonde and medium height brunette got whistles from cruisers. A noisy muffler revved, and we knew we were being watched. They sped past, honking the horn, waving and calling; "Woo Hoo, Chickees! Wowzah!" The chicks waved back, flattered by offhand complements from older boys, in black leather jackets and white t-shirts, stereotype Fonzie. It was big excitement in small town for two girls happy about becoming teenagers.

Barbara and I literally met by accident. A kid in science class started a fire when he got the bunt torch too close to contact paper. The fire alarm went off and within minutes, the entire school was outside in blustery windy weather. Prissy girls complaining their pageboy hairdos were getting messed up. That could never happen, their hair was stiffer than a mummy with half a can of hair spray on it. But Barb was taking the wind in stride, laughing as it whipped her hair around her face. I decided this crazy, funny girl should be my friend. Sometime later we got kicked out of class and sent to the principal's office for laughing. We shook in our boots until her mother arrived. Lucky me, we didn't have a phone, so I was sent home with a letter from the principal for my mother to sign. Lucky me again, mom didn't tell dad. She put me to work scrubbing every floor in the house, then insisted on meeting my new friend before I could hang out with her anymore. I was embarrassed to bring Barb home. Her house was like the cover of Better Homes and Gardens magazine, art on the walls, plush carpets, silk draperies, soft downy sofa, pretty pillows, and flowers on the table. Her bedroom was pink with two beds, one for her, one for her sister. I never imagined a whole bed for one person. I'd slept with two or three sisters since we were little kids. The floors in our house were badly scuffed and worn, in dire need of being refinished. Adding to the lack of niceties, my mother still put those plastic curtains up wherever we lived, which were torn in no time at all. They stayed up despite my requests they come down. Our furniture was even more dilapidated than before. Whenever someone stopped in I'd see the look in their eyes, and remember snooty Lizzy who put us down for being poor. That wasn't going to happen to me again. If anyone turned their nose up, I'd open the door and tell them to take a hike. Nobody was looking down on my family again.

The day arrived when Barb came home from school with me. She took one look around and started talking to my mother like they were old friends. My little sisters came running into the room wearing my half-slip and can cans on their heads, playing runaway brides. Barb bust a gut laughing and passed my mother's test, as well as mine. From then on, we were inseparable, mostly hanging out at her house. Her sister was away at college, so I slept in her bed when invited for sleepovers. At one point I had a crush on Barb's brother Mike, until finding out he was four years older. Gad zooks, he's old! Barb had a big crush on Ricky Nelson, we played his records in her room hours on end, while her younger brother Alex escaped to his room to practice the accordion.

MONKEYS IN TREES

By this time little sisters Nancy and Linda, were climbing trees like monkeys, hanging by their feet. Their agility was astounding, earning Nancy the nickname, monkey girl. One little boy in the neighborhood loved this strawberry blond tomboy, with laughing blue eyes. He called for her at the door. "Naaaaacy....come out and play!"

"Mom there's a boy outside calling for Nancy."

"Ignore the little bugger and he'll go away. That's the same little pest who calls for her when you're in school Pat. Every weekend now boys are coming to my door to talk to one of you girls, but this little kid comes pestering every day. That's what I get for having so many girls. Just ignore him and he'll get tired and go away."

"Naaannnsseeeee! Come out and play Nancy!" The little kid yelled louder, refusing to give up. "He's not going away Mom." Finally, my mother opened the door. "Yesssss, I suppose you're looking for Nancy again." He stood there barely three feet tall, the cutest little freckle face redhead, grinning up at her. "Can Nancy come outside and climb trees? She's the best girl on our street and she can run faster than everybody!" he declared. "Oh?" ...my mother questioned dubiously. "Maybe I'll let her come out and play awhile then." She answered and shut the door on him. "I can tell that little kid's already in love with my Nancy. For goodness' sake they're starting younger all the time." She said, then sighed her long sigh. "I can see the problems I'm going to have with all these girls in this house. Now don't you go getting any ideas Pat, I need you around here. Help Nancy get her shoes on and tie them good, so she doesn't go and fall out of a tree. She's such a little monkey that kid."

"Ok Mom. Come here Rug Rat." "Don't call her like that Pat." "Ok Mom. Come over here Nancy and let me tie your shoes, there's a cute boy outside waiting to climb trees with you, you little rug rat monkey girl." Nancy laughed and ran around the room, strawberry blond curls falling into her eyes. "You want to go outside or not you little rug rat? That boy's not going to wait for you forever." The little charmer ran and jumped into my arms.

FIRST DRIVING LESSON

One night I was putting my hair up in pin curls daydreaming; 'most of the girls in school wear their hair in pageboys or ponytails. Jane Russell has curly hair and doesn't wear penny loafers or saddle shoes or poodle skirts, but she has black hair like mine, and she likes pink too. BOOM... dad busted into the room, interrupting my actress fantasy. "Sum buddy's gotta take me to the peachy parlor. Yer muther don't drive so let's go Patsy."

"She doesn't drive either, you foolish man. She's only 13!" Mom exclaimed.

"High time she larns. Git yer shoes own Patsy, why ya got em off agin?"

 "I'm going to bed Dad, it's almost 11:00 and I have school tomorrow." "Ah sed git yer shoes own so git movin."

"No Leonard you drank too much, you can't go driving the car."

"Ah ain't drivin. Patsy is. Ahm th boss roun here. Ah say when we go n who drives." So out we went, my mother following protesting, me nervous as a cat, dad staggering across the yard. "Git back n th house Stell. Git b hind the wheel Patsy. The hell wif what yer muther sez. Thars nuthin to it. U ben watchin me drive fer years, it's time u drove the car."

The next thing I knew the car was in the middle of the yard. I turned the wheel again and we were on the street in front of the house. "Thas sum good driven Patsy. Nair thot a takin a short cut across the grass."

"I didn't think of it either Dad, it just happened. Don't get mad but I'm not going to drive any further. It's too dark to see and I never drove before."

"Aw go own n git outa ma way. Ahl drive the damn thang." He zigzagged all the way down Ford Road one lane to the other. "Geez Dad, you need to stay between the lines, you just missed that other car."

"What lines? Ah doan see no lines." "There's a red-light Dad you have to stop. STOP NOW! Wait! Don't go yet, there's a dog." "What dog? Ah doan see no dog.... he gone?" "He's gone Dad, but you can't go yet." "What now?" "There's a lady Dad." "What lady? Ah doan see no lady." "She's walking right in front of us Dad! Can't you see her!?" "Ah doan see no lady. Yer a good driver Patsy." "I'm not driving Dad! You are! Wait! There's someone else. Don't go till I tell you." "Ok Patsy... u tell me when." "Go now Dad but go slow. There's a spot in front of the pizza place where you can park." He hit the gas, jumped the curb and just missed hitting the building. "Whoops, good thang Ah got brakes. Go own now Patsy n git us a peachy pie with evarthin." We started back home with pizza in tow, me praying out loud we'd get there. "Don't it beat all, Patsy's prayin fer me." We made it home, but I swear someone was watching out for us.

"Sit down n have som peachy wif me Patsy. Yer muther dun wenta bed. Sed she ain't talkin ta me. Can ya beat that. After all Ah do fer 'er, she ain't talkin ta me."

"I'm not hungry Dad, it's twelve o clock and I have to get up for school in a few hours."

"Sit down Ah said!" Guess I was supposed to be grateful for that slice of pizza, after all he couldn't afford pizza and beer for everybody. But I figured it out for myself. Going in a car with a drunk person wasn't worth a whole pizza.

"Happy ya larnin ta drive Patsy? Me n my bruthers larnt whilst we's kids. Pooshed that ole model t out th road whilst they's sleepin, n drove all nite thru th mountains hootin n hollerin, havin us a time. Good ole days, they sho was. Where's that friend a yourn, that Barbie Ellen girl? Ain't seen 'er roun ere lately. 'Er dad teachin 'er ta drive?"

"Her name is Barbara and she's almost a year younger than me. Her dad won't let her drive because we can't drive in Michigan until were 16."

"Ah say 'er name's Barbie Ellen so Barbie Ellen it is. U girls r big nuff ta b drivin yer muther whar she needs ta go." There was no use arguing so I had pizza with dad, knowing these few minutes of camaraderie with him were not likely to happen again. The next time he'd be lost in a brown bottle he called Johnny. He claimed Johnny was his friend, but he kept him hidden in a paper sack so no one could meet him. Then every Saturday and Sunday morning we'd find him passed out on the dining room floor after Johnny had done him in again. Some friend. If we had to use the bathroom it was at the risk of waking him up. Then there'd be hell to pay. Mom and I would look at each other, trying to decide whether to risk it. Either way he was going to start yelling and throwing things if he woke up. It was our fault he slept on the cold floor. So, we tried to delay all that fun, tip toeing over him to the bathroom for a nice quiet pee. If he woke up while we were in there, he'd accuse of walking over him like a dog. If we were lucky, we could get him to his room before the little kids woke up to see all this fun. When miss smarty got exasperated by it all, I'd mutter under my breath thinking he didn't hear so good. 'Swell, here we go again, another happy weekend. "Whas that ya sed miz smart ass?"

"Just wondering what you want for breakfast this weekend Dad."

"Same damn thang Ah have evar mornin. Beats me why Ah sent ya that spensive skool, cain't even member what Ah have fer brekfus." Other times we'd fix his meal and he'd refuse to eat, a little later he'd demand we make it fresh. After it was all prepared again, he'd pick up the end of the table and send everything crashing to the floor. "Fix me a #@%*#^* decent breakfast!"

POOCHIE

Other times he was way past drunk and wanted to talk to someone. Mom would escape somewhere so I was forced to sit and listen to nonsensical ramblings. He'd slur in my face, breath reeking from whatever whiskey, sour mash, or friend in a brown paper sack. Seemingly unaware they were all his enemies, not a friend among them. "Stop cleanin Patsy n sit yer ass down 'ere n talk ta me. Why ya cleanin s'late. Git yer work dun n th day, ain't spose ta b cleanin n th nite." Obediently I sat my butt down, stomach churning from rancid booze breath. "Ya member first time Ah air saw ya?"

"Geez Dad how could I remember the first time you saw me?"

"She said come n see... lil puppy in diapers...lil Poochie."

Oh brother, what's he talking about now? A diaper on a puppy. How much longer do I have to listen. "I'm really tired Dad, can I go to bed now?"

"Jess like yer muther, cain't set n talk a spell. Go own u useless girl. Git outa my site. U ain't worth a buffalo nickel."

SOMETHING TOLD ME

There were times when he was in a rare happy mood. "Where's my baby girls?" he'd call out and my little sisters ran to be first to sit on Daddy's lap. "Who's baby girl r U?" "Daddy's baby girl," they'd answer laughing sweetly. The oldest watched as they laughed and shoved, vying to be first to sit on daddy's lap to get a hug. She understood waiting her turn, but when it was, he waved her away. "Yer too big ta sit own daddy's lap."

'He's not your real Dad' ...something inside said to me like it was my best friend. So that's it. That's why I'm different. He's not my real dad!

THE INQUIRY

"Mom, I have to ask you something. Is dad my 'real' dad?"

"My God! Why in the world would you ask such a thing!?"

"I can feel it Mom. He treats me different than the others and he never hugs me either. And something told me he's not my real dad."

"What do you mean 'something' told you!? What am I going to do with you? When I tell you to figure things out for yourself, you're not supposed to come up with wild ideas. I don't know what to do with you anymore. Stop being so old and just be a kid."

"Geez Mom, first you say be a big girl and take care of your sisters, now you say be a kid. I just want to know if he's my real dad. It's ok if he isn't, because I don't love him either."

"Don't ever say that! You love your dad, and he loves you too. He just doesn't know how to show it because he was raised bad. His father was never home, and his mean mother beat them every day. He doesn't know how to act, because he wasn't taught right."

"It's not my fault his mother was like the mean old witch in Hansel and Gretel!"

"God help me; what am I going to do with this kid? Why did I let her read all those stories? Now I need to make her stop reading so much. Go out and roller skate awhile Pat."

The next day dad stood watching while I cooked his breakfast, a job we all did with painstaking care because he expected perfection. Biscuits and cornbread were in the oven, home fries were ready. All was good until he started watching, making me nervous. "Who's baby girl are you, Patsy?" "I'm not a baby anymore Dad, I go to work almost every day." "Yer a baby girl longs Ah say so Patsy." "Ok Dad, but would you please stop calling me Patsy? Nobody's called me that for years now."

"Ah say yer Patsy so Patsy u are. Yer muther sed Ah don't hug u. Duz Patsy wanna hug from er daddy?"

"No thanks Dad, I'm cooking right now." When everything was ready, I put the meal on the table. "I have to go to work now Dad, bye." He didn't answer and I didn't care.

BOB'S PIGEONS

Being lonely in a house with ten people was just way it was. My brother and I talked about it one day watching his pigeons. "You're gonna keep finding ways to get out of the house aren't you, Pat? You and me, are loners, we go our own way. That's what dad says every time he hits me. He says he's going to teach us his way. I don't want to be like him. I'm going my own way. You're like me Pat, you think like I do. I've been watching you go to babysit every chance you get. You must be babysitting every kid in the neighborhood now. They talk about you at school, did you know that? They say their mother likes you. I know why the kids like you, because you don't tell on them. Ha ha ha, good for you Pat, good for you."

"Their mothers like me because I cook for their kids Bob. That's fine with me, they pay a lot more. I'll work for them whenever they want, so I don't have to be home."

"What you gonna do with all that dough Pat, getting ready to leave? I am too. Been stuffing it under the pigeon shed. Pretty soon Pat pretty soon. Till then I got my pigeons. I can listen to them coo all day. They sound nice, don't they?"

"Yeah, they sound nice, but they mess all over. I'm using my money for clothes and school stuff, not some shittin pigeons."

"I thought you liked them Pat."

"I do Bob, they're pretty birds and they sound peaceful, but I'm getting things I need, so dad can't gripe about what he has to get for me."

"Me too Pat. I got another job helping the guy stock the party store. He told me not to tell anyone cause I'm underage. Someday I'm gonna make a lot of money and no one will ever knock me around again. You watch and see. What about you Pat? You still want to be an actress like those girls Jane Russell and Marilyn Monroe in that movie we saw. What was it called?"

"Gentlemen prefer blondes Bob."

"Not me Pat. I liked the girl with black hair better. You still wanna be an actress?"

"I don't think so anymore; my play at school was awful."

"That's not what I heard Pat. I heard kids say you were really good in that play."

"They did? Really? How come they didn't clap then?"

"How should I know, maybe they're too stupid to clap. So, what are you going to be if you don't be an actress then?"

"I don't know yet Bob, but I'm going to marry someone nice, have two kids, a boy and a girl, a house with two bathrooms and....."

"Whoa Big Shooter! You're just like those girls in the movie. That's what they were doing, looking for a big shot."

"No, I'm not! You don't need to be rich to have a house with two bathrooms! I just want someone who loves me and will never hit me."

"That's how it's supposed to be Pat. Women should never get hit, they're not strong like men are. Hey, do you ever wonder where Uncle Charlie went? He taught me how trains operate. He said the first railroad tracks were built by Pennsylvania Steel and they made beams for the Chrysler Building and the Empire State Building. Bet you didn't know all that did you? Uncle Charlie taught me a lot about steel, it was interesting. Someday I'll bend steel with my bare hands. I'll be like Superman. Ha ha ha. Wadda ya say Pat, you think I can?"

"I think you can do anything you want to do Bob."

"That's what Uncle Charlie told me. I miss him, don't you?"

"Yeah, I miss him a lot. But I liked his stories about traveling better. Steel is boring to me."

"Not to me Pat, not to me."

THE BUD DAVIES DANCE SHOW

One day a girl at school walked up to me in the hall. "Would you like to dance?" Of course, I started laughing with this funny girl. "I saw you dancing at the Teen Club on Friday. My dad has free passes for a bunch of kids to go on the Bud Davies Dance Show. You want to go and dance with us on TV?" "Sure! That would be cool!"

Boy this is going to be so much fun. How can I get dad to let me go? He'll never say yes. "Oh Mom, I really want to go; pleeeeeeze. It'll be so fun going with these kids from school!"

"Your Dad will never let you go all the way to Windsor with kids he never met Pat. You know you're not allowed to go in cars with boys." "But Mom these kids don't drive yet, they're my age. Their parents are taking us." "Your Dad never met these people Pat. He won't let you go."

"But he never met Barb's mom or dad either and I've stayed at their house lots of times."

"You can go Pat. You should be allowed to do this. It's something special that might never happen again. I'm not even going to mention it to your dad. He won't know if you're working or not. Don't say anything to anybody, just go and have a nice time." "Oh, thank you mom, thank you! You're the best mom there ever was!" "Don't get too excited Pat. Don't count your chickens before they're hatched. You know we always have to wait to see how things go."

Fate worked in my favor and dad wasn't around. I wore my black poodle shirt with a pink blouse, bobby socks and saddle shoes. It was fun being with all the kids, but as soon as the dark cold eye of the camera started following us around on a tripod, I didn't want to dance anymore. Whatever had made me think I wanted to dance on TV? All I really wanted was to hang out with friends, laughing about everything.

ELVIS PRESLEY

In 1956 the most exciting thing on two legs burst onto the scene. Elvis Presley was everywhere so I figured sooner or later he'd get to Garden City and find me. Old people called him 'Elvis the pelvis.' They said his actions were obscene and kids who watched his gyrating hips were going to hell. How could I go to hell just watching a guy wiggle? They're full of baloney. Elvis Presley gives me heart attacks. Come hell, high water or heart attack, I'll die happy when I meet him. He's so good looking he shakes everybody up. Mmm hmm, mmm hmm, ay yay, I'm all shook up. Nobody's going all the way with me except maybe Elvis. After two years of crying over him I finally figured it out. Elvis will never know who I am. Our love is never going to be. There's a million girls in love with him. I don't want a teddy bear or a hound dog. I already took a walk down lonely street, and don't want to stay at heartbreak hotel. I want a one and only love, but I will always love you Elvis Presley.

CARS AND CARHOPS

"Guess what Bob?! I'm going to be a carhop at a drive-in restaurant and get a real paycheck!   The people I babysit for own it. They talked to mom and she's going to sign some working papers so I can work in public. I'll be making 35 cents an hour PLUS TIPS!" "That's really good Pat. Good for you."

The drive in was the size of a couple phone booths squeezed together. Each time I worked there I earned handfuls of nickels, dimes, and quarters. Soon it was time for driver's education at school. Guys wanted to learn to drive on the stick shift. Gals wanted to learn on the automatic transmission. I wanted to learn on the standard shift with a clutch, so I could drive any vehicle after. The guys taking shop classes were learning about mechanics and going to buy a hundred dollar special. That sounded like a good idea to me so over the winter months I got a job at the drugstore. When spring came, I went back to work at the Cubbyhole after school. Then I heard through it the grapevine the carhops at Jack's Drive in, made 50 cents an hour. The word on hamburger road was it was 'the place' to be and the tips were great. But hiring age was 16 years and up. Why should a little thing like that stop me? "Hi, my name's Pat, I work at the Cubbyhole now Sir, but I want to move up to a better job."

"How old are you, Pat?" I answered fast, not wanting to miss this grand opportunity. "I'm 15 sir but I'll be 16 in a few months and I have working papers and references, and my boss says I'm the best carhop they ever had, and I also work three days a week at the drugstore but when school is out I can work here full ti...

"That's enough information Pat if you're finished talking, I want to hire you. My wife and I have saw you working when we stopped there for a sack of burgers. I hire experience with references, age 16 and older, but I'll hire you on one condition. Don't tell anyone your age. If the girls working here find out, I'll have to fire you. So if you want to keep the job keep that to yourself. I have a good business here and don't tolerate cats in my restaurant." Wonder what he means by that? Do cats come in restaurants?

The new job was even more fun than the last. We were so busy there wasn't time to think. Cars rolled in and so did the tips. Hot rods cruised in, radios blasting rock and roll songs like, "Rock Around the Clock" by Bill Haley and the Comets. "Shout" by the Isley Brothers. "Whole Lotta Shakin' Goin On" by Jerry Lee Lewis. "You Send Me" by Sam Cooke. "Searching" by the Coasters. "Long Tall Sally" by Little Richard. "Folsom Prison Blues" by Johnny Cash. "Maybelline" by Chuck Berry. "Only You" by the Platters. "That'll be the Day" by Buddy Holly. "Ain't That a Shame" by Fats Domino. "In the Still of the Night" by The Five Satins. And the hit record ; "Come Lets Stroll" by the Diamonds, caused a new dance craze called, 'The Stroll'.

One day a guy started singing in the parking lot with his buddies. I wondered why they called that guy Smokey. He should be called Sunshine for his sunshine smile and twinkling blue eyes. Rumor said Smokey wrote songs and sang at a house on West Grand River Blvd in Detroit called 'Hitsville.' Smokey Robinson and the Miracles became famous. The house became famous for making many hit records. Barry Gordy changed the name to 'Motown', making legends with The Temptations, The Supremes, The Marvelettes, The Isley brothers, The Four Tops, The Jackson Five, Gladys Knight and the Pips, Martha and the Vandelas, Aretha Franklin and more. And there I was right in the middle of it all, the new carhop at Jacks, having the time of my life. Guys and gals dropped nickels in the jukebox and the music of our generation played, while I ran around taking lunch orders. For a few hours every Saturday and Sunday work was bliss. Happy days! What teenager wouldn't love this job. I was the luckiest girl alive. On top of all that I was making new girlfriends. Or so I thought. In my happy little world everything was a bright, bright sunshiny day, and we were all aboard the friendship train. Until it ended abruptly.

PRINCE CHARMING

He drove in on a Saturday, I'll never forget. We were running to fill orders fast as we could go, when the sudden screeching noise like the braking of a train stopped everyone in their tracks. "There's Walt in that dam hot rod scraping up my driveway I just resurfaced." The boss grumbled. The car continued to scrape bottom as it slowly inched to level ground. Every eye affixed on the midnight black vehicle cruising in like a panther in the sun. Barely inches above the ground, sleek and low, capturing all attention. There wasn't a trace of chrome on it anywhere. No door handles, no bumpers, all the chrome had been removed and leaded in. 30 coats of pearl black lacquer covered the clean, mean, machine, creating a sheen so deep a gal could apply lipstick in the black mirror finish. This wasn't just another hotrod, it was a batman car before it's time. It wasn't a prop on a Hollywood movie screen, it was real life happening in small town Garden City. And wouldn't you know, this was my up. Lucky, lucky me. "Man, oh man, this is the sharpest coolest car I've ever seen in my life!" I blurted out with no forethought whatsoever.

"You're pretty sharp too," one of the guys inside shot back. "Hey Doll, when did 'you' start working here?" questioned a second.

"Wadda ya say chickee? What's 'your' name?" a third guy added, and I blushed to my roots. These guys were a lot older than my friends and too fresh for me. "So, what do you guys want to order?" I asked getting down to business. "Man, I'd sure like to order something from you." That remark embarrassed me to no end, but they seemed to think they were funny.

"All right you guys that's enough. Shut up and tell her what you want." The driver of the car spoke up appearing to be the Big Kahuna in charge, and they laughed even harder. What a bunch of idiots, I thought to myself. "Don't pay any attention to them, they're a bunch of dummies." The Big Kahuna asserted again, and they laughed even louder. That was it. I had enough. "Maybe I'll come back for your order when you little kids can settle down." I walked off in a huff, laughter trailing behind. The boss was waiting for me inside. "I was watching you out there, Pat and heard what you said. You handled them well. I could tell you were nervous, but you don't have to worry about those guys, I've known them for years, they bring their mother's in here. They're buddies who just graduated from high school. They ride around together in Walt's car on weekends. He hasn't been in for a while, and I was hoping he sold that car. Every time he comes in here it tears up my driveway. They usually come inside to flirt with the girls working at the front counter. They're being wise guys because you're the new girl. Go back out there and show them who's boss." That did it. Look out wise guys. You better not embarrass me again. "Ok wise guys. You ready to order now?"

"We're not ready yet, we have to count our change. Come back in five minutes." Phooey on them, I don't have time for this. If they came in here without enough for a burger, I'm not going to that car again. "Do you want to take the bat car's order?" I asked one of the other carhops and she nearly flew out the screen door of the carhop stand. But she was back without an order. "They said if you come back, they'll behave."

Oh brother, I'm missing real tip paying customers because of a bunch of little kids. "All right wise guys I'm back, only because you promised to be good kids. Give me your orders and stay out of trouble and I'll bring lunch. Otherwise, you can forget about me coming here again." "Aww do we have to Mom?" "Yes, you do, and I'm not messing with you either. I haven't got time. I have work to do." "Ok Mom." Happily, confused they gave mother their orders promptly without any fuss.

"All righty then, I'm back with lunch, roll that window up a bit so this tray can hang on it. You kids know what you're supposed to do, so just do it." Now they were all jumping to do whatever mother said. "You know what guys; I have to tell you something funny about this job. Every time I hang a tray on a car window, I remember feeding my sisters in their highchair."

"Sisters! How many do you have? Do you have enough for all of us? How old are they? How old are you? Are you going steady with anybody?"

"Shut up you dummies." The Big Kahuna asserted authority again. "Quit asking her so many questions or she'll get mad at us again."

"It so happens I have a bunch of sisters but they're all too young for you guys, they're still in grade school, and I'm not telling you, my business. Besides your hamburgers are getting cold so Mom will help you; this is the with onions."

"That's mine." "Do you have a name?" "It's Jack." "Say thank you." "Thank you," said the cute blond guy in the back seat who couldn't keep from blushing. "You're welcome, Jack."

"Who gets the one without the onion?" "That's mine." "So, what's your name?" "Smitty." "Mom says you should always say thank you." "Thank you, Mom." "You're welcome Smitty."

"Who gets the regular one?" "That's mine. I'm Bob. Thank you." "Hey, you guys catch on fast. And it looks like I've got you all eating out of my hand." That was it. The four wise guys couldn't help themselves; they were choking with laughter. The Big Kahuna reached out for the last hamburger and for the first time I looked straight at him. Good golly miss molly, this is the most handsome guy I ever saw in my life. Our eyes locked and my heart skipped several beats and I fell into peaceful blue eyes. That was it. The moment I fell in love.

His hand brushed mine and we each got a shock. He jerked his hand back and the hamburger hit his chest. The wrapper opened on impact, and the mess rolled down his shirt and pants to the floor of the car. His face got so red I felt sorry for him, but his buddies thought it was hilarious. Then he made it worse by dropping the nickels, dimes and quarters they'd scrounged up. Coins rolled everywhere and they scrambled to retrieve them, then he dropped them again! He had to be the clumsiest guy ever, I thought trying not to laugh at him, but his buddies had no mercy. "What's the matter with you today Mister Clumsy?" they taunted. Well, someone had to stick up for the poor guy. "Hey, it's not his fault. You're the ones who cracked your piggy bank for all these nickels!" That was it. The wise guys laughed so hard the car was shaking, until a cat came running up behind me screeching. "You've got an order waiting! Or are you still working here?"

NO COMPETITION JUST CATS

The next weekend the sound of scraping on the driveway announced he was back. "I thought you quit because I didn't see you all week." he said, and my little heart skipped again. He was looking for me! "I'm still working a couple days a week somewhere else. I'm only here on weekends right now. So, where's your friends today?"

"I left those dummies home so I could talk to you." My crazy heart skipped several more beats from that remark. "You asked my buddies their names, but you didn't tell us yours." "Oh, it's Pat." "Aren't you going to ask mine?" "I already know it." A shy quiet smile said he liked my answer. "Well, I need to get back to work now Pat, I just stopped to say hello. I'll come back tomorrow."

The cats inside were waiting to pounce on me. "'You might as well forget about that guy, every girl in town wants to date him." They glared and sauntered away and I finally got it. Those are the cat's the boss warned about. Guess I was wrong about them. They're not my friends at all. The realization doused my happy feelings. It's not supposed to be like this. The prince is supposed to be coming for me. I'm not going to be dragged into cat games and lose my job. If they want him so bad, they can keep screeching, but I'm going to wait until he asks for me. If he doesn't, then it wasn't meant to be. But those cats made it sound like I wasn't good enough for him. That really hurts. Why would they say that? I've never said anything mean to them. I should've never tried to be their friend. Aww who cares. If Walt is the right one for me, no cats can take him away. I'll wait and let him prove himself.

The next day the scraping of the driveway announced his return. I plopped myself down on the   carhop stool pretending not to care. "You want to take the bat car's order?" I asked a cat, and she flew out of the carhop station like a balloon. A minute later she was back, deflated but still hissing. "Walt wants 'you' to come out and get his order."

Kat Ching! He asked for me. Be cool. Just wait and see. "Hi Walt, what are you going to have today?" He smiled the same shy, quiet smile, and those blue eyes made my heart skip beats again. "Hi Pat. I'll have what I always get. Tell the cook she knows."

"Ok then Walt, will do."

"So here you are, one Walt special, and a cherry coke and your bill."

"The girls inside don't let me pay for lunch Pat."

"Well, you're never getting anything free from me!" It popped out of my mouth just like that and I felt my face flaming. He dropped some coins on the tray and I grabbed the whole tray in a blind rush to get away. As soon as I stepped back into the carhop stand those cats were there. "Why did Walt ask for 'you'?" the third cat screeched and that was it! I had enough. Three cats against one brave mouse were getting on my last nerve. "I suppose you'll have to ask him that question! And ring up his tab too! He's not getting anything free from me and I told him so!" "Hmmph, bet he never asks for 'you' again."

There's nothing more I can say to those cats. I need this job, so I'll just ignore their sourpusses. And Walt doesn't look so good now either. I don't want a guy who wants something for free. Besides no one ever said anything about the prince showing up in a bat car. There's supposed to be a white horse, a ball gown and sparkly glass slippers. Heck there's no horse, no ball gown, no glass shoes, no bippity boppity boo, or even a fairy Godmother. All I've seen so far is three funny coachmen and some cat girls acting like mean stepsisters. Guess I'll recover from a few skipped heartbeats. Glad he couldn't see my heart stop every time he looks at me. I'm so embarrassed of what I said. Why did I say that? Why does my mouth always open before my head gets in gear? Why am I so blunt? Well, he had it coming for assuming I was like those cats. I'm not like them and now he knows! Guess I need to wait for the right prince. But it hurts so much I don't know what to do. I'm already in love with him. He started his car and drove away without looking back. Sadly, I watched him go and breathed a soft goodbye. It was over before it had begun, and my heart beat a little slower.

The next weekend I was nursing the pain when the loud sound of metal scraping started again. "Go ahead and take his order." I said to a cat and she smiled smugly. Satisfied that I had backed away from a guy who was too good for lil ole me. But I was still learning. Cats don't read eyes and see when they've hurt you. They haughtily continue to claw until they get what they want. They're not like a bear. A bear sleeps on it until she finds her own honey pot. I pretended to be hibernating, soothing a heart that skipped beats at the very sound of his car. Then suddenly that cat was back, screeching her lungs out. "Walt wants to see YOU!"

Before I could bat an eye, another cat brushed past my legs. She streaked out to his car parked next to the carhop stand, and I heard her purr; "Why aren't you coming inside to see us anymore?" His answer didn't travel back. A minute later that cat pounced back screeching at me again. "Walt said to tell you 'pretty please,' come out and talk to him. I think I'm going to puke!"

That poor cat was so wretched I almost felt sorry for her. She looked like she was choking on a hairball. The two other cats deliberately looked me up and down. "What do 'you' have to offer?" They screeched before sauntering off n a haughty huff. Well, what am I supposed to offer? As far as I'm concerned, the prince is the one who's supposed to make the offer. Those cats have it backward. If Walt's the right prince, he'll know there's no baloney for me, just steak thank you. He also won't let some skinny cats stop us from building our house with two bathrooms. Hmm, he said 'pretty please.' I never thought a guy would say something like that. That's so sweet. Maybe this handsome guy who makes my heart skip, really is the right one. Maybe I should go out and see what else he has to say. "Are those girls giving you a hard time Pat?"

"As a matter-of-fact Walt, they are." "I can see that Pat, they're a bunch of cats in there. They insist on giving me free lunch, but I leave the cash on the counter. I'm sorry for embarrassing you the other day. I was testing you. Are you going to stay mad at me for that?"

"I wasn't mad Walt. I didn't know you were testing me. I was embarrassed of what I said to you. Sometimes things slip out before I know it. I'm sorry too."

"It's ok Pat. I'm glad you said it. Maybe I shouldn't tell you this, but those girls only want to go out with me because of my car, I take anybody who wants to go for ride in it, but I don't date them. I was dating someone out of town. Are you dating anybody?"

"No, I don't date. I go to the Teen Club on Fridays with friends. I've been waiting for Elvis."

"Man, you've got your sights aimed high. You think Elvis would mind if I asked his girl out?"

"Seeing as how we haven't even met yet; I suppose it would be ok with him."

"By the way how old are you, Pat?"

Oh, brother I can't tell him I'm only 15. He won't date someone just starting high school. And if the cat girls find out my age, I'll lose my job. Maybe it's ok to tell a little white lie. "I'm 17." "When will you be 18?" "In October." Oh, brother now I've done it. Two lies in one second. In another minute I'll be 21.

"I'll be 20 in August Pat, and you'll be 18 in October, two years difference sounds ok to me, what do you think about that?"

"It sounds ok to me." Oh brother, why did I say that? Maybe I should just tell him the truth and let it go whatever way it goes. It was on the tip of my tongue, but he spoke first. Poof. Good intention. What's that?

"So would you like to go for a ride tomorrow after work Pat," he interrupted my thoughts. "Uh...sure, that sounds cool." "Ok then, I'll pick you up and we'll ride around for a while and talk."

The cats inside were watching. "Did he ask you out?" they screeched. "We're going for a ride tomorrow."

"He'll never ask her out." With that cutting remark they flounced off smugly. The next day there he was, waiting in his car until I finished work. "Would you like to ride out to Ted's today, Pat?"

"That depends, how long does it take to get there?"

"Woodward is a way's out. Haven't you ever been to Ted's?"

"No, I haven't. We better just drive around Garden City."

"Ok then, if that's what you say Pat."

"I might as well tell you; my dad doesn't allow me to go in cars with guys. They come to our house to hang out. And I need to be home early today because my mother needs my help. Hey where's the door handles in this car? How do I get out of here?"

"You don't! I'm only kidding Pat, don't look so worried, I wouldn't hurt a fly. See that button on the dash, just push it. But don't push it while I'm driving, or we'll be high rollers."

"I like how you laugh so easy Pat. My sister is like that too. She laughs at everything. Since you don't have a lot of time, I'll drive by my house so you can see my mother's flowers." His house was five blocks from mine. He pulled in front of a brick bungalow with a yard full of flowers. No grass. Just flowers. A very dark skin woman was watering sunflowers at least six feet tall, on each side of the driveway. "Hi Sonny!" she called over the splashing of the hose. "Hi Ma" he called back. "I brought someone to see your flowers."

"Oh my gosh, they're the tallest flowers I've ever seen! I love them! They look so happy!"

"Sunflowers are Ma's favorite Pat. Let's get out a minute and I'll introduce you."

"Ma this is Pat. She loves your sunflowers."

"Well hello Pat, this is a nice surprise. Let me show you around. Over here are my black-eyed Susan's. Over there are my Daisies. These are pansies, and those are petunias, over there are peonies, and hydrangeas. Everything doesn't blossom at the same time. See here's some more coming up. See the little buds? Each year I have tulips along the fence. My roses have struggled this year, that hasn't happened before. I also have some in the backyard that are doing better than these out front. I have lilac bushes back there too and the fragrance wafts through the house. My garden keeps me busy. Oh, here comes your dad now Sonny."

"Well, who do we have here Son?" "Pop, this is Pat."

"Nice to meet you Pat. Come on in. Today is apple pie day. Erve's got one ready to come out of the oven right about now. She's the best cook ever. I've never had a meal better than hers."

"Thank you for offering sir, but I have to get home, my mother is expecting me."

"Sorry you can't stay longer Pat, maybe Sonny will bring you back another time."

 I left wanting to stay. "Your parents are really nice Walt. Why do they call you Sonny?"

91

"Ma started calling me that when I was a little kid and it stuck."

"Your mother's flowers made me remember something that happened when I was a kid. It was kind of strange. I was walking in a dry field out next to the woods, then suddenly I was standing in a circle of flowers of all different kinds and colors. There weren't any houses around, so how did they get out there? My brother and I went back but they were gone."

"So did your brother think you made it up?" "He said he didn't know how that could be, but he believed me anyway." "He sounds like a good kid to me Pat. What's his name?" "Bob."

"My mother would work in her flowers all year-round if she could. She's out there all summer and my Pop tells her she looks like a colored woman. She laughs at everything he says. They're a good pair. She's Russian Polish and he's Scotch Irish. People come from all over to see her flowers and stop to ask her gardening secrets. Then they see my car in the driveway parked under the sunflowers and they flip out."

"I can see why they would. I thought I was going for a ride with a cute guy, and I met Ma and Pa in a house by Cherry Hill, with flowers everywhere and apple pie in the oven." "So you think I'm cute huh?" "You're ok I guess." It was nice being with him, he was easy going and easy to talk to. We discovered we were both Detroit brats, but as soon as I mentioned St. Joseph's he groaned out loud. "Oh no! Not a Catholic girl!" "What have you got against Catholic's?" I demanded suddenly defensive of my upbringing. "Nothing at all except they're too strict," he answered red in the face.

"Well, my dad's a Protestant and he's very strict so that blows your theory. And actually, I'm not a Catholic anymore but I still respect them. Especially the nuns. They give up everything to serve God and teach other people's kids. They can't get married and have their own. I could never be that good. I decided not to be a Catholic anymore when the priest said we could eat meat again on Fridays. Before that they said it was a mortal sin. All my life I wanted to have a hamburger on Friday because I couldn't. The rule was 'no' meat. Then they changed it. I told my mother they made their own rules, so I didn't believe them anymore. I don't think God made rules so we could change them. Do you?" "Uh..., no. No, I don't Pat. I don't think God wants us to change his rules, that's for sure. So, what did your mother say about that?"

"She's still upset with me. She wants me to believe in her church, but I want to find a new one."

"Boy you sure have a mind of your own. You're different from the girls I've dated."

Hmmm, wonder what he means by that...my own mind. Who else's mind would I get? You only get the one you're supposed to get don't cha? "I can see your wheels turning Pat and can't wait to hear what you'll come up with next." "Give me time to think about it and I will Walt."

"I wanted to tell you something, I work two jobs too. During the week I work for my dad, delivering coverall uniforms. On weekends I do construction work. But I can take Sunday off if you'd like me to go with you to find a new church."

"Sounds ok to me Walt, but what about that girlfriend out of town. Is she still around? How did you meet her?" "She ran into me at Ted's. The avenue was backed up with cruisers and she wasn't watching where she was going and hit my car. We dated a year and decided she was just too old for me, and we broke it off." "How old was she?" "23." "Twenty-three! Boy that's 'really' old!" "I've always dated older chicks Pat. Maybe it's time I date someone more my age. Would you like to go out with me Friday for dinner and a drive-in movie?"

"Ok, but you have to pick me up at my house and meet my mom and dad first." "Am I going to get the third degree from your very strict dad?"

"Most likely. And I might as well warn you, he's not very friendly." "What if I show up and see if he'll let me take you out, is that ok?"

"It's fine with me but I don't know about him." "Can I call you sometime Pat?" "We don't have a phone." "Here take my number and call me from a pay phone. I'm usually home by six."

"Ok, I'll call you. Just drop me off in front of the house now Walt, don't pull in the driveway."

And just like I thought, dad was waiting to see how I got home. "Who's that brung ya here?"

"A guy named Walt; Dad, he lives five blocks from here, the boss knows him, he said he's nice."

"Ahl be th judge a who's nice n who's not so nice." Boy this sure isn't the time to ask to go on a date with him.

The next day cat girls pounced on me soon as I got to work. "How did the ride go with Walt?" They purred pretending to be nice. "We just went for a short ride around town." "What's the matter didn't he like you?" Scratch. Damn cats. "I had to be home early; my mother needed me." "We knew he wouldn't ask you out." They meowed and started sauntering away. "Well actually, we have a date Friday." Well, I just had to tell them. Didn't I? "What does he see in 'you'?" They scratched back over their shoulder as they flounced off.

Miserable cats. How mean can they get? Don't they ever get tired of their own stink? Just ignore them, they were never your friends anyway, besides that, the prince doesn't like cats. You have a bigger problem than cats. You still need to persuade dad to let you go on a date, in a car, with someone he never met. That's going to be like pulling your own teeth. If you ask mom first, dad will blow his top and you'll never get out of the house because he says 'he's' the boss. The only chance you've got is to ask him first and worry about mom later. You need to pick the perfect time. Why can't something ever be spontaneous? Why do you have to wait for every little thing? On Monday evening dad was stone cold sober. It was now or never.

"Dad I have something to talk to you about, because you're the boss in this house." He laughed out loud, and I figured I was off to a good start. "Wadda ya wanna talk bout Patsy?"

"Remember the guy who lives five blocks away who dropped me off from work one time?"

"Ah nare met no boy livin five blocks from ere no time!" his voice went up an octave. "Geez Dad, I'm trying to tell you about him." "So what about 'em then?" "He's a really nice guy Dad."

"Who says so?" "My boss knows him, and he said so." "So, what makes 'you" think e's nice?"

"Cause everybody in town knows him and they all like him." "Ya gunna b leve wht peeple n town say, er u gunna side fer yer sef?" "I'm going to decide for myself Dad if I can go out with him. He asked me to go out on Friday. Can I go?"

"Ain't cha puttin th cart fore th horse? Ya needa side if he's nice befer ya go wif em. What's wrong wif em comin ere like yer otha boyfrens ben doin?"

"They're not my boy friends Dad." "Well what r they then, if they ain't yer boy frens?"

"They're wannabe's, Dad." He laughed out loud, and I figured I was making some headway.

"Walt asked me to go on a real date Dad, for dinner and a movie. Not a walk around the block. The last dummy who came here grabbed my hand and pulled me in the garage after we got back from walking around the block." "U nare tolt me 'e did that. Waddja do bout it?"

"I told him he better not try and kiss me again or I'd tell you. And he better not come back here pretending to be friends with you, so he could walk around the block with me." Dad busted a gut laughing and I figured I was really getting somewhere now.

"Leese now ah know ah kin trust ya now Patsy. How old u gittin ta be theez days?"

"I'm almost 16 Dad and everybody's dating except me."

"If evarbuddy else goes jumpin off a cliff ya gun go do it too?"

"Heck no, Dad, I don't want to jump off a cliff! I just want to go to dinner and a movie with a nice guy before I get old." He laughed out loud again and I figured I almost had it made.

"First off, how'd ya meet this feller?"

"I met him at work Dad, he comes in for lunch all the time."

"U ben missin school ta work n that place? Ow come th boy ain't n school?"

"Schools been out for weeks Dad, I started working there before that, don't you remember?"

"Hells fire n duck shit! Do ah member? Sum days ah fergit what day's here. U ben goin roun wif sum boy Ah ain't met?" He shouted angrily. Uh oh, I'm messing up. Just when I thought everything was going swell, he's mad. "Heck no, Dad. Yu told me you'd skin me alive if I did that." He laughed again and I figured I still had a chance of getting him to see things my way.

"U membered what ah tolt ya Patsy, thas good. Ah'm gonna think own this n see."

E gads, now I need to wait and go through all this again. All this for one date. If this keeps up, I'll be an old maid before I get married. "Geez Dad do we have to wait to see, can't I just go on one date?"

"Ah reckon ya got a fair ta middlin no acountin fer chance."

"Geez Dad what does 'that' mean?

"Go own now Patsy n u'll find out. Doan b questionin me no mo."

The next four days I prayed he'd say yes. Thursday night arrived but still no answer. Time was running out, then he sat down in front of the radio. This is it. Go for it but use a different tactic this time. The last one didn't work so good.

"Hey Dad, I just want to remind you that tomorrow is Friday. Walt wants us to go early for dinner and I hope we're going to have steak burgers."

"Ya aint goin out ths house till Ah meet ths so calt nice feller!" he blustered.

"Sure Dad, he wants to meet you too, that's why he'll be here early. Thanks Dad!"

"Don't go thankin me n puttin th cart fore th horse agin. Ain't met th boy yet. Ahm gunna see." Mother Hen suddenly appeared with her feathers ruffled. "What did I just hear with my own ears? Isn't this a fine thing? No one said a word to 'me' about this!" she snapped indignantly.

"Walt wants to meet you too Mom!" Sometimes this mother of mine pretended not to know what was going on. Whether this was one of those, I really didn't know. But I did know she trusted my judgement, and if I liked him, she would too. "You're going to love him Mom!" My mother smiled with a little frown at the same time. No one could do what my mother did with her eyes. Friday evening came and I was on pins and needles, wondering what would happen. Dad was on his way to being crocked, just not quite there yet. "Wha time u say tht boy's comin ere?" he yelled, pulling back torn plastic curtains to look out. The sound of gravel crunching said Walt's car was arriving. Dad moved closer to the window as though his eyes were playing tricks on him. "What the hell kind contraptions that a comin in here? Nare seen sech a sorry ass lookin thang n all ma born days."

Uh oh here it comes, look out. Run to your rooms before he blows his stack. "U ain't goin no whar n tht damn thang. Jess tell yer hoodlum fren outside u ain't goin fer no ride!"

"But Dad, he's not a hoodlum and it's a custom car! He brought me home from work remember? I told you."

"Ah nair seen no sech thang bringin ya here no time, n no tellin me neetha." He puffed himself up like a teapot, red in the face, steam coming out his ears. A knock sounded on the door and he flung it open and stood there glaring at the young man across from him. Walt ignored all warning immediately rattling off a ready-made speech, without pausing between a single word.

"Good evening it's nice to meet you Sir my name is Walt I hope you're having a nice evening so far it's been real nice weather today hasn't it.... he rattled on nervously without a pause, comma, parenthesis, or period. It was like he practiced all week but forgot the part about breathing.

Dad was thrown off guard. He was expecting a young hoodlum with a greasy duck's ass haircut, (also known as a DA) in scruffy jeans, t-shirt and black leather jacket. Instead, a clean- cut, young man in a sport shirt and khakis, greeted him politely with outstretched hand. Continuing to rattle on nervously without seeming to notice he hadn't taken his hand.

"I hope you're enjoying this nice weather Sir sure wish it would stay like this don't you-I'd like to do some fishing one of these days when I get off work before all the nice days are gone and it starts snowing again and we can't go do you fish sir?"

He finally stopped, seeming to catch a breath, but surprisingly it was dad whose wind was blown out of his sails. This young man actually impressed him! Glory be and hallelujah it's raining men, and it looks like I might go on date with one. Someone has finally impressed mister mean. Oh my gosh, he shook Walt's hand! Wonders never cease.

"What kine a thang's that settin out yonder own ma driveway Boy?" Dad demanded in a too loud voice still holding the upper rein. "It's a completely customized Ford, Sir. Would you like to take a ride in it?" And with that the ice was totally broken. "Jess lemme look at 'er Boy. Ain't nare seen no Ford look like that. A'hm a Buick man ma self."

"They build a good car too Sir."

"Yes siree, they do. Ah worked menny a year fer thm ole boys at GM. What say u n me step out n git a close look at 'er. How menny horses she got?"

"Well, it looks like I'm going out with Walt after all, Mom." "He seems really nice Pat. You already like him a lot, don't you? I can tell. I never saw you look at a boy like that. You know who I think he looks like? Walter Pidgeon." "Walter WHO? Who's that? I think he looks like his self." "He's very handsome." My mother said smiling her sweet demure smile. "I'm happy you like him Mom, I knew you would. I just knew it." "Go and have a nice time Pat."

"Ah bet that dad gum thang set ya back a purdy buffalo nickel. How long ya had 'er?" Dad was still talking cars and Walt was still nervously attempting a grin. My little sisters had gathered to stare at the hunk big sister brought home. My brother stayed on the sideline, coolly taking it all in from the next room. "U kids go on now n git yer sef sum supper. Be back n this house at ten a clock Patsy." Oh no, why did he have to call me Patsy?

"Whew!" Walt let out a nervous breath soon as we got in the car. "It's a good thing your dad liked my car Pat, or I would've never got you out of there." I didn't know how to respond to that. Then he started backing the car up so slow that I wondered if he was changing his mind. The poor guy looked scared silly. He drove without a further word. I figured he probably needed a good laugh after meeting mister mean. So, I started blabbing about my little sister losing a tooth, and how the good fairy left her a nickel. "Which one was she? There were so many! I never saw so many little girls in one house!"

"Lucy's the littlest one, she's the baby."

"They all looked little to me. Now I understand why you had to get home to help your mother. You weren't kidding when you told us you fed your little sisters in their highchair. Did you feed all those little girls when they were babies?"

"I sure did. And they spit it back at me if they didn't like it."

"Where was your brother? I didn't see him. How does the poor kid survive with seven sisters? I've only got one sister and one brother and that's enough. My sister is crazy like you. All my buddies love her, but she's already married to Darwin. The two of you are going to hit it off." Then he was quiet again. I didn't know what to do with quiet. I had to do something, so I started singing along to radio. "Wow, how do you do that? You know all the words!"

"The words are the best part, Walt; they tell a story of things that happen in someone's life."

"I never thought of it that way. I either like the music or don't like it at all. You're a different kind of girl. Where did you come from?"

"Detroit." Boy he laughs at everything I say. Maybe he really is my prince. We rode in silence to Livonia, where he made a left turn on Plymouth Road, and a quick right into Daly's Restaurant. "Oh, I almost forgot to ask you...is this place, ok?" "It looks good to me. I've never been here before." "You've never been to Daly's?! They have the best steak burgers around." "Great! That's my favorite."

"Now you're talking! I'm tired of high for lootin fussy chicks that can't make up their mind."

Boy those girls missed out. I'll go anywhere with this guy. That was my exact thought as he came around to open the door and help me out. While we waited for dinner, he put a nickel in the small table jukebox table and a song by the Flamingos came on; are the stars out tonight, I don't care if it's cloudy or bright, I only have eyes for you. I nearly flipped and almost couldn't eat dinner. Afterwards we talked through the whole movie. I had no idea what was playing at that drive in theatre. "I want to live on a lake up north someday Pat and have a yellow Labrador." Why is he telling me this? Is he the one I've been waiting for? I'm afraid to believe it. "I've never met a Labrador, Walt, I assume it's a dog, don't you want any kids?"

"Labs are good with kids that's why they're so popular. A couple of rug rats would be great with a Lab. I think someday is a good time for kids." Does he mean he wants to have kids with ME? Oh my God! "Someday sounds good to me Walt... just not right now."

"I have a lot of plans Pat. I'm opening my own construction company. You met my buddies; they're all going to work for me when my contractor's license comes through."

"Hey how much are you going to pay those guys? I bet I can do some of that work."

"Man, oh man, my grandmother's going to love you. She's always tearing down walls and moving things around. Whenever I go there, she has me moving the piano or something else. My sister is like that too. You sound just like them. What day is your birthday?" "Halloween Eve." "My God I'm going out with a witch! No wonder you're so crazy."

"I'm not a witch, and I don't like scary stuff. I like lace and flowers and sparkly pretty things." "So, you're a girly girl." "No, I'm just a girl who can kick butt." "Boy, this is going to be fun! Can we go out again next week?" "Next week? Oh no, it got late! I bet they're watching the clock right now. You better get me home fast, or I'll never get to meet your sister and grandmother."

That's exactly what they were doing when I walked in the door at five minutes after ten. This time my mother conducted the interrogation. "You're late Pat." "Yes Mom, there was a long red light." "Did you have a nice time?" "Yes." "Where did you go for dinner?" "Daly's." "Was the food good?"

"Yes." "What did you have?" "Steak burgers." "How was the movie?" "Ok." "What movie did you see?" "I forgot." "What was it about?"

"I don't know." "I thought you said you saw a movie." "We were too busy." Their eyes widened in surprise and they looked at each other. What did she just say?

"Well....did he ask to see you again?" My mother was starting to sound irritated, but my head was so far in the clouds after the prince kissed me goodnight, I could barely answer. "Yes." "Well, what did you tell him for heaven's sake!?" "Yes."

"Oh, good grief Pat, go to bed!" My mother's patience snapped, and I fell off cloud nine. Starting for my room second thought hit. Timing is everything. They're here together, dad 's sober and mom's not working, the perfect time to prime the pump for next week.

"Oh, I almost forgot. Walt said it was nice to meet you. He's sorry he can't call since we don't have a phone. He wanted to ask you if he can take me out next week."

"I think I like that young man," dad replied in an unusually calm voice. "I like him too Leonard," mom agreed. Then they smiled at each other. Oh my gosh. Did I come to the right house? Who are these calm people? "Your Dad and I will talk about this together this time. Go to bed now. Goodnight."

I went to bed to dream about the prince who was coming to pick me up next week. A few weeks later he surprised me. "I went to Orin's Jewelers today, Pat. I want you to be my girl from now on and forget about Elvis." He slipped the silver 'going steady' ring on my finger and I was never so happy. Not even the cat girls who barely tolerated me now, could bring me off my lovely cloud.

Soon it was September, and I was back in school in tenth grade. Ironically Walt still hadn't asked what grade I was in, school was the last thing on our minds. But once I was back there, other kids seemed to know who I was. "Hey, you're the chick who gets picked up every day in that cool black car. What's your name? Is that your brother or something? My name is Dean. You want to walk to the Sweet Shop for a coke after last class today? Oh, this is my friend. He's not going. He doesn't talk much either."

"Nice to meet you guys, my name is Pat, and the guy in the car is not my brother."

"I told you she wouldn't go out with you. You don't have a car." His friend spoke up defining things as he considered them to be, but Dean just ignored him. "Uh, that's cool you have a boyfriend but if you should stop seeing him let me know, ok?" They walked away with Dean chiding his friend; "You were supposed to keep your mouth shut. Next time let me do all the talking when it comes to girls."

Days passed and another car lover came up to my locker. "Hi, I saw you leaving Jacks last weekend in that sharp car. I wanted to talk to you but didn't get a chance. If that guy isn't your steady, would you go to the Teen Club with me?"

"Mom I'm home. Today a cute guy at school asked me to go out with him."

"Oh? That's the second time somebody asked you recently."

"They notice me because I'm going out with a guy with a sharp car."

"Is that why you go out with Walt, because of his nice car Pat? I thought you liked him."

"I don't just like him Mom, I love him. I'd go out with him if he only had a bicycle."

"Good heavens! You love him! Why are you thinking that already? You're way too young to be thinking that. You're not even 16 yet. Who is this other boy? Is he a nice boy too?"

"Yes, he's very nice Mom and I like him." "What's his name?" "Leonard."

"Good grief!! We don't need another Leonard around here Pat! Stick with Walt."

"I knew you'd say that Mom. I only told you about him just to make you laugh."

"Well, I'm not laughing Pat, stick with Walt. He's really nice and he looks like Walter Pidgeon."

"Who the heck is this pigeon guy anyways?"

"Never mind, you silly kid. I'm too busy for this. Go help your sisters fold the laundry before you need to leave for work. I need ten more pair of hands in this house. The work never gets done. By the time I sit down it's time to go to bed."

KAREN

We became friends cooking over a hot stove in Home Economics. Karen's curly red hair matched her vibrant personality. What a blast we had, hands on cooking in a classroom setting. One day I walked home with her after school, and met her mother, her father was still at work. Karen didn't have to tell me what her home life was like. Girls with alcoholic fathers seem to just pick up on it. We formed an immediate understanding bond, and I knew this funny girl was going to be another forever friend.

SANDY

Sandy and Karen were best friends at the time. A sweet funny girl, she was always laughing and easy to get to know, all she wanted was to be loved. Sandy had a memory like a steel trap and knew everyone's name in the whole school. Between classes the three of us sneaked a smoke in the girl's room. Although it made me nauseous and headachy, I felt accepted. A friend of theirs had a pajama party, Beverly invited about 20 girls to her birthday party, and we stayed up all night. Some got cranky and a couple girls got into a silly snit. Then everybody started taking sides and arguing and the party was ruined. Next thing you know we were all walking home at three in the morning. Still crabbing at each other, under a full moon, in our pajamas carrying pillows and overnight bags. Instead of staying with the click, Karen and Sandy locked arms with me, and the three musketeers proceeded down the block. All for one, and one for all, laughing at the moon, friendships sealed forever.

END OF AN ERA

Nothing was ever calm in our house for long. It was still dark out the fateful morning dad busted into the bedroom that Carole and Sharon and I shared. He stood there shouting in a drunken rage. I jumped out of my sleep, my heart racing in fear. "Git out the bed n fix ma brekfus Patsy! Yer muther won't git up, says she's sick. All theez wimen n this ^#%*>* house n evar one sleepin."

Here we go again, another happy weekend. Nothing's going to be good enough no matter what. After all the food was cooked, I set everything on the table. "This is only haf a meal! Where's my biscuits?" Apparently too drunk to see a whole pan of fresh baked buttermilks in front of him he went berserk, throwing food around the room like he was possessed. The pan of biscuits hit the ceiling and blew into bits. Food flew in every direction, hitting the walls like a crazy cartoon movie, gravy and eggs dripping from the window onto the floor. Dismally I stared at the mess. Hours ago, my sisters and I had stayed up late, cleaning everything to please our sick mother. Now it was a garbage mess. "Clean up this *^#+# pigsty n make me a decent brekfus!"

A quiet calm came over me and I had no fear of him anymore. For some inexplicable insane reason, I expected him to agree with what I was about to say. In a calm steady voice, I told him what I considered long overdue. "I'm not making your breakfast again Dad. The way you treat us is wrong and it needs to stop. You made this mess so it's only fair that you clean it up."

"Ahl teech ya once n fer all ya #%^*+^ #* little b----!" His face distorted in anger he rushed forward grabbing the butcher knife off the stove. His arm rose in the air with the knife coming at me in an unreal reality, and every cell in my being screamed … "RUN!!!"

My bare feet felt cold wet ground, and I realized I was running behind the house. Cold cut through the pajamas so I ran into the detached garage, where I hid behind some stored items in the corner. "Please don't let him find me here God!"

Time passed on high alert, then someone was fumbling around trying to enter the garage in the dark. My blood froze. A guarded voice called softly. "You in here Pat?" Sis Carole whispered into the dark, but I didn't answer. Maybe he'd sent her to find me? "You in here Pat?" she asked again. "I brought your coat for you."

"I'm hiding back here behind all this stuff Carole. Does Dad know you're out here?"

"No, he didn't see me leave. I climbed out of the bedroom window. He's still throwing a fit in there. Mom says you should go stay at your friend Barb's house till he calms down."

"I don't have my shoes, Carole; can you bring them to me?" Back she went, climbing in and out of the window again. It was barely light out when I walked away from the house that grew fear, heading south across neighbor's yards, hoping he didn't know which way I went. Watching over my shoulder if he was following. With each step the house was further behind driving me to walk faster. I'm never going back there. But where will I live? Doesn't matter. I splashed through the streets in soaking wet shoes in minutes. Drizzling rain running off my head and under my coat collar. Only three more miles, you've walked there many times. Rain won't kill you. You'll be safe there. I reached into my coat pockets and felt the tip money I'd been saving and forgot was there. How lucky am I? That old man called me a crazy bear. Well, this bear's going to Goldilocks's house with pockets of dough, and good riddance to you too old man.

MRS. G. TO THE RESCUE

Dawn was breaking when I arrived on her doorstep. There were no lights on in the house as I rang the doorbell hoping someone would hear. Minutes passed before my friend's mother peered through the glass storm door, her eyes filled with sleep. Upon recognizing the wet creature on her porch, a surprised utter escaped her throat. She opened the door without a word and grabbed me by the collar dragging me in like a wet poodle. Once inside the warm cozy home I stood motionless, drained of emotion. Mrs. G sprang into action tugging the heavily soaked coat from my shoulders demanding; "Get those wet shoes off now girlie!" She pushed me to the bathroom ordering a long hot shower. Afterwards warm flannel pajamas were waiting, alongside a cup of hot cocoa and biscotti. Sipping and munching I watched her turning down covers on the spare bed in my friend's room. "Climb in Girlie and go to sleep," she ordered. That was her manner. Short and not too sweet. Sarge said what she had to say, combat style. Upon hearing her mother's voice Barb sat up in bed half asleep. Attempting but failing to push her blond hair off her face. "What's going on?" she asked rubbing her eyes in confusion. "How come my best friend's standing in my room in my mother's pajamas? What the hell? Where am I? I must be hallucinating. Pat and my mother are talking in my sleep.

106

Holy shit. How can it be?" She asked her funny self. Amid trauma, this funny friend could still make me laugh.

"Quiet! Both of you. Watch your mouth there Girlie. Cussing in your sleep's no excuse. I'm here in the flesh. Don't wake the dead in the next room. Sleep now. Talk Later. Final orders." That how the Sarge was, she made commands expecting them to be carried out. We crawled under the covers and whispered across the room, then we cried and cried some more. "You were almost killed! What would I do without my best friend?" Barbara sobbed, then we blew our nose and that was it. We were over it. No way would we keep crying. We had to laugh. That's the way it was with us. We began to giggle about the absurdity of eggs dripping from windows, and gravy on the ceiling then we couldn't stop. It wasn't possible to hang out with Barb without a case of the giggles. She could turn a trauma into humor. That was her gift. Her imaginative way with words cracked me up every time. And I certainly needed to laugh now. So purposely she reminded me of the time an old man stopped his car to ask us for directions. "Oh, that's way down by the Boon Docks, mister. Just stay on this road and you can't miss it. Don't stop. Keep going till you run into them." She'd said with a straight face, and he'd thanked us and drove on. Then we'd collapsed in the street howling with laughter.

"Remember that old guy Pat? He was older than dirt. I bet he's still looking for those boon docks two states past puckers knob." That did it. I laughed so hard I had to stick my face in the pillow so Sarge couldn't hear me. "Shhhh, Pat, we gotta be careful. My mother can hear through walls! If we wake her up, she'll call the army and have us dragged off to boot camp." We laughed into our pillows till nearly suffocating ourselves.

 Sometime later I awoke, hearing my friend and her mother talking. Sarge was dressed and wearing her take charge face. "I'll be back Girlie, stay here with Barbara." Then off she went. "Boy your old man's in for it now Pat. My old lady's going to the cop shop. He's gonna get his. That old man's gonna be checking out a whole new row of bars, and not the kind he's used to either." Two crazy teenagers laughed so hard we fell off the couch. That's the way it was with us. Bad things were made funny. We could laugh or we could cry. It was an easy choice.

Nothing came from Sarge visit to the police station. After all, no knew what actually happened. No one except a terrified kid and a raving maniac. A nice policeman paid a friendly visit to investigate. The kid wasn't there to tell her side. The old man said the kid had always been his worse problem. The officer knew there was more to this story. He could smell a crock of rot gut booze and bullshit. He'd seen and heard it all before. He read the story in the sick mother's eyes, and knew they were all so afraid of that old man, they slept with one eye open. What could the nice officer do? No one caught the old man red handed, it was all circumstance. But for the part when the mother got out of her sickbed to see what the ruckus was about. All she saw was food on windows, walls and ceilings. What could the nice officer do under such circumstance? After all he was no Detective Joe Friday. This was a Saturday morning case like none other than Dr. Seuss and the Cat in the Hat, with green eggs and ham splattered all about. So, the officer left without incident. Knowing this case could have been a lot worse. Grateful for people like Mrs. G who made his job easier, taking in other people's wet poodles.

Pretty soon Sarge returned with some of my clothes. "You can't go out in pajamas Girlie!" The lady was funny without trying. Then she left the room and the pounding started. "Uh oh, we better stay in here Pat. I know my mother, and I know when she's mad! She gets out in that kitchen and rattles those pots and pans. It's shake rattle and roll time. I can tell she didn't get anywhere at the cop shop. All that banging out there is what she wants to do to the old man's head." So, there I was, taking cover in my friend's lovely bedroom. Laughing into pretty pillows, safe, sound, and cozy. Drinking cocoa with biscotti while Mrs. G. prepared yummy foods I'd never tasted or even heard of. "We're Polock's Pat, my mother can cook up storms!"

108

That awful but lovely day, all my friend's family let me know I belonged. Mrs. G. was my rescue from the first time she came to our house. Sarge took it all in. She sat in the living room with my mother getting acquainted. It so happened that she saw what she'd hoped not to see. The old man staggered by in the next room. Cursing and talking to himself, so crocked he didn't know we had company sitting ten feet away. That's all Sarge needed to see. "Leaving. These girls visit at my house now on." she said and marched out. From then on whenever I walked to their house Sarge welcomed me. I came to know that her bark was worse than her bite. But this was the first time her shake rattle and roll side came out. After it was over, she came to Barbs room where we'd been waiting for the music to stop. "What do you want to eat Girlie, breakfast or lunch?" she directed at me. Holy pierogies! I was so surprised to be given a choice, I said I wasn't hungry. Without another word Sarge left the room and gave her husband orders. "Go talk to the bewildered girl Emil." Papa G was a sweetheart and a softie. "We want you to stay with us little one. Mike and Alec like having you around too. Rosie's away in college, you'll sleep in her bed while she's gone."

Barbs family was acceptable crazy. They were probably as normal as normal comes. I've never quite figured out what normal is. It's probably different for everybody. For me living in their home was a comfortable, safe, kind of crazy. Though Sarge tried to act strict, she was a walk in the park compared to Dad. She never took credit for all her kind acts. One day she worked at her sewing machine for hours, until finally she got up and pushed a pretty, new skirt into my hands. "For you Girlie." I was amazed! All that time she'd been working on something for me, without even asking my size, and it fit perfect. That was Mrs. G. Always doing good things and brushing it off when I tried to thank her. "Do good. They appreciate. Maybe. Maybe not." She said, chopping her words to save time, making her point brusquely, without sentiment.

After a couple months of living with Barb's family, Papa G took me aside with tears in his eyes. "I have bad news little one. I wish I didn't have to tell you this, but you need to give up Rosie's bed soon, she's coming home from college. Talk to your dad, I know he must be missing you." Dear Papa G was too kind to know that dad wasn't missing me at all.

Footnote: at this writing Mrs. G recently celebrated her 100th birthday. Keep trucking Sarge.

THE TRUTH COMES OUT

"Hi Mom, I'm here! I need to get some more clothes and things. What time is dad coming home? We want to be gone before he gets here."

"Where's Walt? Isn't he coming in Pat?"

"He's waiting in the car so he can honk the horn if dad shows up. I wanted to see you alone first. I've missed you so much, Mom."

"I was so worried about you Pat. I wish we had a phone in this house but maybe it's good we don't. Every time your name is even mentioned he throws another fit. He says you can't come home because you talked to him like a dog."

"Boy he sure can turn things around on the other person Mom."

"Your dad thinks you don't respect him Pat."

"At least he's right about that, I don't respect him! How can I respect someone who acts like a maniac trying to kill me?"

"You shouldn't say things you'd be sorry for Pat. You know your dad would never really hurt you. If you'd tell him, you're sorry it might give us some peace over here. He keeps talking about it and gets mad all over again and takes it out on us. Maybe he'd calm down and let you come home if you say you're sorry."

"Sorry?! Why do you keep telling 'me' to be sorry Mom? He's the one who should be sorry for coming at me with a butcher knife!"

"My God what are you saying Pat? That's not the way your dad told it. He said you talked to him like a dirty dog and made him so mad he threw the food after you left."

110

"That's not the way it happened at all, Mom! He couldn't see his biscuits he was so drunk, so he started throwing food like a madman. Then he told me to clean it up and make it again. I told him nice that I wasn't going to, and he shouldn't treat us like that. Then he went psycho and grabbed the big butcher knife off the stove and came after me, but I ran out the back door. Don't you believe me Mom?"

"Of course, I believe you Pat, now that I know. You'd never make up something like that. It's just that he told me a different story that's all. He lies so much it's starting to confuse me. I can't believe a word that man says anymore. I know how he is and how he gets from drinking days at a time. My God, what if you hadn't run out? I hate to think what would have happened. You shouldn't have sassed him like that, Pat. You know how crazy he can get."

"I couldn't take it anymore Mom, I didn't know he was 'that' crazy!"

"After Barbara's mother came for some of your things, a policeman came here, and your dad told him you ran away from home. I was standing right there and caught him in the lie and wasn't going to let him get away with it. I told the policeman I sent you to your friend's house because there was a big argument. I should've known he was making it all up, but I was so tired that I couldn't think anymore. He yelled for hours after you left. I was so sick I could barely stand. It's a good thing Barbara's mother is so good hearted. She told me before that you were always welcome at her house. I don't know what we would've done if she hadn't told me that. Stay at her house until I think what to do next. Maybe things will quiet down over here."

"Quiet down! Geez Mom, he's never going to change. You can't trust him anymore around these kids. What if he goes crazy and tries to hurt the little one's next time? You have to leave him!"

"Stop Pat. I can't think about this anymore. I know I need to do something because he's getting worse all the time. I just don't know which way to go with all these kids."

"We'll find a way Mom. I'll help you. Some of the kids can get jobs now. You can't let him find out you're planning something or who knows what the crazy nut will do."

"You shouldn't talk that way about your dad even if it's true Pat."

At times talking with my mother seemed useless. She went back and forth contradicting herself without a plan of action. It seemed like she would give up everything to have peace with a crazy man. A light went on in my head. It was the same old thing happening again. This was just a different scenario. I looked into my mother's eyes and saw the truth. "You're not going to leave him are you Mom? I should've known. No matter how much I wish for a happy ending it's not going to happen is it? It's just a fantasy in my stupid head."

"Don't call yourself that Pat, you're very smart. Don't cry Pat, everything will work out. Go back to Barbara's for now to give me time to think. Maybe things will get back to normal and you can come back home."

"Normal! You call this nuthouse normal? I could never come back here. I'd never be able to sleep. It was hard enough before this happened, hearing everything that goes on in this house. I can't take it anymore. I'll quit school and get three jobs before I ever come back here."

What's the point of telling her I need to leave Barb's house soon? What good will it do? My mother can't help me. She has all the other kids to think about. Why should I make her worry about me? She has enough to deal with. They're living with a maniac.

"What are you thinking Pat? I know you. You're planning something in that head of yours. Don't be thinking about quitting school. Go back to Barbara's for now until I figure something out. This is not the way I hoped it would be for you. Things are not turning out right now, but they'll get better. You have to stay in school in order to get ahead later on."

"I was just thinking about getting a different job that's all, Mom. Walt goes out of his way to take me to work every day because he loves me."

"He loves you!? You're just a kid! You don't know what love is yet."

"I know he loves me Mom, we're going to get married."

"Married!? Did he ask you that? You can't get married, you're only 16."

"Geez Mom I know how old I am. He didn't ask me but on our first date we agreed we wanted to have two kids and a Labrador someday."

"What makes you so sure that's going to happen Pat?"

"I just know it Mom. He's the one I've been waiting for since I was a kid."

"How can you be sure he's the 'right' one?" "I just know Mom. I feel it in my heart."

My mother sighed her long, weary sigh, then asked the same rhetorical question I'd heard so many times before. "What am I going to do with this kid?" Then she sighed again. "You've always been too old for your own good. Go out and tell Walt to come in, I want to talk to him."

"I know how she is Walt, she's bullheaded. She'll try and do everything on her own. You need to watch her, so she stays in school. Take her back to Barbara's for now and thank you for taking her to work every day."

"I love her Mrs. D, and I'll make her stay in school, I promise you."

"Hurry and get your things together Pat. Your dad will be coming home soon."

A few days later Walt picked me up after work. "Let's stop and call Barb's mother Pat. Ma wants you to come to our house for dinner tonight. She made your favorite pot roast with brown gravy and onions, and brown sugar carrots and mashed potatoes. She even made you a coconut cake. Wait till you see it! It's a foot tall!"

"We wanted you to come for dinner Pat, so we could talk. Sonny told us what happened with your dad. It's good your friend's family took you in, but now you need to leave again with nowhere to go. We made a room for you here. So, when do want to move in?"

"I'll be taking you to school Pat. I don't want to go steady with no dummy." Everyone laughed, then I cried from happiness. How could I be so lucky.

One day in October Walt surprised me again. "Happy Sweetest Day Pat!"

Sweetest Day? What's that? I never heard of it. He presented a heart shaped box while his mother looked on, watching me open the pretty red box full of chocolates. Plus, a huge silk greeting card he'd signed; "To my sweetheart, Love Walt." Of course, I started crying which made his Ma cry too. "What'd you get your mama, Sonny boy?" She teased and he lifted his five-foot mama off the floor in a big bear hug. "Put me down Sonny before you drop me!"

CONSEQUENCES

It was the end of October. "Let's stop and see Ruth Ann and Darwin before we go out for your birthday tonight."

"SURPRISE! Happy 18th birthday Pat!" Gleefully Ruth Ann led a room full of people in song. "Here you go Pat, have a beer, then you can spend the night here with my brother." Everyone thought that was hilarious; except me. It was my most embarrassing moment. Now what am I going to do? Will he break up with me if I don't stay the night with him? I can't tell him the truth with all these people here. They think I'm an adult.

I chugged down a beer and it chugged back up. Whoops slop, bring the mop. The whole night was an embarrassment. Why did everyone make such a big deal about sex? What was all the hoopla about? It was still a mystery to me. Weeks passed and the lie weighed heavier and heavier on my conscience. It wasn't just a little white lie anymore. It had to come out before I got in big trouble. So, I told my best friend. "I had sex with Walt on my birthday

Barb, now we have to get married." To my horror she started to sob. "Oh no! I'm losing my best friend because she had sex!"

She was no help at all. I had to tell Walt the truth before this messing around turned into a big belly. There was no way I was ready for one of those. The next day he was talking to Ma in the kitchen. "I have something to tell you Walt and Ma should hear this too since I'm living here. The thing is, I lied to you. I wasn't 18 on my birthday. I just turned 16."

For the longest time it seemed he was holding his breath. A strange chalky white came over his face with a look I never expected to see on a prince. Then he blew up. "Oh my God, you tricked me! You're jailbait! You lied to me! I'm breaking up with you right now! I'm leaving here and never coming back!" He stormed out and drove away and I was never so miserable in my life. "I'm so sorry Ma. I'll leave soon as possible so he can come back home. But can you please tell me what that word means?"

"For pity's sake, Pat, didn't anybody ever tell you anything? Jailbait means you're underage. My son could go to jail for dating you, he's 20 years old now!"

"Oh my God I didn't know. I never heard that word before!" At that very moment Pop walked in the front door, home from work. "What's going on in here?" he inquired with authority.

"Pat just told us she lied about her age Louie, and Sonny broke up with her. He left madder than a hornet, saying he's never coming back. Pat never heard of jailbait, so I was explaining to her."

"Is that all? I thought somebody died the way you two look. What's for dinner? Let's talk about this later when Sonny gets home. He has to come back, he lives here."

Hours later when everyone was asleep, I lay awake until I heard the bat mobile. Walt went to his room and was gone the next morning before I woke. I took the bus to school then walked to work afterward. Then walked back to their house, expecting to be kicked out. By the time I arrived it was past dark. Everyone was waiting in the living room. Walt's face was stubbornly set ignoring me. Pop

115

started the conversation. "We all need to talk so we'll start with you Pat. What do you have to say for yourself?"

Was that a trick question? No one ever questioned me like that before. Someone was asking me to explain myself. In the house of fear there was one judge who convicted without inquiry. He presumed you were guilty even if you weren't and punished harshly. This time I was guilty as sin. "I lied Pop. I hurt everybody when you were all so good to me. It's the worst thing I've ever done. I'm really sorry and I'll leave as soon as possible."

"Nobody's going anywhere until we decide the right thing to do. I had a hunch you might not be as old as you said, but Sonny swore you were turning 18, so I trusted his judgement. Now I'm sorry I didn't check on it myself."

"As for you Sonny you really should've known better. You've always dated older girls, so I assumed you got your lesson. Then you brought Pat home and said she was the right one, because she was naïve about these things. Don't you think you should be asking more questions of someone you're caring a lot for Son?"

"I suppose so Pop."

"I want a straight answer Sonny. Is there any chance that Pat could be pregnant?"

"No Pop." Walt shuffled his feet and looked down, embarrassed.

Then Pop turned to me, and I wanted to go through the floor. "What do you have to say Pat?"

"No Pop, I started my period yesterday."

"I see," he said his face flushing. "Thank you for the straight answer. Sorry to put you on the spot but I had to know if we had a bigger situation. As for you Son, if this is the worse Pat has done, you'll get over it. When you forgive her, you'll be lucky if she forgives you too."

"If she forgives me!? What for Pop? I thought she was legal age!"

"Her age is not the only issue here Son. You knew she was naïve. If you would have gotten to know her better before rushing things, this would not have happened."

"I suppose you're right Pop, but she lied to me. I thought she was a good Catholic girl and I trusted her, but she tricked me and it's too late now. I don't trust her anymore. I hate liars and I don't want her around anymore."

"Are you going to sit there and tell me you didn't just lie about being with her?"

"I didn't lie Pop. She told me yesterday morning everything was ok."

"What you just did Son is called skirting the issue to avoid telling the truth. I taught you better than that. So do you think I should just put her out now?" The prince didn't answer his father. "I see you have more growing up to do before you see your fault in this Sonny. You have to be able to forgive before you talk about marrying someone."

"As for you, Pat, if you want to leave, take whatever time you need. If you want to stay, you are   still welcome here. Erve and I will not put you out. It's your decision. As far as you and my son are concerned, there's only one certainty. You have a lot more growing up to do and shouldn't even think about marriage, until you're out of high school at the very least. Maybe you kids will patch things up, or maybe you won't. You might get married someday, or you might not. But if you two don't know how to forgive, marriage should never happen. For the time being, you might have to go your separate ways to keep peace is this house. That's the only rule we have here; the peace must be maintained. That's enough about this. Mistakes have been made that are not irreparable. Life will go on."

"Erve and I decided earlier that we want to tell you our story Pat. You had a troubled childhood, but history is there to teach us. If we ignore the lesson, we get nothing but the pain. We lived in poverty as kids. The First World War started before I was born, and my father didn't make it back. The whole country was unstable. The

117

rich owned most of the assets, limiting growth in the economy and wages plummeted. The stock market crashed on Black Tuesday in 1929. People gathered around their radio listening to prices fall. I was 12 years old, but my mother wouldn't let me leave the house, because she heard people were jumping out windows to their deaths. The great depression went on for over ten years. Banks lost people's savings, so no one trusted them, and hid what little they had in their mattress. Jobs were scarce. Hundreds of thousands lost their homes. People farmed their children out to be fed under someone else's roof. Despair was everywhere. When farmers in the southwest lost their farms, the land went uncultivated, and the great dust bowl formed. Topsoil blew so thick daylight looked like night. Average working men became hobo's hopping on boxcars, riding across the country searching for work. Cities became Shantytowns. People stood in soup lines for a slice of bread, or a cup of coffee. I was often asked; brother can you spare a dime? If you had a buffalo nickel in your pocket, you were a lucky fellow. I couldn't see a future for myself, so I joined the Navy. When Franklin D Roosevelt came into office, he had a plan to jumpstart the country. His 'new deal' went into action, and systems were set up as safety nets to guard the economy. The Federal Deposit Insurance Corporation was formed to ensure the banks wouldn't lose people's savings. Unemployment was set up to keep people from losing their homes. Social Security was set up to keep the elderly from becoming homeless. World War Two lasted over six years. Over 60 million lives were lost. When it was over veterans returned home and bought homes for zero down on the GI bill that Roosevelt initiated.

We say we fought for our freedom, but we will never be free until we stop killing each other. If we don't find ways to keep peace, we're going to destroy ourselves. The United Nations was formed with that ideal in mind. For countries to come together to resolve their differences and keep the peace. Perhaps one day you and my son will make a trip to Manhattan and see flags of all nations flying together. It's a beautiful sight. History has taught Erve and I, above all else, to keep peace."

"How did you meet her Pop?"

"I got out of the Navy with a bum leg and answered an ad for a temporary bookkeeper. When I got there, I learned it was an orphanage. There was a young girl in the yard, struggling to hold onto a younger boy. He kept trying to pull away, but she wouldn't let him go. I didn't get the job but couldn't forget those kids. I went back to find out about them and was told they'd been there for years. Their parents were immigrants who became homeless and wanting the children to survive, they took them there. When I heard their story, I couldn't walk away; the right thing to do was give them a foster home. In time the girl told me she was in love with me. I could hardly believe my good fortune, that this beautiful young woman could love a homely guy like me. We were married as soon as the law allowed. It was the happiest day of my life. Her brother lived with us until he went in the service. That's our story Pat. Now we find out the girl our son brought home was only 15 years old too. You need a family so we will be your family."

"Now hear me out Pat, I have more to say and it's about your dad. You might think I don't know him, as we only met once when Sonny's car acted up in his driveway. I've known many troubled men like him. Your dad's drinking is beyond his being able to help himself alone. I've got a drinking problem too; it started in the Navy. I've been in recovery many years. At one time it was hour by hour. Your dad was in the Army. His habit might have started there since you remember him drinking all your life. Drinking is a sickness for many people Pat. Your dad's sickness has gone on so long his judgement is nearly destroyed. No man in his right mind would put a daughter your age out to fend for herself. Deep in his heart your dad loves you, but he's too sick to see what he's done. Hopefully one day he'll get the help he needs. When that day comes, you can begin to build a relationship with him. Someday when you're older you'll see your parents differently. You'll be able to see that they're just people with faults. Until then we'll be here for you. Because we love you, don't we Erve?"

119

"That's right Pat, we love you like a daughter. Whether you and Sonny make it or not, you will always be a daughter. Tomorrow I'm going to bake your favorite, pumpkin pie. What should I make for you Sonny?"

"Don't make me nothing Ma, I won't be here. If Pat is staying Pop, I'm leaving home."

"You're a man now Son. If you decide to leave, so be it. My door will always be open to you." "Don't go Sonny," Ma cried. "Forgive Pat and be her friend if nothing else." He got up without answering and went to his room, minutes later he came out with some of his things. "Good by Ma," he said quietly walking out.

The weight of his departure fell heavy, crushing down on me. A lie had cost more than my innocence. Walt left his family's home because of me. I took the bus to school every morning, choking back tears, holding back more in classes. Afterwards I walked to a job that was no longer fun; customers stopped leaving big tips, the star carhop had lost her magic charm. "What's the matter Chatty Patty? We don't see Walt picking you up anymore. He broke up with you, didn't he? We knew it wouldn't last."

Smug cats were happy, and I couldn't say a mean word, or I'd lose my job. I was in a sad sour pickle mess, and I'd created it myself. What if Walt's parents turn on me after they start missing their son? You know you can't count on anybody. Please God, don't let me end up back there with dad. I can't go back. I won't. I'm keeping this job and no cats can force me out. I'll leave when I'm ready, not before.

The long days and tearful nights passed slowly. Weeks went by and then the phone rang. "I thought it was only right to let you know that Walt's been staying at my house Pat. He wanted me to call Ma to tell her he's ok, but he doesn't want to talk to you."

"Ma's not home right now Smitty but I'll tell her."

"I'm sorry this happened between you guys' Pat, and I wish you good luck in whatever you do. You're a nice girl and I want to help you, but Walt is my friend so I'm helping him."

"I understand Smitty, thank you for being a good friend."

Time passed slowly. Ma kept feeding me to cheer me up. Weeks seemed like years to a sixteen-year-old with a broken heart. One afternoon I was walking home and there was the bat mobile in the driveway. Walt was back! My feet wanted to run, but my heart raced in ahead of me. For one reason or another, Ma and Pop happened to be gone. I passed Walt's room and he was sitting on the bed, sorting through things he'd taken from his closet. His clothes were piled in neat stacks, ready to go. So, this was it. He was leaving for good. If I didn't say something now, he'd be gone forever, and we'd never speak again.

"You don't have to leave your home Walt! This was my fault and I'm very sorry. I'm going to see my dad and beg him to let me stay until I find another place to go." He jumped up dropping a stack of clothes and grabbed me in his arms.

"I missed you so much I couldn't stand it. I'll never let you go back to that house. I won't let you live with that old man so he can hurt you again. I'd really end up in jail over you then. I love you Pat and want to marry you someday. I just hope you don't drive me crazy. That old man made you crazy and I'm the guy who's going to be stuck with it. Just don't ever lie to me again, no matter what happens. Promise you'll always tell me the truth. I can take it. I swear I will. We have to be honest with each other if we're going to make it."

"I promise I'll always tell you the truth even if you don't like what I say Walt. I love you with all my heart."

"I'm going to get you an engagement ring, I must like that you're crazy because I only came back so I could be near you."

"Why are you taking everything out of your closet then? I thought you were leaving home."

"I'm just cleaning my closet. I'm taking some things to Smitty. He doesn't have anything, and I have too much. I left his house mad because he told me what he thought. He called me a damn fool and said I was wrong for not making up with you. I didn't want to hear it

121

and cussed him out, now I feel bad, he didn't deserve that. He was only telling the truth, Smitty's a good man."

"Yes, he is Walt, he's a real friend."

"Smitty is always going to be my friend so don't try to scare him off."

"Why would you say that!? I love Smitty; why would I do something like that?"

"Because you're a crazy kid that's why. You scared Jack and Bob away and I don't want you to scare Smitty away too."

"Don't blame me if you're not seeing your buddies, they have girlfriends now, that's why you don't see them. I love Jack and Bob too. All those guys are the greatest thing since sliced bread. They're the nicest guys around. Ask them to double date with us. I feel weird being the only girl with a couple other guys along. They're not my brother's you know. I grew up with six sisters. I'm a woman's woman."

"Well, I'm a man's man and I like having my buddies around. They like you a lot too, but we want to get together to do manly things."

"So go fishing and hunting with them sometimes but save some weekends for us alone."

"That sounds great to me Pat."

The next week he surprised me again. "I went to Orin's Jewelers again Pat. This is all the cash I had but someday I'm going to get you a real nice diamond." The tiny chip sparkled in the blue velvet box, but not on my finger. That was ok. It said we were engaged.

THE SIGNATURE CHRISTMAS

And so, it was Christmas, and what had we done. Another year together and we'd only begun. Nothing had changed inside me; just because I was engaged to a prince didn't mean I felt secure. I was the same emotionally insecure little girl I was when we met. If he wanted to go someplace without me, I panicked. Nothing would make me feel secure unless we got married. Despite the fact I was still in high school we set the date for the coming January in 1961. We would start our lives together in a New Year. All I needed was my mother's signature. And so it was Christmas and there I was, nervously going back to that house, thinking about the last time I'd seen dad over a year and a half ago. Knowing that a welcome mat and cookies wouldn't be waiting for me. Quietly I slipped through the back door hoping mom was in her usual place. Luckily, she was doing the laundry in the small room by the back door. "Shhhh, be quiet Pat, he's right there in the dining room with his head in the radio. I'm so happy to see you. I was just thinking about you and here you are!"

"I came to tell you Merry Christmas and bring a little something, a box of chocolates for the kids and your favorite fruitcake, with lots of nuts. I have some good news too; Walt and I are getting married next month. I need your signature and my birth certificate."

"You just turned 17 two months ago Pat!"

"Geez Mom, why do always tell me how old I am? Don't you know that I know that?"

"You silly kid. All I'm saying is it's too young to get married. How can you be sure about this?"

"I've never been surer of anything in my life Mom. Oh, and I want to ask you something else before I forget. Was Dad in the war when he was in the Army?"

"For goodness' sake! Why in the world would you be asking that now of all times?"

"Because I barely see you anymore Mom. When do we ever get to talk? I started wondering where Dad was during the war, because Pop has been telling me stories about how they grew up during the depression, and how those bad times affected them."

"We grew up then too Pat. I told you a little when you were a kid, but you were always such a worrywart I didn't want to tell you more."

"So, was he Mom?"

"Was he what?"

"Was he in the war... Geez O Pete, Mom!"

"Don't be so impatient all the time Pat. I don't remember all that. He didn't talk about it. I don't see how he could have been because you were born then. He had to be out of the Army. He kept that old uniform in the back of the closet for years. Remember when he put it on one time to show you how he looked in it? You kept asking him, so he did. Maybe you don't remember that. You were just a little kid."

"I remember a lot of things Mom. He was proud that it still fit. I told him he looked handsome in it, and he got drunk and mean again that night."

"You remember things you should forget Pat. I can't believe you want to get married already. Why do you want to get married so soon?"

"Geez Mom, I know that look. You don't have to wonder about it. We don't 'have' to get married. We just don't want to wait anymore. We've been together over two years. That's long enough to get to know each other. We're not having kids right away. We're going to wait."

"That's good Pat. Wait till you're older to have kids. You must promise me you'll stay in school. I like Walt a lot, and you know that. It's just that I can't believe you're old enough to get married. You always thought you were older than you were. You're too old for your own good."

"Whatever that means Mom. Anyway, we have a plan. I'm staying in school and still going to work. We're saving for a house."

"That'll be nice to have your own home, it makes me happy to know you kids have a plan. Wait here and I'll get your birth certificate. I'll only take a minute."

Wouldn't you know dad decided to go to the bathroom that minute. At seeing the ghost, he thought he chased out long ago, he stopped dead in his tracks. There she was again. Looking him in the eye defiantly. "What the hell am ah seein n ma house? U ain't welcome here no moe!"

"I just came to get Mom's signature then I'm leaving."

"We ain't signin nuthin fer u, yer on yer own."

"I'm not asking for anything Dad. All I need is Mom's signature. I'm getting married."

"Married! Who the hell'd marry u? No man n his rite mind."

"Damn you Leonard! Why would you say a thing like that to hurt her on purpose? God will punish you for that!" my mother yelled.

"Aww go own n sign th damn thang Stell, she ain't gun mount ta nuthin n her life so makes no differnce. Sign n git 'er gone frum ere."

"Stop it, Leonard! She's never done a thing to hurt you and she doesn't want anything from you so get away from us! We don't need you in here. I don't need your permission to sign for my own daughter. I already signed her paper so get out of my kitchen!" Feisty little mom pushed past him, and he lost his balance, stumbling backward. Green eyes flashed in wild anger.

"Go Now Pat! Take your papers and go marry Walt! God sent you a decent young man. Go marry him and be happy! Come and see me when your dads at work."

"She ain't nare comin n ma house agin!"

"Shut your mouth Leonard, it's my house too, and I'll see my daughter whenever I want!"

"Git yer ass gone ya sorry thang. Sorry fer eny feller marryin u. E ain't gettin nuthin."

His words followed me out ringing in my ears. Why does he hate me so much? Who cares? I'm getting married and Walt will protect me forever. Woman child revved the motor on a mean batman machine and was away from that house in seconds.

WEDDING DAY

Papers in hand we planned a wedding on a shoestring. There would be no ball, no ball gown, or sparkly glass slippers. I had won the prince. He was my prize. He was all I needed. The wedding was to be held in the home office of the Justice of the Peace for a small pittance. I found a tea length dress at rock bottom clearance, borrowed my sister's Holy Communion veil, completing my ensemble. Necessity is the mother of invention. We scrimped and saved coins in paper rolls from the bank to make a wedding happen. As the day approached sis Carole finally told me what Dad said, "nobody in this house is going to that thing, your mother don't need a dress, she's staying right here where she belongs." A couple days before the wedding he passed out drunk and mom went to the corner pay phone. "Pick me up Saturday morning Pat, he's not stopping me from going."

 "I thought he wouldn't get you a dress Mom." "I'll starch my housedress and wear that." "Don't worry Mom; I'll get you a dress."

Flowers were crossed off the list. We didn't really 'need' them. After roaming through stores for hours I finally found something. It wasn't what I really wanted for her, but it was the last roll of nickels. With the package under my arm, I took it to her, so she could hide it under the bed until Saturday. She opened the big green box from Federal's department store, folding back white tissue papers. A look of disappointment came to her eyes, but she managed a smile and thanked me. Then I made a wish, that someday I'd be rich enough to give my mother everything she ever wanted.

The morning of the wedding the weather was below zero. Yet there she was, waiting in freezing cold on the street in front of the house. She jumped in the moment we stopped. "Go Walt hurry!" That's when I knew what it cost her to go with us. "Thank you for coming for us today, Mom."

"You kids had to know I wouldn't miss this day no matter what happened." She said managing a smile and sunshine skipped across blinding white snow into the car. The sun continued to shine that cold January day as she stood behind us with my friend Barb. "Who gives this woman to be married to this man?" Justice questioned, and she stepped forward in her official navy blue, white-collar dress. "I do. I am her mother." She said in a sure steady voice. Forever after I owed a debt I could never repay. At the expense of her own safety, my mother had made it possible for me to marry the love of my life.

MARRIED LIFE

We continued to live with Ma and Pop saving for a house. Every evening after dinner the whole family sat around laughing with one of Ma's homemade desserts. Cream puffs filled with custard and topped with chocolate sauce. Chunky chocolate chip and nut cookies served warm with vanilla ice cream. Pound cake topped with fruit and whipped cream or ice cream, your choice. Fresh baked apple and cherry pies served warm with a scoop of ice cream. Chocolate fudge cake with fudge icing, topped with cherry ice cream. Everything made from scratch and guaranteed to add a couple pounds. Ma's birthday cakes were famous at kid's parties. She put half dollars inside the layers. Inspect before you bite. Into the batter she mixed walnuts, bananas, maraschino cherries and coconut. The three-layer cakes were topped with butter frosting and whipped cream between each layer. Her cakes were enough to knock a sweet tooth dead. Ma, the gourmet cook, and extraordinary baker, a happy, chubby, little chef. That was Erve. My dear kind and laughing mother-in-law. A little orphan girl who grew up and taught herself the secrets of chefs, showing her love for others with food and flowers.

A FULL TIME JOB

One afternoon I sat in history class trying to listen, while the same bunch of silly kids kept interrupting. This is so ridiculous. I'm not getting anything out of school anymore. When class was over, I walked out of the building and caught the public bus. Within the next hour I had a full-time job at the mall and went home to tell my new husband. He blew a gasket like I figured he would, but it was too late now. What's done is done. "You need to get your butt back to school and forget about that job. I promised your mother you'd stay in school and graduate. Now you've broken my promise. You don't have to work; I'm making plenty and we're saving most of it by living here."

"I figured you'd say that Walt, that's why I didn't tell you beforehand. I'm going to go to night school with adults."

"So, I guess you're saying you're going to do what you want and tell me later, is that it, Pat?"

"No not really, it's not like that. My job will give us 40 extra dollars a week, so we can rent our own place."

"Forty dollars! That's only a dollar an hour! I make that much in a few hours! What were you thinking Pat, taking a full-time job for only 40 dollars a week!"

"It adds up to $160 a month, we can rent something and not be living off your parents. I want to pay my own way and not be a mooch."

"It's not being a mooch, that's what parents do for their kids. Your family now Pat, they love you and want to help us get started."

"I know that Walt, and I appreciate it I really do. I love them too. They're the best in-laws I could dream of getting, but I want my own place. I've never had privacy in my life. Now we're sleeping together, and your folks are in the next room. Don't you understand?"

"Ok I get that. But we'd have to rent a dump for that amount. I'm not going to waste our savings on rent. The plan was to buy a house within two years."

"It's still the plan Walt, but a dump is ok until then. We can go to thrift stores for a few pieces of furniture to get started, we're going to need it anyway."

"I guess I have no choice then, do I Pat? You've got it all figured out. I better go along with honey bear, or I'll come home to listen to her growling. Is this the way it's going to be? You make up your mind first, then tell me before we can talk about it?"

"Now I feel bad after you put it that way. I'm sorry Walt, I'll talk to you first next time I promise. The thing about high school is I don't fit in there anymore. Ever since we went to bed together, I don't feel right with a bunch of kids just flirting around."

"Don't kid yourself Pat, those kids aren't just flirting around. They're having sex."

"That's a mean thing to say about kids you don't even know! They're just going to dances and parties and making out a little. They're not going to bed like we did."

"Ok Pat whatever you say. I really don't care what they're doing, it's none of my business. Let's just go find our own place and make our own fun."

So we moved into a little rental and within a year. Surprise! "Guess what Walt, I'm pretty sure I'm pregnant."

"I didn't think that stuff we were using was going to work. Looks like I'm going to be a father. I know you'll be a good mother. I see how protective you are with your brother and sisters. Wait till Ma and Pop hear this! They're going to be happy. Wonder if we'll have a boy or girl."

"It'll be a boy."

"You can't just put in your order like that Pat."

"Why not?"

"Aren't you going to get bored sitting around waiting for the baby to come?"

"Why would I get bored, I have no intention of quitting my job."

"Can you work when you're pregnant?"

"Of course, I can. Why not, I'm healthy as a horse so why would I quit working? Besides, I want to get my sisters party dresses and shoes for their junior high school dances."

"Whatever you want to do for your family is fine with me Pat. But why are you so sure we're having a boy? Maybe science will come up with a way to know but it won't be in time for us. How do you know what's in the oven?"

"Because I want a boy first to watch our girl."

"That doesn't make sense Pat a girl will do that too. I'd like to have a boy, but a little girl would be nice too. What's the real reason you want a boy first?"

"Because I always wanted a big brother. Bob protected us but there'll never be another little kid like him. We have to have a real big boy, and that's all there is to it!"

"Aww don't cry Pat, here let me hug you. It'll be ok if we don't have a boy first. If it's a girl she'll be a tough little nut like you. She'd beat the hell out of anyone who bothered her brother or sister. Oh my God what'll I do with two like you? And why are you talking about the next one already? You have to let me know these things ahead of time."

"I am letting you know. We agreed on our first date that we wanted two kids. So, let's get it over with and have them close together. That way they'll want to do things together. Besides, I don't want to be pregnant all my life."

"All your life!? It only takes nine months Pat. Even an elephant only takes a year. But it would be good for our kids to be close in age. So, when can we get started on the next one?"

"First we need to make one rule. No one can babysit our kids except our mothers or sisters."

"That's a good rule Pat, let's keep it. Can we go to bed now?" Hmm why not, I'm already pregnant. What else can happen. You can't get pregnant on top of pregnant, can you?

THE LONG RIDE HOME

One particularly pleasant day I felt pulled to see my family and acted on it. As I approached the back door, I heard a muffled sob coming from the pigeon shed. My brother was inside with his pets, trying to recover from another beating. The day suddenly turned a mean red and I turned and ran for the house. I got one foot inside the back door before my mother was in front of me. "Stop Pat! Don't go in there. It won't do any good. It'll just make things worse. I'm glad you showed up though. I don't know how it is but you always seem to have good timing. Bob needs you right now. Take him out for a nice long ride and talk to him. It'll be good for him to get away, and he likes Walt's car so much."

We went for a long ride all right. It was a doozy. The first of many excursions my brother and I would take throughout our lives. That afternoon two angry kids headed for Telegraph Road, where all the hotrods went to race. I had no intention of racing. I was just going there to drive all hell out. We hit Telegraph and flew south breaking every speed limit, putting distance between us and that dreaded house. We flew past the Ohio State line and never even noticed. Windows down, wind blowing in our face, the miles passed along with our anger. By the time it dawned on me how far we'd traveled, a sign said Kentucky. "Where the heck are we Bob?"

"How do I know? I figured you knew where you were going since you're the one driving. I'm just enjoying this car. Boy, it sure does fly. Walt should've painted it green and named it the Green Hornet. Green is my favorite color, you remember?"

"How could I forget you've told me a thousand times. Do you remember when I told you we would get out of that hell hole someday? It's about time don't you think? If you want to come and live with us, I'll ask Mom about it when we get back."

"I've been thinking of leaving for a long time. I'm going in the Army, already talked to the recruiter, but he can't take me till next year. When we get back to the house I'll talk to mom. If she thinks she can handle dad without me, I'll tell her I'm ready to go live with you and Walt."

The long ride home took several more hours. Mom was waiting anxiously in her usual spot in the kitchen by the back door. "I was so worried about you kids! It's been dark for hours now."

"Sorry Mom. We lost track of time. Pat was headed in the wrong direction a while. We want to talk to you about something."

"So, talk Bob before he wakes up and wants to know everything we're talking about."

"Yes Bob, I know what I have to do to get around him. You don't have to tell me that. I wasn't born yesterday you know. It would be better if you left home now, that way I won't have to worry that he'll hurt you bad the next time."

"It's getting worse all the time Pat. He acts like a crazy person anymore, jealous of his own son. What a shame. What would it come to if you stayed here Bob? I can't take a chance on that. . Start packing your things and put them under the bed, so you're ready when she comes to get you. I'm glad you and Walt are doing this Pat."

"Me too Mom. I'll be back soon. Maybe even tomorrow."

As I pulled into our driveway Walt was coming out the door with his coat on. "My God, where have you been so long?! Look what time it is. I called Pop to pick me up and he's on his way. We were going out to look for you. I was imagining all kinds of things, afraid the old man hurt you or something. Please don't go there without me from now on. I'll wait in the car so I don't have to see his face, or I might punch him. Promise me you won't go there alone again."

"Ok Walt but..."

"Someone called tonight on the ad in the paper to sell the car. They wanted to see it, but I had to tell them I didn't know where you were. I started thinking you might have wrecked it and were afraid to come home. You've never done anything like this so what was I supposed to think? I was going out of my mind wondering what happened. Now Pop is on his way here and there's no way we can reach him."

"I'm sorry Walt, I really am. You know what...you just gave me an idea. There should be phones in cars so people can call each other!"

"That's not a bad idea Pat. But why would you make me worry about you like this, when we have a new baby coming?" After I explained what happened, he understood why Bob and I went for a mad dog drive. "We've talked about your brother coming here before this, so let's just go see your mother tomorrow while the old man's gone and ask her if Bob can live with us. We need to get him away from there. No kid should be treated like that. It makes me sick to hear it. I get so mad at that old man I could spit nails at him. It's too bad we can't bring your sisters too. With a new baby coming and no health insurance we can't afford it. The hospital wants five hundred dollars beforehand, and the doctor wants his three hundred up front too, it's a wonder anyone can be born these days."

"At least we got to take my sisters to the Ford Rotunda in Dearborn for the Christmas display. You have the best ideas, Walt; I love that about you."

"Those little girls never saw anything like that Pat, they're eyes got so big. They had such a good time and you were the biggest kid of them all."

"I loved it, Walt. It was the most beautiful Christmas display I'll probably ever see. I'll never forget it. It was Christmas in fairy land."

The next day my husband came home with a frown on his face. "Guess who I ran into today? I was on the job in Bloomfield Hills and who showed up but your old friend Crazy Johnny from Jacks Drive In. He was looking for some extra work and stopped to talk to me. He said he saw my car going down Telegraph yesterday like a bat out a hell."

"Ok Walt it's true. I was driving too fast but not as fast as Crazy Johnny said. Boy he's got some nerve to talk. He passed every hot rod on Telegraph Road when he gave me a ride in his brand-new two-seater. He scared me half to death that time, the car lifted off the ground! You thought I was exaggerating until it was your turn. He even scared you. You're the one who named him Crazy Johnny after that. Then everybody started calling him that too. He shouldn't be talking about other people's driving. He's the original Go Johnny Go. That song wasn't about some kid with a guitar, it was about Crazy Johnny and his flying, powder blue, T- Bird!"

LIFE WITH A KICK

We were watching TV one evening, when it happened. "Holy Moley, something weirds going on in my stomach! It feels like something's moving! You think it's the baby?"

"How would I know Pat? I never had a baby. Does it hurt? Should we go to the hospital? I'm calling Ma to ask her what we should do. Stay right there. Don't move!"

"Ha ha ha ha ha ha. It's never a dull moment with you is it, Pat? Ha ha ha ha ha ha ha ha. Ha ha ha ha ha ha. That's the funniest yet. I can't stop laughing at you two. Didn't your mother ever tell you anything? Tell Sonny to bring you over so we can see how big you got since last week. Ha ha ha ha ha ha ha ha, Oops I laughed so hard I gotta go pee. Here talk to Ruth Ann, I gotta run!"

I'm glad I didn't know in advance about my baby moving inside me. The first time it happened was magical. Not expecting it, made it even more so.

MOTHERHOOD

The greatly anticipated day arrived. When the labor pains started I called Doc who told me to go directly to the hospital. After 24 hours of pain a very young nurse told me it was 'light' labor. "Light my ass! I'm telling you this is bad pain. Plain and simple really bad pain!"

"I'm sorry but your baby isn't ready to come yet. We're sending you home."

"No way. You're not sending me home. Call my doctor and let's get this boy out of here!"

"What makes you so sure you're having a boy?" Sweet little nursie poo, questioned.

"Because we're only having two kids, so the boy has to be first to protect his sister."

"So, what if it's a girl?"

"Well, I guess she'll just have to be a tough nut like me then, won't she?" Sheesh where'd they get this nurse ...out of a Cracker Jack box? "Please call my doctor. I'm not leaving unless he says so." As I figured he had a different opinion about this. "I want you to stay put Pat. This is your first baby and sometimes they can surprise us. I want you at the hospital where we can keep an eye on you. Go out in the hall and walk. Walk up and down the stairs and let's see if we can get some action out of this little sleeper. If that doesn't wake it up, we'll let Walt take you for a ride down a bumpy road. Ha ha ha ha ha ha ha ha ha ha."

Sheesh, glad everyone thinks this joy ride is so dam funny. After 24 hours of fun, I'm exhausted but the show still must go on, can't stop in the middle of it.

A couple more hours of walking up and down the stairs, my labor increased to the point of 'Shriek.' They finally put me out of my misery with a shot in the spine, with something called, Saddle Block. Boy there's a name. Sounds like an old cowboy song. After that good stuff I was ready to watch the show. Overhead mirrors were set up and waiting. There's something else I didn't know about. Mirrors. Nobody told me anything about those. Guess you're just supposed to keep asking questions everywhere you go. The delivery room was akin to an assembly line, a lot of smooth operators working in there, it's really something. Watching my baby come in the world was nothing short of phenomenal. They held her up in the air with the cord still attached, screaming at everybody with a beet red face. Arms and legs kicking like she was ready to take on the world. Why'd you pull me out of my nice, warm, hibernating sac? "Ok little girl, we're going to take care of you right now!" The entire staff took notice of baby bear's demands to be back in a warm cozy spot. When the little bundle of pink was laid in my arms I was overwhelmed with emotion. She was the most beautiful baby I'd ever seen. Mother love was nothing like I could have imagined. It wasn't like when I held a new baby sister and fell in love with cuteness. This baby was mine. Protective mother love took over. If anybody ever tried to hurt one of my babies, they better fear mother bear.

I took to motherhood like I'd been doing it all my life. It was as natural as breathing. Long before I ever got pregnant, I knew what my babies' names would be. Twins Michael and Michelle were the cutest kids at St Joseph Elementary. Someday I was going to have two children and name them Michael and Michelle, in that order. But now I was finding out that nothing in life is a sure thing. While still pregnant I decided it might be better if I waited to meet the baby first, to see if the name suit the little person. After all, you don't name your cat and dog until you meet them, their personalities tell you who they are. So, I held my newborn baby and talked to her. Looked into her big blue eyes, and sweet round face framed with black hair, and I knew. 'Michelle Rene' was the perfect name for this little Irish French girl full of spunk.

OFF TO THE ARMY

Shortly after Michelle was born, Bob was ready to leave for the army. Mom signed his papers and he was excited about his first big adventure. "Wish me luck Pat I'm off to the Army. You and Walt have a new baby and your first home coming real soon now. Lots of action going on Big Shooter. Little Michelle looks more like you every day. Matter of fact she looks just like you. Did you do that by yourself too?"

"Aw go to the army Shortie and let's see what you can do. Wish you weren't leaving." He stood there grinning, his six-foot two frame towering above me, a duffel bag slung over his shoulder in a devil may care attitude. My little brother had grown up. "I got to go Pat, there's no backing down. The decision's been made. Goodbye for now."

THE SUGAR SHACK

We bought our first home In Plymouth and moved in. The Sugar Shack was almost ugly, but we chose it for the property, three acres of land, within visible distance of Lake Pointe water tower. At that point in time, the area was sparsely populated in a peaceful country setting. It seemed the perfect place to start out with a few months-old baby, and Crazy Dog. The yellow Labrador was rescued from the pound, and ran like crazy, hence he got his name. All the flower seeds I planted never came up. Crazy Dog dug them up, as well as every little seedling.

The house was very old. After long dreary winters, creaky old windows barely cooperated to let fresh air in. The door off the kitchen, opened into a huge room addition on the back of the house. The room never warmed up enough to use until summer, hence we put no furniture in there. It became the playroom for Michelle to ride her tricycle and run with Crazy dog all year round. There were continuous problems with the old water pump, the well, and septic system. We often had no water when one of them defaulted again. Dishes had to be stacked in the sink and meals delayed. Laundry piled up waiting for available water. The access to the pump was through a door in the floor in the recreation room. A few stairs led down to a small, musty smelling, dark space. Walt hated working on those antiquities. Every time he thought he fixed one of them, the other didn't work. But on the plus side the acreage yielded several huge cherry trees. Each spring they blossomed in splendor, and before summer came, they reaped a bounty of the best cherries ever. We had more than enough for all our families and the friendly elderly couple next door. Ma taught me to bake deep dish, cherry pies, that turned out as good as hers.

BABY STEPS

When Michelle started walking, she didn't bother with baby steps. She stood up and toddled across the room, picked up her toy and plopped down to play with it. I couldn't believe my eyes. My baby wanted something, so she went and got it. She was going to do everything herself. Little did I know, her first strike for independence had already begun. I taught her the only way I knew, so we continued to butt heads. Until I realized it's ok to cut the umbilical cord, sometime around 30 years later.

One gloomy day the phone rang. "Hey Big Shooter, how's that baby girl doing? She take any baby steps yet?"

"Hey Bob, it's good to hear your voice. Michelle just got up and walked on her own the first time. She has a pet rabbit named Puff. They play in the rec room with Crazy Dog. She rides her tricycle round and round with them. It's a real circus over here. How's the Army treating you?"

"It's all good Pat. I got a little news, I moved up a bit, and happy about it. I made rank Spec E4."

"That great Bob. What does it mean?"

"It's a rank above Private First Class, below Corporal, but pays the same as corporal. It'll put a few more bucks in my pocket. I'm not going to make this a career. I just wanted to achieve something while I'm here."

"Congratulations Bob. I'm proud of you. This makes me happy too."

"I have to go Pat. Take care of that baby girl and give her a hug for me. Bye for now."

THE THINKER

Hearing from my brother meant a lot, his timing was perfect. I was going through something that I didn't understand. It would be years before it was given a name. Postpartum Depression lingered long after my baby was born. Doc referred to my headaches, nightmares and gloominess as woman's issues. If only there was a magic slate pad like we had when we were kids, just lift the page and wipe troubled thoughts away. Why did I have to be a thinker? What's wrong with me? I have a husband, an adorable baby, and my own home. Tonight, I'll fix a nice dinner and tell honey bunch the good news. Doc says our second baby is coming. Another dream is coming true. He'll wrap me in his big arms with a big hug and talk about big plans. We're going to get a bigger house with a big yard, mister big will say. Then he'll ask about the MDOT again. "Did you call about the letter we got from the Michigan Department of Transportation? It's good that they want to buy our house to put an expressway through here. We won't be stuck with that old well and septic anymore. But it's sad for the old couple next door, they're losing the only home they've ever owned. They wanted to die there someday. Their nice old barn is coming down too. Got to make way for the new. That's progress for you."

The blues wouldn't leave me alone. On top of that I was overly possessive. It made me crazy when my husband wanted to spend time with his buddies. Why couldn't I have him to myself? Why should I share him? For the first time in my life something was mine alone. He was never going to see the pyramids along the Nile or watch a sunset on a tropic isle unless he took me with him. You belong to me... just like the song says. In my world the prince didn't go out with buddies. Cinderella and the prince lived happily ever after without them. Snow White was the one with seven little buddies, Dopey, Sneezy, Happy, Doc, Grumpy, Sleepy and Bashful. Cute as they were, who needs them. Not me. I assumed after we married, his buddies would disappear into 'buddy land' somewhere until they got a wife. He was all I needed, why wasn't I all he needed? He might get in trouble fishing and hunting with single buddies who wanted to stop for beers afterward. Why didn't his buddies get married, then it would be ok if they went out sometimes. Why should a prince go out with single buddies? I always heard you can't trust men to begin with. So why is he going to be different? They're supposed to be fishing and hunting. Does that mean I have to believe everything he says? Trust isn't something I know about. I got married for love. Now I'm suddenly supposed to know about trust. Here comes trust into the fuzzy wuzzy picture. Hi, my name is Trust, you must trust me because we're married. Oh really? Somebody should've mentioned that little tidbit before. Why should I trust you? Isn't loving you enough? Well, it's just too bad that I don't get the trust thing. Nobody's perfect buddy.

He knew I was crazy from the get-go. No way I tricked him on that one. That's what he said he loved about me. He knew from the start and married me anyway. Guess he got what was coming. Prince Walter found me on a carhop stool and shooed away some cats. He got past a mean man who smoked like a chimney. Then we drove away in a bat mobile to meet his jolly mother and father in a righteous flower garden. My fairy tale came to real life baby. It's me and the prince who're supposed to live happily ever after. Not me and the prince and a bunch of his buddies.

"Ok Walt, I'm telling you this for the last time. This trust thing is a whole different ball game. I know about work and responsibility and taking care of babies. Read my mind about the rest!"

"Ok Pat ok, whatever you say, just calm down." So, I did, but I still clung to my handsome prince for dear life. Afraid he might vanish in thin air. Poof, and my fairy tale would be over. Hold on tight kid. Don't lose what you got.

MOTHERHOOD AGAIN

We were still living in the sugar shack when a baby cherub was born. Here's how that story goes. In the middle of the night, I went walking in my sleep to pee, but it wouldn't stop. Since there wasn't any pain yet I figured it couldn't be the baby. So I got in the tub and stood there letting it drain out. Efficiency is the word. Why mess up a clean, freshly waxed floor? After a nice warm shower, I was wide awake. Now what was I supposed to do in the middle of the night, prego and big as a house? Why go back to bed when I couldn't sleep? Why go to the hospital when all they would say is you're not in labor? No kidding. Already figured that out. The only thing left to do was clean the house again. That's always a good thing to bring on pain. So, I mopped and waxed everything but still no pain. Then packed Michelle's diaper bag with everything Ma would need. By that time, I'd worked up a ravishing appetite and decided to make a good hearty breakfast, but first I better pack a bag for myself. I tiptoed into the bedroom and the big guy stirred in his sleep. "Whatcha fishing for in the closet Pat?" he mumbled through a snore. "My water broke and I'm starving so I'm making breakfast."

"Hmmmff ...sounds good...breakfast... in the closet... something broke...whaaaaat?" He shot straight up in the air and popped out of bed like he'd been poked with a live wire. "What's that? You've got to be kidding me! We gotta go! I gotta call Ma and tell her it's coming! God my clothes are gone! What did she do with my pants? Don't tell me she's washing them again! I just put them here last night!"

"Calm down Walt. My labor hasn't even started. And I didn't take your clothes."

"If you didn't take them how'd they get out of here? Help me find them. No, sit down! I don't want the baby to fall out! Let's go Pat! No. We can't go I need pants! You find my pants and I'll go wake up Michelle!"

"STOP WALT! Listen to me. Can you hear me now? Calm down. Do not go in Michelle's room and wake her up, she's two years old, she doesn't have to wake up for this. We have a long time yet. My labor hasn't even started."

"Oh."

"Sit down Walt, I'll find your clothes. You probably knocked them under the bed when you were spinning around like a top. Sheesh, what else can I do for you, when I need you to be calm?"

"Ok Pat I'll sit down, but this is all your fault, every bit of it. Always washing my clothes. Cleaningest woman I've ever met. We need to get you to the hospital. I don't know about babies coming and don't want to see it happening either!"

"Stop being a chicken shit Walt. I watched Michelle being born and it's the most amazing thing anyone can see. Don't worry Chicken Little, the baby isn't ready to come yet, we have plenty of time, remember how long Michelle took? Besides, I have a feeling it's another girl, and we still don't have a girl's name picked out. You don't like any I suggested, so pick one and we'll go."

"I'll think of one on the way Pat. I'm too nervous for this right now. Let's just get Michelle to Ma and Pops house, so we're closer to the hospital."

"There's no need to rush, my labor hasn't even started."

"I'm going to wrap Michelle up, and you better be in the car when we get out there, or we're leaving without you. We can eat breakfast at Ma and Pop's, I'm not taking any chances on that baby dropping out!"

Half hour later we arrived, and Ma took one look at my face and shouted; "Get her to the hospital   now Sonny before that baby is born right here in the living room!"

"But he hasn't picked a name yet Ma, and I have a feeling we're having another girl."

"Just go, you crazy kid. Sonny can decide on a name later!"

"I just thought of one Pat, let's name her Holly!"

"Oh my gosh I love it! It's so happy. Let's go have our baby now. YOU BETTER HURRY!"

Within the hour I was watching my baby come into the world. "Push down Pat. You're doing good...keep going... push...keep going...push some more...here it comes!"

The head came through and the baby was out. I fell back trying to breathe normal. After a few minutes I realized everything was just too quiet. My baby's not screaming. They took my baby aside and no one's saying anything. Why aren't they holding my baby up so I can see it? Why isn't my baby screaming like Michelle did when she came out? The nurse and doctor are hovered over the baby. I can't see what they were doing. Why are they taking so long? Tears streamed out of my eyes. Oh no! Something's wrong and they don't want to tell me! "Is my baby, ok?!" I shouted out loud. "Your little girl is perfect." The nurse finally spoke, and I cried uncontrollably with relief. They held her up for me to see her and little Holly smiled. There she was, naked as a jaybird, smiling about coming into the world. They wrapped the little cherub in a pink blanket and laid her in my arms, and she lay quietly content. A shy crooked smile passed over her sweet face, as she slept. And I knew the name her father had chosen was perfect for this happy little angel baby.

Postpartum depression came again. Maybe the saddle block anesthesia had something to do with it, who knows. At times I was so sad I cried at the drop of a hat. Other times it felt like there was a fog in my head. There were days when I was so tired, I had to choose which baby got a bath. Who needed it most, the new baby or the two-year-old? Lucky for me, Holly was the easiest baby I'd ever taken care of. She was content to just be. Her nature was always easy going. When she started walking her and Michelle were inseparable. Unable to pronounce her sister's name, she called her Mushy, and the name stuck forever. As Holly grew, she was a kind and loving little child and got along with everybody. She loved animals and for a long time she told us she was going to be a veterinarian.

THE AFTERNOON VACATION

"I've been trying to think of someplace to take you Pat. A change of scenery might help get rid of your depression. This ad in the paper says the horse races are going on in Canada now. It's harness racing season. Let's take an afternoon vacation. We can drive there in an hour, have dinner in the clubhouse watching the races, and be home in time to put the girls to bed. We've never seen horse racing; we might like it. What do you say?"

"Sounds good to me Walt. I'll ask my mother if Rose or Linda can babysit Michelle and Holly."

"Maybe you should take your birth certificate with you Pat, in case they ask for it." My mother told me when I picked my sister up to babysit. Then off we went to Canada. Crossing the border was no problem, an officer waved us thru soon as we approached. The clubhouse was exciting, the horse races even more. We didn't stay for all of them, wanting to get home to our kids. But at the border, re-entering the U.S. became an anxious situation. The border patrol officer continued asking questions, then told us to park and come inside. At long length, we were told I wasn't going to be allowed back into the states. "Where did you get this document Ma'am?"

"My mother gave to me when I got married Sir."

"Pat is my wife Sir; we've been married five or six years I think." Walt offered, nervously squeezing my hand so tight it hurt. They ignored him as he didn't appear sure of it. "And we own a home in Plymouth" He added as evidence, but they still ignored him. One of the officers kept going back and forth to another room, relaying a message to the other discreetly. The time dragged on, until it was getting dark. We'd planned to be home hours ago. Finally, I began to cry from anxiety. "Why are you keeping us here officer? We have two toddlers waiting for us, and my teenage sister is babysitting. They're all going to be scared because we're not home yet. We told them we'd be back before they went to bed. We were supposed to be back hours ago. I have to get home to my kids!" A fresh rush of tears poured out in my distress.

"We're still checking Ma'am. Where was your mother born and where does she live now?"

"My Mother! What does she have to do with this?"

"Just answer what he's asking you Pat." My husband of questionable years said, suddenly being   strong and affirmative.

"Of course, officer I'm just upset that's all. My mother was born in Canada. She's lived in Michigan as far back as I can remember. I have her address if it's needed."

After another while the other officer returned. They stepped aside speaking discreetly again.

"We've decided to allow you to re-enter the U.S. tonight, so you can be with your children, but it is imperative you talk to your mother soon as possible. You will receive an official notice on this matter at your home in Plymouth very soon."

We got out of there as fast as we could. "What was all that about Walt? What am I supposed to talk to my mother about?"

"How should I know? You better tell her everything tomorrow to see if she can make sense of it. Let's just get home now to see how your sister is doing with the kids. Some vacation this turned out to be. We already had more than enough on our plate, now this."

"A scary thing happened at the border Mom. They asked for my birth certificate like you said they might, so I gave it to them. They kept us there for hours. They weren't going to let me come home! They kept going back and forth checking who knows what, then told me to ask you about it. I don't understand about immigration, I never even heard the word before!"

"They just made a mistake Pat. Don't worry. It'll all be ok."

Now Walt was reconsidering his stance. "I don't know about this Pat. I've thought about it and something is fishy here. Those border patrol guys don't make mistakes. They know what they're doing. Something isn't right with what your mother said, but I don't know what to do about it."

Did I pay any attention to what my husband said? No. I believed my mother. She was my mother for God's sake. I believed exactly what she told me. "They made a mistake."

A short time later an official letter was delivered registered mail. In bold black letters it read. "Urgent. Deportation." I flew to the phone. "I can't believe it Mom they've sent a letter saying they're going to deport me!"

"I got the same letter Pat. I'm going to call and make an appointment for us. We'll have to go downtown to find out what's going on and get this mistake cleared up."

I must have been the most naïve person ever born. I should've suspected when my mother said she'd call. She never took care of business; she'd always let me do it for her, but having my hands full with two toddlers, I was relieved she was finally taking care of something herself. She called back later saying we had an appointment at the Immigration Bureau, downtown Detroit. The day of the meeting I picked her up. On our arrival a distinguished gentleman introduced himself as Doctor B. He asked me to wait in the lobby, as he wanted to talk to my mother first. Shortly after, he came to escort me to his office. Through glass wall partitions, I could see my mother inside and she was crying! "What's the matter Mom!? Why are you crying!? She wouldn't answer.

"Your mother has been keeping a secret." The gentleman answered for her. "She wants me to tell you, so you won't think bad of her." What is he trying to say? Why would 'his' telling me affect what I think of my own mother? What's so bad she can't tell me herself? We tell each other everything, don't we?

"The man you always thought was your father is not your father." BOOM! It was out of his mouth like a sledgehammer, and he was staring at me waiting for a reaction. The hell with him, he's not getting one my brain said. Reeling in shock, relief, and hurt in the same minute. Is this a surprise or am I relieved? Or am I mad? Which is it? I once thought he wasn't my father, so why does this hurt so bad? Dammit my mother's been lying to me all this time.

Aww, poor mom, I can't stand when she cries. I know how she is. She's embarrassed that a stranger knows this personal thing that happened in her life.

"So now you know." The doctor confirmed. "How do you feel about this Patricia?" How does he think I feel? He pulled the rug out from under me, and now he's asking how it feels. I really don't like when someone asks a stupid question like that. It's like they don't have any feelings themselves. How would he feel if I said your father is not your father Doc. That's what I ought to tell him. See how he likes it. But of course, I won't do that. Instead, I told the man with doctor in front of his name, exactly how I felt.

"In a way it's a surprise. In another way it's not. I wondered about it when I was a kid. And one day it came to me that he 'wasn't' my father."

Now it was the Boom man's turn to be surprised. "How could that come to you?"

"He treated me different than the others. I felt his indifference and figured it out."

"Did someone tell you he wasn't your father?"

"No. I felt in my gut."

The good doctor seemed shocked. What did he expect? He kept insisting on knowing how I felt. He had degrees up the ying- yang hanging on the wall behind him, including a doctorate, but didn't know squat about intuition. After more staring he added another.... BOOM! "Do you want to meet your father now Patricia?"

Anxiety rushed in. Hold on Doc. What's the rush? I turned to look over my shoulder, not ready for any long-lost daddy hugs. "Your father is not here Patricia, but I can arrange it quickly. Do you want me to?"

Who 'is' this guy anyway? Is he so important he can put a person back in someone's life after all these years? Of course, I want to know who my father is, but how does my mother feel about it? "Mom would you ever want to hear from my father again?" She shook her head a vigorous no and that was it. My mother won. "No, I don't want to meet him. I have a husband now. He's all I need. I needed a father when I was a kid. If my real father didn't want me then, why would he want me now?"

The Boom man stared at me like I was a bug under a microscope. "How do you feel about your mother after learning this, Patricia?"

"Same as always, I love her. She's lived through hell, and I don't want her to ever be hurt again." Doctor B turned his attention to my mother now.

"This is remarkable. And to think you worried about this all these years. Now you know."

My mother did not respond. She said absolutely nothing. She had a million chances over the years to tell me but let a stranger do it. Oh my God, she's ashamed of this fatherless child. My thoughts wanted to run rampant, but the Boom man gave me no time to absorb anything.

"There's more to inform you Patricia. You believe you were born in the United States. That is not true. You were born in Canada; therefore, you are a Canadian." BOOM!

No! This can't be! I've lived here all my life but I'm not an American! What's going to happen to my family now!?

The boom man continued.... "After you were born your mother brought you to Detroit. She later met Leonard and they were married. After more children were born, he adopted you. Your name was changed to his so everyone was one big family. Now you know."

Can this man be any more irritating? He just wiped away my identity as I knew it, and all he can say is, now you know. I want to scream at him. Of course, I won't do that. Don't shoot the messenger. He's just trying to deliver today's old news.

The boom man continued... "Now that you know, we can address the real problem we have today. You and your mother have been in this country illegally all these years. When she brought you here as an infant, it was ok to be here temporarily. If she wanted to live here, it was necessary that she apply for permanent residence for you both. Over the years your mother has repeatedly been notified of being in violation. Now we have orders to deport you both back to Canada. I was asked to assist because you are an adult who was unaware of your own history. So now you are informed."

My heart was jumping out of my chest but I responded calmly; "Thank you for informing me."

"The officer at the border is the one who deserves your thanks, Patricia. If it weren't for him, you would already have been deported. He took it upon himself to research the document you provided. When he was finally able to talk to someone at the courthouse, he learned that you were adopted. The court sealed the record of the adoption and gave your mother a record of your birth. The document you have, is not your birth certificate. It is simply a record. The court left it to your mother to inform you of the circumstances surrounding your birth."

My mind was racing, trying to take it all in, terrified they might take us away now that I was told everything. Up to today I'd never given a thought to immigration. It didn't concern me. Now my family could be subjected to being torn apart.

"Now that you are informed Patricia, I must formally ask; do you wish to remain in the United States?"

"Yes, of course sir. I want to stay here with my husband and my children."

"And you mother...do you wish to remain in the United States also?"

"Yes, I do," my mother finally spoke.

"All right, then we shall proceed in preparing the necessary documents right now to apply for permanent residency for each of you. After that is approved you will each receive a green card as proof of your right to live here indefinitely. If you want to become a citizen, you must take all the necessary steps to become one."

If you want to become a citizen. The words were a slap in the face. Not a citizen! My entire life I believed I was an American. Now a few words from a perfect stranger said I wasn't. Who are you? Do you 'really' know? Imagine someone you never met before, telling you these facts; 'you're not who you think you are...you don't belong here...you don't even know your birth name.' Think about it. How would you feel?

It's not about someplace you love to visit, whether it's Canada or any other place in the world. It's about the thing you feel when you put your hand over your heart and sing the song of your country. Your chest swells and tears catch in the back of your throat. It's your home dammit! What if someone took all that away from you in a hot minute? How would you feel then? You might just feel a bit ticked off like I did. My mother was still crying, and I wanted to ask why the hell are 'you' crying? I'm the one who lost something today. You were always a Canadian. I'm betwixt and between now. I don't belong anywhere. My whole life I believed I was from Detroit, proud of being from the Motor City and Motown. I was the little kid who sang the Star-Spangled Banner so loud it hurt people's ears. You didn't take care of business Mom so now it's a big freaking deal. Everything that matters in my life is at risk. They could separate me from my kids!

That's what I really wanted to say. Instead, I was conflicted by loyalty and pity for my mother's embarrassment. Feeling betrayed by both her and dad. And the fear of being taken from my family. It all ran amuck like a whirlwind tornado in the Wizard of Oz, where's Toto when I need him. Realization hit that my mother was never going to tell me. She had every chance after I got married, yet never said a word. Long ago when I was a kid, I thought I saw through this, but I believed what she told me, and learned to doubt myself. Ok, ok, so get over it. Don't hurt your mother's feelings. You know what a terrible life she's had. She's a good woman, bless her heart. Just give Boom man the information he needs and get these papers filled out. E gads, is there anything they don't want to know? It's a wonder they don't ask the size of your underwear. Grin and bear it. The future of your family being together, depends on not making any mistakes on these papers. Why would mom be so careless about something this important? Didn't she think about my kids? She still has kids at home too. Bob is in the army and Carole and Sharon are married now, but Rose and Linda and Nancy and Lucy are still at home. What if the immigration authorities had come and taken her away before this? What would've happened to them? They would've been stuck alone with mister mean because they're all Americans! Didn't she think about that? Hello? It's planet earth calling. What planet are you on Mom? If she would have told me this herself it wouldn't have been half as bad. Doesn't she trust me? I would've taken care of it and not told the family if that's what she wanted. It could have stayed her secret. But I was so upset I spilled the beans to Carole and Sharon. Now what am I going to say? Am I supposed to make up a lie to protect a lie? What a lousy can of worms. Now I must put old smiley face back on for Doctor Boom. Well excuse me all to hell if I can't find the dam thing this time.

"Here's your original birth certificate Patricia. It's no comparison to the record of birth you have in your possession. I'm very surprised it was accepted when you married Walter. It seems your marriage to him was meant to be."

"Walt's going to get a laugh out of this one isn't he Mom?" My mother didn't acknowledge in any way whatsoever, that I'd spoken. Invisible was left to read her 'real' birth certificate alone. Name...Patricia

Number of live births...two.

Are the parents married... Illegitimate birth.

Father's name... Unknown.

What kind of archaic certificate is this? They tagged an innocent baby illegitimate! An insulting demeaning word, insinuating this gift of life is inferior. The question is a yes or no answer. Are the parents married? No judgmental answer was required.

Oh, go soak your head kid. Don't get yourself wound up worse than you already are. You're never going to change the world. It is what it is. Wait a minute. Hold everything. This certificate seems familiar. How can that be? Did I see this before? Oh my gosh, I remember now. I was a little kid changing sheets on the bed and a paper fell out...what's this? Something about Patricia. I'm Patsy but I'm Patricia at school. This says there's 'two' live births. What does that mean? How could I be born two times? Confused little kid went to the fountain of knowledge to ask.

"A paper came out of the mattress when I was making the bed Mom, so I put it back. It had a big word I don't understand, about someone named Patricia. Was I born two times? How can that be? Is there another Patricia?"

"You're being a silly girl Patsy imagining things. There's no paper in the mattress." Of course, nosy little kid went back to look but there was no paper. Silly me, guess I imagined it Mom. Well, here we are today at the Immigration Bureau and I'm sure not imagining this time.

The entire time the documents were being prepared, my mother looked away. Not once did she acknowledge my distress, or the infamous piece of paper in my hands. Silly girl folded it quietly and put it in her purse. Big girls don't cry in public.

"Do you have any questions for your mother now Patricia?" the Boom man asked. "My mother and I will talk later Doctor B." There was no need for him to know any more of my mother's secrets. Couldn't he see she didn't want to talk about this? "Are you ready to go Mom?" She looked away from me again.

Oh swell. This is just great. All these booms dropped on me this morning, and all you can see is your shame. It's not just all about you Mom. Don't you think this affected me at all? How can you be so indifferent? You're my mother for God's sake. Guess I'm just supposed to stuff it all down again. Where's my smiley face when I need it? Sorry if I can't manage to make one again.

"Thank you, Doctor B, we're grateful for all your help. Now I'm going to take my mother to lunch and make her laugh, if you don't have any more surprises up your sleeve." The dignified gentleman rolled back in his big leather chair and laughed out loud. "Who does she take after mother?" He inquired merrily.

"Oh, she's always been a crazy kid." My mother replied poker faced, waving it off. Sheesh, glad I could make somebody laugh. I used to be able to make my mother laugh too. We're so different I'll never understand how that can be. I'm not going to be so trusting now. Why should I be? The people who were supposed to teach me trust, lied to me all my life. And I have to act like there's nothing wrong with that. Isn't that ducky.

Now here I am driving Miss Daisy and she decides to break her silence, saying she doesn't want to go to lunch with me. What did I do?! What's going on now that I don't know about? I waited a few minutes before testing the water. "Can I ask you something Mom?" "No! I don't want to talk about it." That was it. I was shut down. My mother always let me go quite far, but when she shut me down that was it. I better respect her. My brain could run rampant, but my mouth better shut itself up. Isn't this double ducky. I can't believe it's not a bad dream. We continued in silence all the way to her place. "See you later Mom. I love you." There was no response. Invisible person wasn't looking for a lot. The smallest something would have meant everything the day she got lost.

Months crawled on in painful confusion of being ignored. It didn't make sense. Why wouldn't she talk to me? Somehow my mother had disappeared in that glass office. I didn't know this woman. Why would my own mother be mad at me for something I had no nothing to do with? I didn't ask to be born; or did I? Now I understood why dad called me the black sheep. Another man was my father, and it rubbed him the wrong way. I was the little pain in the ass with all her questions he grumbled about. Maybe I should go over and tell him thank you for adopting me. Boy that would get him. He wouldn't know what to do with that. Maybe I should be grateful he adopted me and tried to do the right thing. Maybe it would make peace between us, and everybody would be happy. That would be just ducky...for them.

Mom acted like nothing happened. She mentioned nothing about that day at the immigration, except she didn't get her green card yet either. She didn't seem worried a bit. Dad acted somewhat awkward when I thanked him for adopting me. I hadn't expected it to be so hard to do but held back tears and said it sincerely. And just as I thought, he didn't know what to do with it. Yet there was something in his eyes; could it be that he was pleased? I'd never know. Mom was fine. Dad was fine. I was supposed to be fine too. Yet every time a car drove slowly by our home in Plymouth, or a knock came at the door, anxiety struck. The fear of being separated from my children was near unbearable. Doctor B had said they shouldn't come to deport us, BUT... he couldn't guarantee it. That was enough to scare the hell out of me. I needed a guarantee.

The day the green card finally arrived months later by registered mail, I started jumping up and down like a rubber ball. "Thank God! It's finally here! Look Walt, it's here!"

"Yes Pat, that's nice. Maybe now I can get some sleep."

Happily, I called my mother. "I got my green card today, Mom! Did you get yours?"

"Yes Pat, it came today."

"I want to talk to you now Mom. There's a lot of questions that only you can answer. First, I need to know what you want me to say to the rest of the family?"

"Oh for heaven's sake Pat, tell them whatever you want." Then she hung up on me! Now I did it. But what did I do? I can't believe this, she shut me down again. Who am I going to talk to about this? My husband says I'm driving him crazy. How are my sisters and brother going to feel when they find out I'm a half-sister? Will they tell me the truth? What is the truth anyway? Something people only tell when it makes them look good? Someday I'll find out who my father is. What if I find him and the secret hurts someone? I don't want to hurt anyone. Maybe I should forget about finding him. But what about my grandparents? Are they alive? I've always wanted some grandparents. What's my nationality? I'm not just a plump little nut who fell off a chestnut tree.

"Wake up Pat, you're crying in your sleep again. Is it never quiet in that head of yours? Doesn't it ever sleep? You got to quit waking me up. I need my sleep so I can climb on a roof tomorrow and not fall off. I know this has been hard on you, but you'll get past it. You don't have a father, but you've got more than a lot of women. You've got me."

"Oh swell, lucky me. Sorry I woke your insensitive butt. Go back to sleep mister macho."

When everything is supposed to be fine, you have no choice but to play the fake it till you make it game. When that game gets too much, you have a bag of coconut chocolate chip cookies and chocolate milk, that makes everything warm and fuzzy. But the wondering still goes on. Wonder where my father lives? I could be talking to some old chap in the grocery store, not knowing he's my father. This is ridiculous. I'm going to see mom and tell her how I feel. She'll never know unless I tell her straight out. We think so different about things. Sometimes I think the only thing we have in common is she's my mother.

"Surprise, I'm here Mom! Let's have an old hens party!"

"Don't be silly Pat. I don't have time for silliness. I still have to finish washing the clothes and get dinner made."

"I'll help you Mom and we can talk at the same time. Efficiency is the word."

"You crazy kid, what do you want to talk about this time? You always want to talk, talk, talk."

"Don't be crabby Mom. You work too hard, and it makes you a crab. You never told me about my father, and I've been waiting patiently. I need to know who I am and where I came from."

"That's silly Pat. You know now that you were born in Canada. And you grew up in Wyandotte with the rest of them. So, what are you saying, what more is there to tell? What's done is done."

"Geez Mom, there's lots more. Think about it. Your father died when you were a kid. Remember how much you missed him? What if you never met him? Wouldn't you want to know about him? I want to know about the person I never met. I didn't have a real dad, and you know it. It wasn't your fault Mom, you tried to get me one, but it's like you said; what's done is done. But I still need to know about my real father and my heritage to know who I am. You and I are very different, there's more to me than you. Laugh Mom, that was quite funny!"

"Oh you." Instead of smiling she became pensive, so I waited. This time there was no turning back. I was going to get it out of her, one funny way or another. "I understand you're embarrassed about having sex when you weren't married Mom, but that's not so bad. You could have done a lot worse thing. Nobody has the right to look down on you. If they do, they're just being a hypocrite. I'm glad you had sex. If you didn't, I wouldn't be here. It must have been a good thing, because you got me out of it!" My mother couldn't keep from laughing out loud. "You're such a crazy kid!"

"That's right Mom, I'm the crazy kid who doesn't understand why you're so embarrassed about sex. Everybody does it. If we didn't do it, no one would ever be born. Who would go through the pain of childbirth without having some fun first?" This time my mother doubled over with laughter. "You must take after your father because you're sure not like me!" she exclaimed holding onto her sides. "Heck Mom we always knew that. Now that we've got all the sex out of the way, tell me about my dear ole pappy."

"Oh, you and you're silliness. I never saw anything like you."

"Yes Mom, I'm an original. Now tell me about my father.... pleeeeeeze!"

A small smile traced my mother's mouth as she remembered her first love. Almost bashfully she began to speak. "His name was

Bernard," she said surprising me. The name I'd picked for my confirmation was Bernadette. Ironic that I'd come so close yet was still so far. She said they knew each other quite a while. Though I wondered how long quite a while was, I didn't ask. She was finally talking, and I wasn't going to interrupt. She said they were in love and talked about getting married. When they found out she was pregnant they went to his parent's home to get permission to marry. They refused, saying he was too young. He was 20, she was 23. Bernard argued with them about it and became very angry. He left and went to join the Army. She had no means and stayed in Canada to give birth to me. "Why does it say two live births on my birth certificate Mom?"

"They made a mistake Pat." She said with finality, and I let that subject close. Despite what I'd told myself about not trusting, I believed her. People think a lot of things when they're hurt. She was my mother and I trusted her, no matter what happened. She was whispering like it often was when I was a kid, when we were confidants. There was a lot I wanted to ask her that I'd wonder about later, but all that mattered now was being close to my mother again. But strangely it seemed as if our roles had somehow reversed; and I was the mother now and she was my child.

"So why did we leave Canada then?"

"It was very different in my day Pat. People thought you were a bad woman if you had a baby and weren't married. They still think like that but pretend they don't. They looked down on you and called you a bad name and the baby too. I knew people would never forget, and it would follow us forever. Nobody knew me over here. Your Aunt Marie and Aunt Bella took turns watching you so I could work. I was a waitress in a very nice, expensive restaurant."

"That was smart Mom, getting a job where the big spenders go, they leave bigger tips."

"Maybe I wasn't so smart after all Pat, look what I ended up with. Leonard." She looked at me and I looked at her and we burst into laughter, in a moment between girls.

157

"So, what happened to my father then Mom? Did you ever see him again?"

"He came to see you after you were born and brought his sister with him. She was so nice. I liked her a lot. She came back to see you a few more times, but I never saw him again. Years later someone told me he married a pretty lady who could have been a model."

"You were pretty too Mom, I've seen pictures of you back then, you were beautiful, still are."

"Stop Pat, don't be silly."

"How did you think you were going to keep me without any money? Weren't you scared not having a husband or your own place to live?"

"They put you in my arms the minute you were born, and I knew that somehow it would work out because I loved you."

Somewhere inside a dam broke and all the emotion I'd held came rushing out in a flood of tears. The little girl inside was at last acknowledged, in the love my mother had for her newborn baby. "Don't cry so hard Pat, you're making me cry. I was so glad I kept you. You made me laugh so much when you were a baby. You still do, you silly kid. I'll tell you the rest of it now, so you don't have to keep asking me questions later. Leonard started coming into the restaurant and was so nice looking in his uniform. He came back every day to sit in my section, being a gentleman. He kept asking me to go out with him and I finally said yes. When I brought him home to meet you, he named you Poochie. We were in love when we got married. It wasn't always like it is now, we had such good times in the beginning. We used to laugh all the time. Everything changed when he started drinking. I didn't know when we got married that him and his brothers drank when they were just little kids. They would sneak out at night looking for stills in the mountains and drink moonshine. He must have become an alcoholic way back then. I keep praying he'll change, and things will go back to how they were when we first got married."

Surprise, surprise. They were in love at one time. That was news to me. I never heard them speak of love. My mother believes he can change. What do I know? Maybe he can.

THE HOUSE THAT JACK BUILT

The Michigan Department of Transportation finally bought our Sugar Shack and Walt found a house 'for sale by owner'. The seller had added a very large addition onto the house, but personal problems forced him to sell. Lucky us, we got a 2300 square foot home for $9000. That's right, nine thousand dollars. In 1964 you got a lot for your money honey. The four bedroom and second bath addition were only roughed in, needing to be finished. We moved in with our little girls even though half the house was a shell with sub flooring and exposed two by fours. Excited that our daughters were going to grow up in this big house. Walt did all the work himself saving us a ton. The wiring, the plumbing, the insulation, the drywall, the mudding, sanding, and painting. The bathroom fixtures, the tile, the wood floors. He did it all. It was the perfect set up for a prince who by now had become a mere man. That was just fine with me. Now he was my carpenter and jack of all trades. But whenever a job had anything to do with plumbing, he cussed like a jack hammer. "The girls are talking now talk Walt. It's going to be problem when they start repeating your favorite words."

"It's this house that Jack built. How could he do this before the plumbing went in #!@#* %^* Eventually the construction neared completion and I was eager to start decorating. "I want to decorate the girls' bedrooms to suit their personalities, Walt."

"Ok Pat, do whatever you want to do." I wall papered the first bedroom halfway up with pink and white stripes, and painted the bottom half, light pink. A pink check bedspread, ruffled curtains, was perfect for feminine little Michelle who clomped around the house in her mother's high heel shoes. I wallpapered the second bedroom with yellow and white daisies. A pale-yellow bedspread and ruffled curtains were perfect for sunny little Holly. The decorating bug bit hard and I was just getting started. The décor in the master bedroom had to say romance, so red it was. I covered one wall with red flocked wallpaper, then the red carpet was rolled out. A red velvet bedspread with red pillows looked good in the Sears catalog so I ordered it. The final touch, a red rose in a silver vase, then I stepped back to look at my handiwork. Uh oh, maybe I overdid it. It looks a bordello. My carpenter thought it was great.

ON BEING A KID AGAIN

Maybe we give our kids what we wanted as a child. I set the fourth bedroom up as a playroom for the girls, with child size furniture. A little pink refrigerator and stove, little table and chairs, highchairs for baby dolls, and talking dolls, and dolls of all kinds. The girls played house mixing tiny packages of cake mix and put it in the easy bake oven baking tiny cakes. They made big messes and Patsy played with them, throwing flour in the air that Pat could clean up later. We were having fun, reading the story of Snow White, and eating tiny cakes. Their little friends came over for pajama parties. We sat on the carpet and had pizza. I told them stories till they crawled sleepily into sleeping bags, and little Julie said; "Stay and sleep with us Mama Pat." Then we all went to sleep, happy little girls.

THE BOXER

On returning home from the Army, my brother was surprised to learn that mom had left dad and taken our kid sisters, Nancy and Lucy. They were staying with our Uncle Joe's family in Canada. Uncle Joe's daughter, also named Nancy, was a young teenager at the time. She recently shared a very short story of my brother's visit to her home. "There was a knock at the door. A soldier was there. He'd come to visit his family. He was so handsome! It was the first time I'd ever met my cousin Bob." My cousin Nancy told us that story with such animation, I visualized it as though I were there. After a while, my mother and sisters left Uncle Joe's home and went to Uncle Willie's to stay with his family awhile too. Then came the call heard from another country. Dad had shot himself. The superficial wound grazed his underarm. Was it an accident? I never thought it was. But it worked. Mom and the girls went back to him.

Meanwhile brother Bob, always a Detroit boy at heart, was living downtown. At this point it seemed my brother's childhood dream of bending steel with his bare hands had taken a turn. Bob decided he become a boxer. He trained in the same gym with Tommy Hearns, and they became friends. Tommy went on to be a famous professional fighter in the 1970s, but boxing wasn't what our mother had always hoped her son would do. The very thought of Bob fighting brought tears to her eyes. Our family prayed that he would find what was right for him. Whenever we talked, I asked my brother again why he wanted to keep fighting. "It's like I told you before Pat. Boxing is a sport. There's big money in it when you become good enough to beat your opponent."

Time went on, and one day he called and asked me to come to a fight they'd scheduled for him. "I can't do that Bob; I don't like fighting and blood flying all over."

"I thought you'd want to come to support me Pat."

"I'll always support you Bob, it's just that I couldn't stand to see you get hit. I might do something crazy like jump in the ring and try to stop the fight."

"You wouldn't do something that foolish Pat; you'd get caught up in the sport."

"You don't understand. I just don't want to see my brother getting hurt."

"I won't get hurt Pat I know how to protect myself. I'm ready for this fight. You should come and see a real fight. You might like it."

"There's no way I'd like it. We think different about this. I can't understand why you want to keep fighting."

"It has to run its course, so I'm giving it my best shot. You've let me down Pat, I thought you'd come for the family to see my first fight. I have to go now, say a prayer for me to win." So I prayed my brother would win and decide to quit boxing.

161

Sometime afterwards, sis Rose and I were driving to an event downtown with our husbands Mark and Walt and happened to spot our brother walking down the street, in the vicinity of the gym. As we sped past, he disappeared inside somewhere, and Rose and I nearly came to tears at the thought of him off to another fight. Sometime later still, to the family's great relief, our brother quit boxing. His short-lived career had run its course. He'd walked his own walk and did what he had to do, and I finally understood.

LIVES SAVED

A couple years later the phone rang in the middle of the night. A Detroit policeman was calling to inform me that my brother was in a bad accident. He went through the windshield and was thrown out of the car. They found him sitting on the curb where he gave them my phone number before passing out. He was with our cousin Jim Bob. They'd both been drinking, apparently a lot. They were taken by ambulance to the nearest Detroit hospital. Walt stayed home with our girls while I rushed through empty streets to the hospital downtown, dreading what I'd find when I got there. My brother's bed was raised to sitting position, his head heavily wrapped in bandages, his handsome face bruised, and badly swollen, tracked with stitches. "What woman is ever going to look at me now Pat? I'm a freak! ...he ground out bitterly.

"You're lucky to be alive! You need to slow down brother! Life is short."

"What makes you the expert all of a sudden?"

"I might not know much, but I know enough not to drive drunk with drunk people! You two dummies should be thanking God you're still alive!"

"I never thought you'd yell at me Pat, or I wouldn't have given them your phone number to begin with."

"I'm mad because I almost lost you! You're the only brother I've got, I love you, you dummy!"

"Yeah, I know Pat. I love you too Big Shooter." For a while Bob wore a full beard. The scars faded and no one would even think it happened.

WHEN GRAND MAW DIED

During a family discussion someone happened to mention 'when Grand Maw died.' The fact is, I thought no one had told me she'd died. Then I remembered. They told me. I just didn't want to hear about it, she was none of my concern. My only thought at the time was, buzzards were probably tap dancing happily on her grave. Sorry Grand Maw, but that's all I had for you at that time. Now here I am, remembering a person who traumatized me so bad I totally buried it and forgot all about her. Grand Maw is back to haunt me because I never forgave her. I've carried that old baggage around for decades. That's heavy stuff on a heart, believe you me. Its way past time to deal with it. Just when I thought I was doing ok, Grand Maw's back. You really don't know what you're holding inside do you? Staying in the spirit is hard work.

Once again I've stopped writing and put myself on time out to do the work. I'm learning that this is what it takes. Self-truth takes me through yet another long dark corridor to reach the light of forgiving. I've come to terms with another ghost of the past. I finally let you go Grand Maw. Rest in peace.

A YOUNG ANGEL

Just before Easter the call came from a family member. They said there had been an auto accident involving our cousins, Margaret, Eva, and Terri, and a couple of their friends. At that point in time, they were all young teenagers, with exception of little Terri. I immediately called aunt Drexie, who was so distraught she could barely speak. At length she managed to say Margaret and Eva were going to be ok but little Terri died; and she didn't have the means to dress her baby girl for her funeral. I picked them up at her home in Detroit and we all went shopping. At the funeral I prayed that God would give them strength and I'd never have to see another mother burying her child. From then on, I would have never wanted Aunt Drexie, Margaret, Eva, or little Terri in heaven, to call me any other name than Patsy.

TIED IN KNOTS

Everything was supposedly going fine. Happy wife and mother, having fun with my girls. Playing hostess, giving parties that everybody loved. All Walt's buddies and their wives, Ruth and Darwin, Carole and Mel, Sharon and Art, the more the merrier. Amidst the fun my depression lingered on. Mood swings at my cycle, awful headaches preceded by the dark blur, the recurring dream; a bright white light, water dripping on a red window, dark shadows, and I wake up in a sweat. I brooded over why my father walked away after seeing his baby. Who does that? You can't count on anybody. Look what dad did to mom. Why did he cheat on her? Why do some men stick, and others stray? I questioned my husband to the point of crazy, testing him. "I'm never going to leave Pat. You're my wife, that's all there is for me. I'll never do what your old man did to your mother. I love you. You have to believe me."

"Do you really love me Walt or are you just saying that?"

"Why would I just say that? I'd leave if I didn't love you. Doesn't that make sense?"

"I don't know, I want to believe you but I'm afraid to."

"What am I going to do with you? Maybe you are crazy."

"Sometimes I think I am."

"What did that rotten old man do to hurt you so bad? Oh my God, I'm so sorry Pat, I shouldn't have said that. I don't know what I'm saying anymore. Try to forget what happened to you. Don't think so much. I feel awful when you're sad. I promise I'm always going to be here. I'm not like your old man. I'm here to stay."

Finally, he went to talk to his mother. "I talked to Ma this morning Pat. I told her we're having problems and she wants you to come over and talk. Go see her now and I'll stay here with our girls."

"Why did you tell her our problems Walt, I don't want people to know."

"Ma is not just people; she loves you like a daughter Pat. I'm not going to lie to you. We promised in the beginning we'd never do that. I told Ma you're driving me crazy, and we need help. Maybe she can help us. She went to psychiatrists for years to deal with being an orphan. Let her try to help. I don't know where else to go, we don't have that kind of health insurance."

To make him happy I went to see Ma and talk. "I'm glad you're here Pat, I was hoping you'd show up. I'm your mother now too, and I have something to say. Sonny was here this morning at his wit's end. You're about to lose the only man who's ever loved you. How can you think he doesn't love you? Everyone can see it, why can't you? He thinks you're more beautiful than the women we saw on Miss America last night. Why don't you see that in yourself?"

"Because it's not true Ma. Those girls have done things in their life. I haven't done anything."

"How can you say that? You don't give yourself any credit Pat, you were working two jobs and going to school when Sonny met you. Most young girls couldn't do that. What ever happened to make you see so little in yourself?"

"I don't know Ma."

"You have a man who loves you dearly. Don't you know how many women would be jealous of what you have with my son?"

"Why would they be like that when he's 'my' husband? He married 'me."

"Because they want that too Pat! Why do you keep trying to tear it down?"

"I don't know Ma. I never thought of it like that."

"You're still a naïve kid who thinks no man could love her. You're holding onto something that makes you think that way. Talk to me and let it out."

"I can't Ma. There's so many things that I just can't remember them anymore." Erve started to cry but I couldn't find a word to console her. "My son would give his life for you," she sniffled. "He's not just your husband. He's my son too. I don't want anything to happen to him. I'm worried about my grandchildren too. You've got to learn to be happy for all our sakes. Whatever is holding you down needs to come out in the open or it's going to tear us all apart. You have to see a psychiatrist and get it out so you can be happy!"

"I don't need a psychiatrist Ma. I just needed to know he loves me, and you've convinced me."

"My God Pat! Why would you believe me and not your husband?"

"I don't know Ma."

"Don't you trust him? Did something happen after you got married Pat?"

"Nothing happened Ma, Just all of a sudden I didn't know if he loved me."

"Did you believe he loved you when you married him?"

"I think so, but later I started to wonder. Remember when I lied about my age and we had sex, and he said I tricked him into loving me? After that I was never sure how he really felt. All I knew was I loved him so much I couldn't bear to lose him."

"Sonny fell in love with you the first time he saw you. Why do you think he brought you to meet me as soon as you got in his car?"

"I figured it was because I didn't have time to go for a long ride that day Ma."

"Why are you still holding onto that lie Pat? You must forgive yourself. Sonny forgave you because he loved you. You can't trick somebody into loving you, they either do or they don't. There's a reason why you don't believe in yourself. Something happened that's causing you to think this way. You don't want to see it because you were hurt so bad. But you need to see it Pat. You have to grow up now! You have two children who need you. See a psychiatrist to find out what's hurting you. Do it for your kids if you can't do it for yourself."

"I don't need a psychiatrist Ma. I can do it myself. I already feel better from talking to you."

"Do you Pat? Or are you just saying that to make me feel better because you know I'm worried?"

"I really feel better Ma. I promise to work on myself. I have to get home now to my kids."

Erve gave a long sigh of resignation; "Ok Pat, do it on your own if you insist, but you have to get started. Anything you do to help yourself will be better than it is now. Come see me when you can talk about it. I know you can't talk to your mother, she has too many troubles of her own. Pop and Ruth Ann want to help too, so talk to them if you can't talk to me."

It wasn't that I couldn't talk to Erve. I couldn't talk to anybody. My husband's family was there all along, and not once could I bring myself to talk to them about what I felt inside. They lived on the bright side of life. Why tell them my problems? Ruth Ann was the funny older sibling I always wanted. She kept me in stitches with one funny episode after another. One time she came up with the idea of a catering business with me helping of course. Darwin bought her a catering truck and painted it pink. I went to her house every morning and we cooked while our four daughters Laurie and Darla, Michelle and Holly played in the next room. We made huge pots of chili, sloppy joe mix, macaroni and cheese, or whatever concoctions she came up with. Then off she'd go to construction sites, dressed in pink to sell lunch while I watched our girls. When that business became too restricted by the Board of Health, she got another idea. She wanted us to drive in the Ladies Demolition Derby. I wasn't having any part of driving around in circles, in a banged-up wreck, banging into other wrecks. It was hard enough to drive in a straight line in Michigan winters. Another time she and I we were on the expressway and a tire rolled by in front of us, going full tilt boogie, dancing in front of us like a BF Goodrich commercial. I no sooner got the words out of my mouth; where did that tire come from, the passenger's side of the car dropped to the pavement, sparks flying everywhere. Something obviously broke, which she expertly determined was the axle, and managed to get the car off the road. And we lived to tell the story.

Another time she called me saying she was coming to pick me up. She needed help packing. She was ticked off at Darwin for some silly reason and wanted to make him think she'd left him. So we dropped our girls off with Ma, then went to her house to pack her clothes. Without nothing else to use, we stuffed them in paper grocery sacks. Then off we went on the way to Ma and Pops house, singing in the rain. Suddenly we had another blow out and of course she had no spare. The wheel and tire were out there alongside the highway somewhere. She'd forgotten to get another. After the rain stopped, we got out to walk, each taking a couple sacks of clothing, thinking no problem, it's only another mile to Ma and Pops. Then the rain came down, and there we were. Paper bags soaking wet, clothes falling all over the street, wet hair in our eyes. Ruth Ann and me in trouble again, laughing ourselves silly. A car stopped and a bewildered kind soul offered to help. We threw the muddy wet clothes in the back seat, and he drove us to Ma and Pop's. No doubt wondering what these crazy girls were up to. Gathering all her wet things out of the back seat, he couldn't help but notice the towering sunflowers in the front yard. No doubt wondering as he drove away, about the unusual encounter on his otherwise normal day.

No.... Ruth Ann and I never talked about anything serious. Why ruin all our fun? Every time she called, we got in one mischief or another, dragging our little girls along laughing with us. The garage sale queen taught me the ropes. Everyone should have a Ruth Ann to teach the do's and the don'ts for this kind of 'sailing'.

Ma and Pops house was always fun, feast and laughter. Why bring up bad memories and spoil everybody's fun? They'd never understand the craziness that went on in my childhood. Nobody would. Besides, they couldn't change it. Maybe they wouldn't feel the same about me if they knew. They might not accept me. Better to keep it to myself.

When Pop wasn't working on another 1000- piece or more puzzle, he told corny jokes. Or stories about history, which weren't told the way it was taught in school. He was delighted to discover that little Holly shared his love for puzzles. Pop also loved miniature trains. After setting it up for Christmas one year, he decided to leave it up all year in the living room. His great sense of humor was always ready with a new joke. "Glad you're here Pat. Just told this bunch a good one but they don't get it. Explain it to them." Seems Pop and I had the same funny bone.

On the other hand, Ma's insight had scared the hell out of me. She'd broken through a layer of my shell and got my attention. I was filled with new resolve. No way was I going to lose the most precious thing I ever had; my own family. Common sense said no one could fix me but myself. I didn't need a psychiatrist to tell me that. The thought of a psychiatrist terrified me. And why not? Look what they did to Ma. They strapped her down and fried her brain with electric shock treatments, like in the movie, one flew over the cuckoo's nest. When she came home from Eloise mental hospital, she was like a zombie for two years. One day she seemed to snap out of it and cooked and baked all day. Then she went out and worked in her flowers till dark. The next day she did the same thing again and every day thereafter. It was like she forgot the whole terrifying electric shock episode. But I didn't forget it. If those shrinks could do such a barbaric thing to a dear, kind, lady like Ma, what would they do to me? Nobody's doing that to me! Besides, I don't have a couple years to unscramble my head. My kids need me now. I can do this, and I will, so help me God.

First, I talked to our family doctor, the one who delivered my girls, that Ma thought so highly of. Doc L was telling me, some women have depression for years after childbirth. It didn't sound very encouraging, and my mind wandered to a sign on the wall. It's something I do. I read signs, billboards, advertising, whatever. Sometimes a sign can save your silly life. On that day Doc's sign was quietly arresting; 'Physician heal thyself.' I filed it in my do not forget zone, as Doc gave me some little white pills saying they'd make me feel better. Those pills caused the worst nightmares of my life. Dreams so wild and grossly vivid I was afraid to go back to sleep. I threw them in the toilet remembering the sign. 'I'll be my own physician and heal myself. Doctors use drugs, I'll use mind over matter.' Off I went to the library. It was good to be there, akin to being back in school again. Except this time, I was gathering books on mental health, psychology and spirituality. Every available minute I read to improve crazy, or at least reduce it.

"I'm proud of you Pat. You're always reading to help yourself and it's working. You're doing a lot better already. Don't go back to that part time job, stay home and take care of the girls."

"They're both going to be in school soon, Walt so I've been thinking about what I want to do. Just because I didn't go to college doesn't mean I can't have a career. I'm going to be an independent contractor like you, in business for myself. I've decided to be a realtor. It gives the flexibility of taking time off to do things for our kids. The real estate course will take a few months at night school. After that I need to pass the state exam in Lansing to get the license. Then I can choose whichever real estate office I want to work for."

"You're a big help to me in our construction business Pat. I need you. Maybe you should wait until I can handle it myself. Sounds like you've already looked into it, and I think it suits you. You like everything about home design and you're a natural salesperson. You're the extrovert, I'm the introvert. We go together like Mutt and Jeff."

"Very funny Waldorf."

"It's good to have my wife back, you're like your old self again. You're fine until your mother calls. Then you get all worked up over something the old man did again. Sometimes I wish I'd never put a phone in over there so she could call us. I've been thinking about her situation. Maybe we should bring her and your little sisters to live with us. That way she wouldn't need the old man. I get along fine with your mother, and it would be nice having her here. We could take them in and not have to hear what the old man's doing anymore. Think about it Pat. Whatever you decide is fine with me."

"Hi Mom, we have something for you to think about. Walt and I would like you and the kids to come live with us. The house is big enough and you'd like Plymouth. There's good schools and the kids can get jobs for the summer. It would be a relief for all of us."

"You and Walt have such good hearts, but I can't do that. I can't take the kids away from their dad. Maybe I could tell him it would be nice for the older ones to go to your house to find jobs for the summer. He might let them do that. He thinks Walt is a good man, and he's not mad at you anymore since you came and thanked him that day. It made him happy. You know how he is; he didn't know what to say back to you that's all. I can't ask him to let the kids go for the whole summer, it would just cause a big fight. He'd never let them be gone that long. He loves them too much."

"Good grief Mom, he sure has a terrible way of showing love. Don't you think what he does to you is hurting them? I thought you'd be happy to get away from him. Every time we talk, you say he hit you again. I'm not talking about the kids coming here for the summer. I'm offering you a way out. Why would you want to stay there? Do you still love him, is that it?"

"I don't know any more Pat. He's not as bad as he used to be when you older kids were home. Sometimes he's not bad at all. Sometimes we even laugh a little. Maybe you should forgive your dad for the things he said to you. That was years ago. He didn't mean them."

"For God's sake Mom what are you saying? Have you got so used to being hit you forget when he did it? Just last week you said he hit

171

you, and now you're telling me to forgive him for 'saying' things! Did you forget that he chased me out of the house with a butcher knife? What about all the times I saw him beat you and my brother up? Am I supposed to forgive those too? Am I supposed to forgive someone who tried to make me think I wasn't worth a buffalo nickel? That's what he told me; don't you remember? I can't forgive that! I'm not a saint! I'm a mad woman n.... "Stop yelling Pat or I'll hang up on you!"

"Ok Mom ok. It just makes me so mad that you're still going through this. It's a wonder I can force myself to be nice to him. Do you know how hard it was to thank him for adopting me? I was only trying to make peace so I could see my family; don't you understand? I'm forced to kiss his ass because you can't come visit in my home. You're living in an f-ing prison, and my little sisters are seeing it. Now you tell me he loves them! What kind of love is that? Its stinking rotten .s...

"Stop Pat! Stop talking that way or I'm hanging up for good! How can such a nice person talk so bad? Where did you learn to talk like that? What would people think if they heard you?"

"I don't really care what 'they' think. Real friends accept me for who I am. I respect you and love you with all my heart but your situation is driving me out of my rabid ass mind! I can't believe you asked where I learned to talk like this. Hello? Are you still there...?

"I'm here, I'm listening, but you still shouldn't talk that way, no matter what 'he' says. People think bad of a woman who talks like that."

"Oh, I see Mom, so it's ok if a man beats a woman up but I shouldn't go crazy and call him out on it...is that it? Maybe I'm wrong for thinking like that too, eh?"

"Oh Pat." My mother sighed her infamous long sigh, before asking her same old rhetorical question. "What am I going to do with you? Why do you always think different than what I say?"

"The funny thing is I do understand what you mean Mom. I just wish you'd hear me too."

"I hear you Pat."

"Ok Mom thank you for that. The other day I took the kids to visit Karen's kids, Susan, Kelly, and Paul, and there was a poem on her wall, called 'Desiderata'. I'll get a copy for you. Maybe it will help you to see how I think. We have the right to live in peace. You deserve a lot more than what you're getting. I really worry about you Mom."

"Sometimes I worry about you too Pat. You're the one who's sounding crazy these days. You should realize that your dad is doing much better since half the kids are gone. He doesn't have so much to worry about. All I'm saying is you should forgive him and maybe those headaches you get all the time would go away."

"And maybe my little sisters will live in candy land since it's all so lovely over there now, except for an occasional punch in your head. Why do you say I 'sound' crazy Mom? I 'am' crazy! Everybody knows it, why don't you?"

"Oh Pat, I wasn't saying you're crazy."

"That's ok Mom, I understand. I was trying to help but maybe I'm wrong. If so, I'm sorry. If you change your mind our door is open. Otherwise please don't tell me what he's doing anymore. I have to keep my sanity for my own family."

There I was again. Back in the library gathering more mental health books until one fell off the shelf and hit me. Obviously, I needed this one. 'My Mother Myself.' That's a sign if there ever was one. I consumed them all and thought about the unusual relationship I had with my mother. From the beginning of time, she and I were partners, raising babies. My mother had always let me get away with more than the others, which I assumed came with the territory. Being the oldest meant I got more freedom. Now I could see there was a lot more to it than that. Leonard tried to make her feel guilty about my birth. She had a baby out of wedlock, so he continued to shame her. Often repeating vile comments about a kid that wasn't his, though none of us knew which kid he was talking about. I was the thorn in his side he adopted from societal pressure. He didn't

173

do it from the heart and my mother knew that. So, she tried to compensate for his cruelty. For every action there is reaction. It is the law of the universe. Naturally, it applied in our house as well. The dynamics of ten personalities created a house of mad bears. What kind of boundaries did I learn in a house like that? Boundaries to me were tracing the outside edges in coloring books, making everything look brighter. After being pushed out into a new life I feared for those I'd left behind. Still caught in the middle of my mother's war. Still trying to make her change her life. Ever since I was a little kid. God help me. I was a little control freak. So, what am I doing now? The same dam thing.

"Maybe I love my mother too much Walt. I'll never stop wanting to protect her. I can't help it, it's in my soul. She's never going to leave, and I'll never understand why she stays. It's never right to let someone abuse you. I'll never accept what he's doing to my family. Never!"

"You don't have to accept it Pat. You just need to live your own life. I thought your mother would jump at the chance to leave but she can't. She feels trapped. He has her so brainwashed she's afraid to leave. She probably thinks he'll do something worse if she does."

"How can I not worry about her? If only she'd come here and let all the kids be happy together."

"Maybe bringing them here wasn't such a good idea. Maybe your mother would be better off taking the kids to Canada. I don't know what's best for them. She needs to decide that for herself. It's her life. All I want is for everyone to be happy. If she changes her mind, I'll go along with whatever you want, because you're a good wife. You hardly even yell at me anymore. You're a good mother too. Someday our kids will know how hard you worked to not be crazy."

"Please don't ever tell our kids I was crazy."

"They already know Pat, they're smart kids. They take after me. I'm so glad I can still make you laugh. We're all going to laugh about it someday. You'll always be a little crazy, that's what we love about you. Our kids will love you no matter what because they're good kids. They know how much you love them. Just stop taking those diet pills. They make you mean. You're not yourself when you take those things. You move furniture around all night, and I wake up in the morning and think I fell asleep in the wrong house. Then you clean like Mrs. Streak and yell at me all day. We can eat off these floors. They don't need to be that clean. You need your sleep. Stop taking those pills before they kill you. They're poison!"

"I have to lose weight, I gained 60 pounds when I was pregnant with the girls."

"I don't care about the weight, there's just more of you to love Pat. I'll love you if you get to 200 pounds. When you don't eat, I don't eat, because you don't want to cook. Feed me and take me to bed and I'm a happy man. Just stop taking those pills!"

"Ok, ok, I'll stop taking them. I didn't know they made me act so bad. I don't want to upset you Walt, I love you so much."

"I know how much you love me; you still don't like when I'm out of your sight. You must really love my ugly ass. Love me a little less so I can breathe kid."

Then off he went, fishing for perch, trout, smelt, walleye, salmon or whatever fish was in season. Ice fishing took over soon as it was ice. Fishing is good no matter what weather. There's always another fish to catch. When he wasn't fishing, he was hunting with one or more buddies. I had no choice. I learned to trust. It no longer bothered me that he was with his buddies on weekends. His buddies were all married now. They were all great guys and I trusted them all. I stayed busy with my kids, took ceramic classes with my friend Barb, read voraciously, constantly re- decorated the house, took in ironing, re- painted the house inside and out, went to real estate school. In short, I was too busy to miss him. He came home with dead things, fish, partridge, pheasant, deer, and one time a little rabbit.

 "Get that dead rabbit out of here before the girls see it and think you killed Puff's friend! And don't bring any dead ducks, home either. You're going to traumatize our girls. Bad enough the neighbor kid jumped on their pet duck and broke its leg. The poor thing had to be killed and they cried over for an hour about that, now you bring a dead rabbit in here."

It finally dawned on me that my husband had all this free time, while I on the other hand was working nonstop like a freight train. Boy that ticked me off good. By the time he got home, firecracker was lit and exploded. After that he stayed home a few weekends. Time passed in happy family land. Then my husband hired a new worker. From the start I sensed something about the guy. Frankly, he gave me the creeps. I told my husband, but he pooh-poohed me. "He's ok Pat, you just have to get to know him." Seems that's exactly what the guy had in mind. When I angrily told my husband his new hunting buddy made a dirty pass at me, he didn't believe me! Then I told the guy's wife why I didn't want to go out with them as a couple anymore, and she gave me an ear full. She already started to divorce him after finding out that he'd done something far worse. So, I told my husband exactly the kind of guy he was, expecting he'd fire him, and get him out of our life. Instead, I was astonished when he insisted the jerk was his friend. It was a stab in my heart. He made his choice. I saw him as he really was. He'd stopped being a prince long ago and became a selfish man who took me for granted. Why was I staying home to run the construction business? Why wasn't I starting the career I wanted? Why didn't my husband fire someone who approached his wife in her own home? I wasn't safe in my own marriage. My husband didn't care anymore. This marriage was soon over if that's the way he felt. The good old boys club was alive and going strong. Why did I think things would be different than they were in my mother's time?

CAREER TIME

A career in real estate was more than a job, it was a means of expressing myself and I loved the work. As soon as the girls left for school every morning, I was multi-tasking. Between handling construction calls, and real estate business, I was swamped with

176

floor time at the office, showing homes, taking listings, writing contracts, and getting back home before my kids got there. In the beginning I built my real estate contacts networking through family and friends. Being a realtor was gratifying work. What better job could I have than helping people make the transition into their new home. Back then we used the multi-list book, it was inches thick with listings for each city. At times I wrote an offer on the hood of my car. It was a simple way of doing business. A person's word was their bond. A handshake meant something.

The first real estate office I worked for was in Garden City. Going back to smalltown meant driving from northwest Plymouth, passing other offices on the way. I wanted to start with first time buyers. It was a time when there was a thing called red lining, where real estate offices steered people to certain neighborhoods, based on race. I walked into the office on Ford Road to interview, and told the manager if redlining happened in his office, I'd turn them in.

"When do you want to start work Pat?" I knew I'd found the right broker. Rick ran the office, with his wife Marlene, they were a good team. He taught me the real estate business from the ground up. After the business grew, they moved to another office in Livonia. I went with them. They had no problem if I wanted to take time off to help at my kid's school. I was the teacher's helper at various events. Christmas parties Mrs. Claus showed up in a Santa suit stuffed with pillows, hair dusted with flour under a red cap, reading glasses on the end of her nose, telling tall stories. Children listened in rapt attention to what was happening at the North Pole, how Santa was busy with the reindeer, the elves wrapping presents and baking cookies that I brought for this party. Mrs. Claus was a big hit.

Many years later Holly played Santa for our office Christmas party in that same suit, she was an even bigger hit.

A MAN NAMED ED

A fellow realtor came rushing in the office one day and changed my life in minutes. Although we'd only spoken in passing, it's hard not to take note of a man who's always brimming over with happiness. You wonder what he's so gassed up about when you're struggling to make it without jumping off a cliff. It was starting to grate on my nerves. He needed to share his secret with us mere mortals who manage an occasional smile. His exuberant, bubbly champagne attitude was something we all needed to know about. "What's with you Mister Ed? Why are you always so happy?" I blurted out, disgruntled by his bouncing through the office like a happy kangaroo.

"I am filled with the spirit of the Lord!" He declared and blew my everlasting mind. "God, I need some of that." The words came spontaneous from my heart and were heard. Immediately Ed and Rick put down the contract they were reading and walked to my desk. There in the window of the office they prayed for Jesus to come into my heart on a morning I will never forget. "What a wonderful way to start my day!" Ed declared joyously. "To think I only ran in here to pick up a contract. Praise the Lord! God is with you Pat."

I did not cross paths with the man named Ed afterwards, but the faith of a mustard seed had been planted. My business continued to grow as I continued to learn from Rick. Some people say a man and a woman can't be friends without being sexual. How sad for them. True friendship is a rare thing. As it was with my brother, Rick was a lifetime friend.

BETTY JO

Betty Jo came to work for Rick when he opened a new office in Farmington. A highly respected experienced agent, she would become the pivotal person of my lifetime. When the student is ready the teacher will appear. I watched and learned from everything she did. She taught me ethics and integrity in business and became my mentor. She often used the expression; 'rise above it.' There was an air of class about her that made you feel good just being around her. She dressed to the nines with impeccable taste, but not expensive. A smart hat often completed her outfit. Betty Jo was mother earth; always had time for everybody, a few kind words with the busboy, the waiter, the janitor. All were treated like the president of whatever establishment we were in at the time. It was easy to understand why she had so much repeat and referral business. Betty Jo was my role model, someone I aspired to be. From her I learned confidence, something I may not have developed had I not met this West Virginia lady who sang 'Country Roads' one night at a piano bar and brought the place down. With her I went to the best places, places I wanted to go with a husband who wouldn't take me. Betty Jo and I traveled to real estate conventions in Hawaii, New Orleans, Texas, Ohio, and other professional meetings in our home state. In Hawaii we stayed with her daughter Nancy and son in law Greg, at their home/ nursery, of exotic tropical plants. We took a helicopter to Maui, me hoping my stomach would land when we did, Betty Jo her adventurous self. Though the view was incomparable, no more helicopters for me.

Betty Jo gave me positive thinking books. "Become the most positive person you know Pat." A force for change and betterment had come into my life. This amazing woman with her own family of four, took me under her wing. Despite being a decade older than her oldest, she recognized my need to be nurtured. God had sent another mother, and from then on, everything that was to become good about me, was learned from her influence. Betty Jo was there for the big storm. Her wise brown eyes saw it coming.

THE STORM

At this point we'd been married about eight years. The storm had been brewing ever since my husband took the word of his part time worker, over his wife's. Clouds kept forming on the horizon and I kept warning that a flood was coming. "I've really had it with your weekend fishing trips with that new buddy of yours. You better listen because I won't keep telling you the same thing over and over. I'll do something about it. I'm not like my mother who stayed home all her life."

"My mother never had a car and neither did yours Pat. You have your own Lincoln and can go wherever you want, anytime you want. I've never stopped you from doing whatever you want."

"You're absolutely right about that, but I need a husband who wants to be with me sometime. I want to go on dates with you and have some romance in life. I love music and dancing and want you to take me out, is that too much to ask?"

"I'm home every night of the week, on weekends I want to relax with my buddy. I don't like dancing. Dancing is for sissies. You knew you married a man who can't dance."

"Ok, so we don't have to dance, but you can put your arms around me and move your feet a little, can't you? If you can't stand that, we could go to a movie, a play, bowling, or whatever!"

"I don't like movies or plays, that's girl stuff. I'll try the bowling."

"Ok, so we've gone bowling a few times. Now you want to quit going, because you're tired from working all week. Why aren't you too tired to go with that jerk? I'm tired of fighting with you about this. I'm going to leave your selfish butt and I'm not just threatening! I mean it! I need to be with my husband sometimes!"

"Stop going crazy on me Pat, just go and stop bothering me. You want to dance so go dancing with your girlfriends and let me do what I want."

"You really don't care anymore, do you? Married people don't go out dancing alone."

"Just go Pat. Leave. Quit bothering me!" It broke my heart. Words like that can't be taken back. He proved that he couldn't care less. Our marriage was over. I opened the yellow pages and found the first lawyer in the book. Then called my girlfriends to go dancing.

"What's this that came in the mail? I don't believe it! YOU'RE DIVORCING ME!?"

"Why are you surprised? I told you over and over what was happening to us, so why don't you believe it now? You wanted to be free to hang out with jerk. You told me to leave and that's what I'm doing. I'm not staying with someone who doesn't care about what I need."

He didn't say he was sorry. He didn't ask me to stop the divorce. He didn't say anything. After the initial surprise it was like nothing happened. It was every day all over again. We went to work as usual, except on weekends. Friday nights I went dancing at the club with my girlfriends. Saturday nights he went to the same club with jerk, aggravating me even more. He wouldn't go listen to music with me but would go with him. Like little kids we went on trying to get back at each other. Too immature to see the battle would never win the war. Someone needed to be the bigger person. It wasn't us. We needed a real hero.

"Hi Pop, it's good to see you, it's been too long. Come on in. Sonny's not home, he went to finish up a job."

"Sonny doesn't know I was coming here today. I came to see you. He told me you filed for divorce. Will you let me talk to you about that?"

"Of course, Pop. I'll always listen to whatever you have to say. You're the father I never had."

"Thank you for that Pat. I always thought you and I were close, so imagine my surprise when Sonny told me about the divorce. Erve and I could see you kids were having problems again, but never thought it could come to this. And we don't want to know what happened to bring it this far. The only reason I'm here is I don't want to see this divorce happen. It would be a grave mistake. Marriage is hard work. It might look like Erve and I always get along but we've had our times when we wondered about sticking it out too. Marriage is forever Pat, especially when two people have a love like you two have. I've seen the way you look at each other. That's not something everyone gets in marriage. I know my son can be very selfish and stubborn, but I've taught him well, and he's a good man."

"I've been asking myself why you two would stay in the same house when you can easily afford not to. Sonny said you haven't even spoken about dividing things up. Is that right Pat?"

"Yes, it is, Pop."

"Why do you think that is?"

"I haven't even thought about it Pop, maybe we're just tired of fighting so we don't talk at all."

"Well, I've thought about it a lot and keep coming up with the same answer. The two of you want to get back together but you're both too blind stubborn to see it. Neither will take the first step. You're a fighter Pat. Don't quit now. My son deserves a strong woman like you. My bet is this marriage is not over no matter what you're thinking now. If you would tell him, you've changed your mind, I believe he'd start over. That's my bet and I'd put all I have on it. Forgive each other and start over. Don't let go Pat. Real love like you have with my son will heal itself. Your girls need their father by their side. I wish you'd heed my words and give them good thought. Don't let this divorce go any further. That's all I have to say."

Pops words stayed with me, I thought about them a lot. Never had a man been so open and honest with me as Pop, not even my own husband. Why can't we talk? What happened to us? I want my girls to have their father with them. Walt is a good father, and he loves them. Why does Pop think I'm so strong? I'm not strong at all. I can't even ask my husband what's wrong with us.

Then the lawyer called. "When do you want to come in to prepare the property division Mrs.?"

"I'm not ready."

"You've been delaying, have you changed your mind?"

"I haven't figured it out."

"I'll have to charge for the delay."

"That figures."

"Pardon me?"

"When I figure it out, you'll be the first to know."

Miserable uncertainty lagged. One night I ventured to ask. "I'm going to meet some of our old friends to listen to music Walt, do you want to come along?"

"No, I'm never going to that place again."

"Well, I guess I should go, since they're expecting me."

All the way there I was miserable. Thinking about the showdown we had weeks ago when it all came to light, and he'd made an admission. Something inside told me to go back. Go back to what? He still hasn't said the words. Words of remorse. Words of regret. I need something from him. I need to hear the words. The door of the club opened, and I went in. Found the friendly group of happy, partying faces then announced; "I'm leaving."

"What? You just walked in! You haven't even sat down. Sit for a minute crazy lady, then you can surprise us again," they laughed.

"I have to leave; this is not where I'm supposed to be." I turned from faces that clearly said I'd lost my mind. All I knew was I had to get home. A block away I saw the brightly lit telephone booth and stopped. "I'm calling to let you know I won't be there tonight when you arrive Karen."

"I was just going to call you; I'm not going either. I'll be at your house early tomorrow to see Walt."

"What are you talking about? Why are you coming to see Walt in the morning?"

"Oh my God you're not at home, are you? You haven't heard. Walt's father just died in an automobile accident. He had a heart attack while driving home from the fishing trip up north. Darwin was sleeping in the camper but he's ok. Wasn't Walt supposed to go wi..." the phone dropped out of my hand. Somehow, I made it home, only God knows how. I was beside myself. I stepped inside the house and a strange thing happened. I saw myself from above turning to lock the door. The click in the lock brought knowing that I wasn't going out again without my husband. Whether he would try again or not, I was already home. Quietly I hung my coat and went to find him. He was standing in the living room waiting, his face ashen. He opened his arms, and I went straight into them. Words were no longer necessary. Pop's last wish was bigger than the both of us on the eve of Thanksgiving, 1969.

They say the good die young, it must be true. Remembering Pop, I am reminded of what he taught me about war, and how he played his individual part of keeping peace. It so happens that my Daily Word booklet addressed the same topic today with the following verse.

"Nation shall not lift up sword against nation, neither shall they learn war anymore." Micah 4:3

A NEW BEGINNING

Losing our beloved Pop was totally unexpected. He was 52 years young. Walt was shattered by the loss of his father. Pop was his rock. As for me Pop was the person who came closest to being a real father. He was in my life for 11 years and will live in my heart forever. For all intent and purpose, he was my father. After a while we did what Pop wanted us to do. We started over. My husband took me out on regular date nights. He was not a romantic, he simply expected me to know he cared. So, one night on our date, when he took my hand under the table, I waited to see what was up since he rarely expressed amorous feelings vocally. "You have to help me with it!" He squawked.

"What are you doing under the table you goof, somebody could be observing what kind of shenanigans are going on over here."

"I can't get it on with these big clumsy fingers of mine."

"What in the world? Get back up here Walt, this is getting embarrassing."

"I promised you this a long time ago Pat and I'm finally keeping my promise."

There on my hand was the most beautiful ring I ever saw, a heart shape diamond twisted halfway up the wrong finger. Of course, I had to cry about it. "Oh my God it's so beautiful! This is too much. You have to take it back, it's too expensive!"

"Ok Pat after seeing it on your hand I think it should have been bigger to show up more."

"No, no! It's fine! It's fine! Really! It's fine like it is!"

"Whatever you say Pat. I want you to wear it to Las Vegas. I'm taking you on the honeymoon we never had. We're staying at Caesar's Palace. We'll go to every show you ever wanted to see. Except Elvis, he sold out months ago, but we'll see him when he comes here. I rented a car so we can see the Grand Canyons too."

Las Vegas, the home of glitz and glamour, bright lights and illusionists, high rollers, and every kind of gambling you want to throw money at. Plus, the best entertainers. Walt's favorite show was Les Folies Bergère, near naked showgirls in elaborate feather headdresses and little else. Of course, it was disappointing to see Elvis name on the International, marquee and there was no way we could get in to see him. But we did see him later in Michigan at the Pontiac Silverdome, with sis Rose and her husband Mark. Not long after we got home from Vegas, we had a surprise. Most people know where they were born, but not many know where they were conceived. So, here's to you Michael, what happened in Vegas, did not stay in Vegas.

IRISH HILLS

Soon after we got back, we bought a cottage on a lake in Irish Hills, where family were always welcome on weekends. One afternoon we climbed aboard Walt's new speedboat. After a while he dropped anchor on the sand bar. "All you goofy sisters go jump in the lake!" That was Walt being Walt. As for me there's nothing better than feeling earth beneath my feet, even in a lake. When time came to get back on board, the lady carrying a watermelon couldn't do it. The harder I tried to pull myself over the side, the funnier it got.

So, Walt came up with another bright idea. He got down on all fours and I was supposed to climb on his back and my sisters could pull me aboard. As soon as he started blowing bubbles underneath me, I laughed so hard I couldn't climb on his back to save my soul. He popped out of the water, and I promised not to laugh again but soon as he got down on all fours, those dam bubbles came bubbling up and I was a goner. Laughing so hard I couldn't move and my sisters howling too. He popped up out of the water blue in the face. "Get off my boat! All of you! You're trying to drown me so you can take it! Well, I got a better idea. I'll stay up here where I can breathe and instruct you sisters how to get the lady with a watermelon back on board. Ok, everybody ready? Stop laughing you bunch of lunatics, or we'll be out here all night. Ready on the count of three, one, two, three, heave ho!" The team rolled watermelon lady over the side of the sparkling, gold flake speedboat. That had to be a hilarious sight for everyone on the lake.

Through all the fun the rest of us were having, poor mom was in dire pain. She finally admitted after much prodding, that it had been going on for months. We insisted on making a doctor's appointment. Afterwards the specialist told her to bring the whole family in so he could talk to us. We all showed up, all ten of us. Doctor M wasted no time letting us know the severity of her upcoming surgery. Our mother would be in the operating room for many hours. She had ovarian cancer that spread to other parts of her body. They were going to remove her vagina and her rectum, plus do a total hysterectomy. Hopefully, they'd be able to remove it all. If it went well, she would be in the hospital a minimum of two months, probably longer. She would not be able to travel for a year. He did not mince words. "You should be prepared. Your mother will need the support of all of you. This operation is new, it's only been performed twice in this country. I lost my wife in one of them. Pray for your mother. She's going to need many prayers."

The room was quiet, overwhelmed by information foreign to our ears. I looked around and saw what had to be a reflection in my own eyes. Fear. Followed by united strength for our mother. Across the room sis Sharon, also pregnant, caught my eye and I knew mom would fight like the fighter she was. She was excited about the approaching birth of our babies, both due in July.

As I said we were all there, the ten of us including dad, which would soon become a point of curiosity, as to the way his mind worked. What he did after hearing this news should not have come as a surprise. But it did. Either during the surgery, or while she was in critical condition, he had his own agenda. He walked into the local real estate office and sold their house on a cash out basis. By his own hand, my mother and two youngest sisters no longer had a home. After the fact, I remembered the day he'd picked my brain. I'd taken Michelle and Holly to see Grandma before she went in the hospital. From out of the blue, he'd asked. "Ah seen a sign n th real estate winder Patsy, ya know what it means?"

"They buy homes for cash at a big discount to re-sell them at market price for a nice profit. Why did you ask Dad, were you thinking of selling?"

"Jest wandered by n seen th sign thas all Patsy, u dun sprize me, dint thank ya'd know nuthin."

Of course, it struck a nerve. That I wouldn't know the business I was in, was a direct insult. I took pride in every closing, knowing that I'd made a difference in someone's life. For ordinary people, a home is the biggest purchase they ever make. They were happy so I was happy. But not him. He had to insult the person who led him through getting a second VA loan. The house in Wyandotte had been repossessed. The red tape involved to reinstate his eligibility took several months of work for which I wanted nothing. Except his approval. Just once.

"We couldn't even think of moving now Pat. Your dad just saw a sign and wondered that's all," my mother had answered for him. Bless her trusting heart. "Of course, Mom I understand," I'd answered back then forgot about it. Sign, sign, everywhere a sign, did you read the sign? Of course not. I was busy praying for my mother's life. Not for a second did I think he was up to something. Who would think like that? Who would ever think he could be such a cold-hearted son of a bitch to lift a hand against her at a time like this? Not me. And certainly not my mother. Her blissful theory was if we all prayed more, he'd be redeemed. Oh goodie, let's all dream the impossible dream.

Meanwhile by other hands, a team of highly skilled surgeons worked to remove the cancer, along with my mother's anatomy. Who knew such things could be done and the body could still function? Certainly not me. How could they remove body parts that were used several times a day? Weren't they necessary to survive? It was mind boggling to me. I never even heard of a hysterectomy, much less a colostomy and a cystectomy. There weren't any medical encyclopedias laying around our house, or computers to research things. I was freaked out by all this. Miraculously the team brought our mother through the surgery. She was in the critical care unit for days afterward. God's hand was on her, feeding a strong will to survive. By his grace she kept making it through another day of touch and go. Eventually we were allowed to go in, one at a time, for a couple minutes.

She lay there pale and semi-conscious, while I tried not to focus on the countless tubes running in and out of her small frame. She was such a paradox to me. This woman I blamed when I was a child, and thought was weak, because she let him get away with wrong. God forgive me, this woman is the strongest person I've ever met. Look what she's gone through and she's still suffering. It's so unfair. And there's nothing I can do but sit here with my baby kicking inside me and watch her suffering again. I feel so helpless. 'She's in God's hands,' the voice inside whispered. Please hear me God. Help my mother to make it. She's only 52 and suffered so much already in her life. There must be something better waiting for her. Please bring her through this and give her some happiness before she leaves this planet.

Then I left the room so the next sibling could go in. But where oh where was her unseen husband? On one of those precarious days two young sisters were first to realize his actions. Nancy and Lucy woke up to a moving van in their front yard. Thank God I was still at home when the telephone started ringing off the wall. And thank God that Michelle and Holly were already in school. I ran to pick up the incessant phone and a barely audible voice whispered across the line; "Come and get us Pat! Dad said we have to go to Kentucky with him, but we don't want to leave Mom. He's loading the furniture right now. I've got to hang up. he's coming back in. Please Hurry Pat!" I nearly flew to Garden City clenching the wheel with white knuckles. Blocking the moving truck in the driveway I ran in the house with the baby inside me kicking excitedly.

"Wow what's going on in here Dad!?" It took everything I had not to give Sis' cover away.

"We're leavin this state," he ground out. "What do you mean Dad? The doctor said mom can't travel for a year, and these kids won't want to leave her right now either."

"Ah'm doin what's bess fer this family."

That was it. I lost it. Caution went with the wild wind. "Best for 'who' Dad? That's what you're telling these young girls, but I know better. You're running out on our mother like you always did!" He came toward me with his fist in the air ready to strike.

"You hit me, and you'll be in jail so fast you won't know what happened! You hit a pregnant woman before and always thought I didn't remember that didn't you?" He stopped short. The truth could not be denied. His eyes filled with surprise, then recognition. It even surprised me. Where had it come from after all those years?

"U take em then, n take yer muther too! Ah'm on ma way out a here n ain't lookin back!" With that my sisters ran down the stairwell from where they'd been listening. We rushed out of the house and drove away with only the clothes on their back. He loaded everything else on the truck. Furniture to underwear, he took it all. With every dollar he got from the sale of their home, he left the state. While his wife of 27 years lay in a hospital gown fighting for her life.

So, there it is. That's what big sister remembers. Somehow, my sisters had it in them to be more forgiving. My perspective comes from the role I was given to play. There was never time for cry me a river. Big sister had a specific job. Stand back. The oldest and meanest will make sure everybody's ok. That man doesn't care. He ran for the hills soon as he saw the sign that said, 'Road closed. No more sex.' Cynical big sister knew the score of that game. Was I bitter? Hell yes, I was bitter. You better believe it. The greatest thing a man can do for his children is to love and respect their mother. This man left my mother and innocent sisters in the darkest hour. From where I stood this last cruel act was unforgivable. There's a thin line between love and hate. All my life I walked it for my mother's sake. Now big sister was picking up pieces of hearts when she hadn't found her own pieces. Where was justice for my mother after giving him all those beautiful children? And all the pain endured from him? Him and his so-called justice went to Kentucky, leaving my mother the victim again. He was no longer dad. He wasn't my dad and never was. He was just he. He had no name. The truth door opened, and I allowed it in. Speak the truth. I hated this man with a vengeance. And felt I had every right to do so. And God knows I paid for it. Hate is like cancer. It spreads to consume one's happiness. Peace was only an illusion. It was out of the grasp of the tough cookie who thought she had all the answers. Ah, the brash intellect of youth.

In the meantime, back at the hospital, someone had to tell our mother the cold hard facts. That her husband, her home, and every material thing she had in the world was gone. In my mind's eye I still see that person standing to speak.

"I don't know how Mom can take this after all she's been through, but she has to be told. I'm going to tell her but let's wait until she's a little stronger; ok girls?"

I never loved my brother more than that moment. The time came when she had to be told, and the strength of my mother's faith blew me away. "Thank God I'm alive with all my good kids." That's all she said.

Mom continued to recuperate. We all visited daily, passing each other in halls coming and going. The trip from the east side of Plymouth to Ann Arbor, was a long drive on a winding country road. The front seat pushed back all the way making room for the baby giant that was coming soon. One sunny morning I waddled into mom's room and there she was, sitting up in bed smiling! "Why are you here again so soon honey? You were just here yesterday. The nurses are with me all the time. You don't have to worry about me anymore. They take such good care and pamper me so much; I'm going to be spoiled by the time I leave. You have to quit coming all this way alone, look how big your stomach is!" Evidently, she thought I didn't know there was a huge watermelon sticking out above my feet. "The baby's going to come while you're driving on that lonely road alone, and there won't be anyone out there to help you."

"Good grief Mom, nothing like that's going to happen. The baby's not due for almost a month."

"My goodness I've been here so long I forgot what month it is. You know Pat, I was never big like that before any of you kids were born."

"That's because you're a little pip squeak Mom. You're not a Renaissance woman like me."

"Don't make me laugh Pat, it still hurts a lot."

UNIVERSITY HOSPITAL - ANN ARBOR, MICHIGAN

This hospital went above and beyond. They were absolutely, wonderful. Mom was there two and a half months. When she was finally ready to leave, her caregivers gathered. Sometimes words are inadequate. How do you say thank you for all this? All who had taken such good care, and called her, the miracle patient, were there. Mom was radiant with gratitude. We drove away in a flurry of doctors and nurses waving. A heartfelt tribute goes out to U of M Hospital. Thank you for the additional time we had with our mother, she lived for 25 more years.

MOTHERHOOD A THIRD TIME

 Now that mom and my mother and sisters were staying with us, I was overwhelmed with all the careful instructions. Her medical supplies could not be contaminated, otherwise she could become very sick. Mom had to wear 2 colostomy bags, one for her bladder to empty into, the other for her bowels. She showed me how it worked one time and I got weak in the knees. I'm not a nurse. I'm the talker. The one who holds a hand. If a nurse is needed, call sis Nancy, not me. Thank God Nancy and Lucy were 17 and 16 at the time and helped with everything. All in all, 1971 was a year of blessed events. Mom full recovery. Sis Rose married Mark. Sharon gave birth to a boy July 5 th. And I became Joey's Godmother. On the 15th of July, Walt and I left for St Mary's hospital, leaving Mom in charge. After waiting all night for the baby to come, he left at dawn exhausted. Seems Mom had also been awake waiting at the kitchen table for hours for some news. Walt crept in quietly, assuming everyone was still asleep, and didn't see her sitting there. She took one look at his tired, drawn face and became alarmed. He looked so bad she was afraid to ask. Minutes passed before she finally blurted; "Is everything ok Walt?" He nearly jumped out of his shoes. "Good God Mom! I didn't see you there! You're like a ghost in that white robe, next to those white lace curtains. Throw that robe away so you can't scare me again and I'll get you a new one. Everything is great, we have a 'boy' this time! Wait till you see the size of this kid. Don't cry Mom, it's all good news. Now I see where Pat gets her happy cry."

It was quite a busy time with a new baby in the house too. Our little guy got a lot of attention between his grama, two aunts and two young sisters. Walt kept repeating the story of how Mike got his name. Of course, he had his own version but the way it actually happened went more like this. Initially we somewhat agreed that if we had a boy we'd name him Walter Louis, for Pop. But the more I thought about it, it didn't seem right. Because Pop had called himself Louie, and the whole family called Walt, Sonny. It didn't make sense to name a kid something, then call him something else.

"I've been thinking Walt. If we have a boy, maybe we shouldn't name him after you and Pop, because neither of you like the name Walter."

"I thought we already settled this Pat."

"Well, it was a nice idea to start but a person should change their mind if it turns out not to be, don't you agree?"

"Let's leave it like we said so you can't change your mind again Pat. Besides, we could be having another girl and I don't like the names you picked so we still have to decide that."

Maybe he was assuming we'd have a Walter the third, but I wasn't thinking anything of the kind. All I wanted was to push this baby out first, then we could talk about the small stuff. The only thing that really mattered in this third pregnancy, was that the baby was healthy. I had a scary pregnancy. Early in the pregnancy I started throwing up bile one morning, which kept repeating into the afternoon. Something told me this was not just morning sickness. Something was wrong. I drove to the hospital and was rushed into the operating room for emergency appendectomy. Afterwards they said I was a very lucky lady. The baby could have been poisoned if I'd waited any longer.

When the time came for the birth, I was determined to watch again. Labor was harder, a couple extra pound baby made a difference. When they said it was a boy, I couldn't stop crying I was so happy. Finally, a boy! He was not only healthy he was the cutest little boy I ever saw. They laid him in my arms in a blue blanket and I was overjoyed. Eight pink bundles had preceded this one. Six sisters, and two daughters were put in my arms in pink blankets. When the nurse came to take him back to the nursery, I wouldn't let him go. "We do bring them back you know. All right, I'll give you a few more minutes then.

"Hello little Walter," I said to my baby boy, and he screwed up his face intentionally. "The little guy doesn't seem pleased about his name Walt; look he's ticked off."

"He's just got gas Pat, that's the way the men in my family look when we do that."

"It's not gas, I can tell. He's not happy with that name. Besides, he's too small to be a Walter."

"For God's sake Pat, he was over nine pounds! The kids already a linebacker, look at his shoulders. My grandmother had five sons and none of them were that big!"

"I'm serious Walt, the name isn't right for him. We made a mistake naming him that."

"We already did it Pat. We can't undo it. Maybe we should've named him something else but it's too late now."

"It's never too late. His name should be Michael. It suit's him. Michael means next to God. He's the miracle we thought we'd never have. He'll do good things with his namesake from Saint Michael. I loved that name all my life."

"I like it too Pat; I really do, but you should have said so before we gave the name to the nurse, and she recorded it. We can't change it now so forget about it."

"Let me think about this."

"Stop thinking Pat, his name is Walter. What kind of drugs did they give you anyway? I knew I should've warned them you can't take aspirin without getting goofy."

"Stop making fun of me Walt. I didn't say anything because we only lost Pop a year before I got pregnant. Now I know the name is wrong for this little guy. I can feel it in my bones. He's not a Walter. He's his own self and he needs his own name."

"Well let me know what you decide. The hospital won't let you go home for three days, so he'll have to be Walter until you find out how to change it. I know when you make up your mind to do something, you'll do it no matter what. Hello little Michael, it looks like your mother is changing your name and you don't get to say anything about it. That's how she is son, you'll get used to it like I did. You sure are a cute little guy, you look just like me you lucky kid. We're going fishing soon as you start walking, so hurry up and walk little man."

For a short while, Mike was called little Walt. Although I went to the courthouse and changed it, mom was still calling him' little Walt.' She insisted he looked like Walt so he should be Walt. "No Mom, he's Michael."

 "But he looks just like Walt, Pat." "That doesn't mean he's Walt, Mom, he's himself, so, call him Michael or Mike." "But he looks like Walt, Pat." "I know Mom, I know."

Poor Mom with all her kids and grandkids, she was like the little old lady in the shoe who had so many children she didn't know what to do. She didn't call any of us by our name. She couldn't get us right. She went down the line calling us every name in the book but our own, unless she got lucky and hit on it. Sometimes she got so flustered she just stomped her foot and said, "You know who I mean, I'm looking right at you. Just answer!"

When little Mike developed bronchial asthma, the doctor said he would grow out of it, but it was frightening when it flared up. Walt would take the heavy little guy from my arms and walk him back and forth, with the vaporizer blowing steam in the room to help him breathe. "Go check on the girls Pat, I hear them waking up in there. Don't worry. Mike will be ok." That was the Walt I loved most; the man who was my children's father.

LIFE IS EVER CHANGING.

We sold the cottage in Irish Hills; not having time to go there anymore. Eventually the time came for mom to have her own apartment and the whole gang chipped in. Over the years everyone made sure she was taken care of. When mom even mentioned something, sisters were on the phone calling each other, and all the guys delivered it. "You need anything Ma, just call us," they told her. A tribute to all the brother in laws who were around between the years of 1972 to 1996, wherever they are, who made it happen. And yet there was one thing mom wanted that we could not replace.

She wanted the family album. John told her we'd make new memories. And that we did. For the first time in her life, mom was living it up, vacationing in Florida, California, Las Vegas, Niagara Falls, and in Canada. Also at Linda and John's summer home. We had the best parties, singing and dancing, the guys singing doo wop. On New Year's we got busted for being too loud. We sent mom to the door to talk to the police; what nice cop would be hardnose on a sober grandma just dancing around? "Ok mam, have a good time just keep them a little quieter."

SMOKEY HOLLOW ROAD

We found the old house near the end of Smokey Hollow Road, after driving over 400 miles with our three kids. The lot was on an incline, leading down to about 200 feet of beach frontage on Lake Michigan. The house needed a new roof, but the clapboard siding was in surprisingly good shape, only needing to be scraped and repainted. The roof extended over a welcoming and charming front porch. Inside the rooms were small, the kitchen a disaster; the bathroom no better, with an outlet someone once called a toilet. The only upstairs room was also small. Despite all that it lacked, we dreamed of building an addition on the east side of the house, with windows overlooking the lake. It was the 'someday' house promised on our first date. Someday it would be finished, and we'd sit on the porch watching the swans on the lake. We bought the dream.

This time we bit off more than we could chew. Roughing it, is putting it mildly. Camping is the taj mahal compared to the toil we put into that dream. Every weekend, after working all week, we commuted the 400 miles with three kids to get there. Worked on the old house two days, then drove 400 miles back to our 'real' jobs. The dream became a nightmare. We slept on a mattress on the floor upstairs, as downstairs was in an filthy state of renovating, used the old toilet after a quart of bleach was poured over it, went in the cold lake with a bar of soap to bathe, ate sandwiches from our cooler on the porch. The house yielded its history when Walt inspected the attic and found old letters dated in the 1800's, and cherub valentine cards.

One day something scary happened to Michelle when she was upstairs; the vision of an old lady appeared in front of her. She ran down and told us and we were all scared. How do you explain an unexplainable strange phenomenon to young children? Yet through all this, they fondly remember the beach front on the lake, and walking to the 'picture perfect' country store a mile away. One day while Walt and I were toiling on the house, they were at beach edge, Michelle playing the piccolo she'd found, Holly and Mike skipping rocks across the lake. He managed to hit a swan and it trumpeted loudly and flew out of the water chasing him through the yard, angrily trying to nip him. What a commotion! Everyone running after the swan trying to stop it from catching Mike. The snoop sisters from next door came running and yelling too. Lucky for Mike, the swan turned and flew back into the lake, frightened by a barrage of humans screaming at the poor creature. I went back to painting the exterior of the house, even though it was a bit premature since we planned an addition. I had to see at least that much done. Gutting the inside could be done over winter months. The house called for a smokey blue color. While Walt painted the second story on a ladder, I did the bottom portion. When the painting was finished the house on Smokey Hollow Road, came back to life with its new coat of smokey blue.

Eventually the dream wore us out physically and mentally, as well as financially. Over the winter months business at home slowed to a crawl. Walt's buddies had long ago taken other jobs. Roofing is brutal work to begin with, and even worse in winter when ice is on a roof. Rainy day savings only go so far, then you're in trouble, and we were forced to give up the dream. A single investor purchased the house through the local realtor we used. I felt a strong dislike for this man at the closing. The bank treated him as though he were royalty, barely speaking to us. After all was said and done - we were forced to let our dream go to save our credit, for a paltry $39,000, barely covering our expenses. There's been many properties since then between our family, that I've loved, but never has one affected me like the lakefront on Smokey Hollow Road. There was something about that house. Perhaps I lived there in a previous life? At times I wonder about reincarnation.

Many years later Mike took me on a special trip up north, just him and I. As soon as we found the house I started to cry and couldn't stop. It had an addition with windows overlooking the lake, the way Walt and I envisioned. I was still crying when we got to the historical country store in Old Mission. It still looked like a picture out of time. Mikey bought his mommy an ice cream cone to make her stop crying. Then he got into a conversation the way he does with everyone he's never met. So, I trailed off to talk with the clerk, still licking my ice cream cone, and asked about the job posted on the wall. The next thing I knew they offered it to me. "Thank you but it's a little too far for me to drive." Mike and I left, whereupon I cried even more, finally letting the dream go to wherever broken dreams go.

THE THINKER

No one knew me like Walt. At times it was unnerving; him reading my mind all the time. "Uh oh she's got that look in her eyes, she's thinking again. In another minute I'm going to be in trouble for something her dad did." Of course, I got peeved at him for that. "See what'd I tell you kids, she's mad and I didn't even do anything. I better get out of here. Let's go kids!" He had pet names for me. If I was sewing, he called me Sara Spunda. When I was cooking, it was Betty Crocker. If I was cleaning, it was Mrs. Clean Streak. "You streak through this house faster than Mr. Clean. I guess it's a good thing you're not like my mother. The dust bunnies can choke a lion over there."

"It's a good thing I'm Mrs. Clean Streak, because you're sure not Mr. Clean."

"Uh oh, Halloween's coming. I better get my witch a new broom for her birthday."

"Oh, goodie I can't wait Mr. Cheapskate."

"Mr. Cheapskate has an idea Pat. I'll take you and the kids for hamburgers on your birthday and a drive-in movie. The "Snow White" movie is playing now, the kids will love it."

"What a great idea! I can't wait to see it. I've only read the book. I love your ideas, Walt."

"I know Pat, that's what I love about you; a hamburger and a movie and you're happy. Except in the middle of the month when the witch comes out and scares me to death."

"Stop calling me a witch. I don't like being one, but sometimes you make me do it."

The decorator in me loved changing things, which meant 'honey do' projects for my carpenter. "Uh oh, she's thinking again, I know that look, she's planning to knock down a wall. She's like my grandmother. That woman had me moving the piano and knocking down walls every time I visited. She stood next to me swinging a sledgehammer at 80 years old. I was hoping I wouldn't marry a woman like that but looks like I did. I see your wheels turning Pat. Bet I won't be going deer hunting this weekend, maybe next week either, depending on what's in that mind of yours. I'm afraid to ask. What do you want me to do this time?" I didn't want hubby to be able to read my mind all the time, so I tried to confuse him. "I've been thinking, maybe I should go hunting with you."

"HUH? You're kidding me. Well, aren't you?"

"No, I'm not kidding. You made it sound like so much fun when you said it was a thrill. Maybe I could use a thrill too."

"Well ok then. You can go with me if you want to try it. I'll take you this weekend." So off we went to sit in the middle of the woods waiting for a deer, until I thought my frozen bottom would fall off. I didn't have a rifle, so what was I to do if one showed up? My job was to watch for one and NOT talk. Oh goodie, what fun. At long last I finally started speaking my mind about how cold it was, and it just so happened at that moment a deer showed up. It stood there looking at me with big brown eyes, so I went on talking to it. Evidently it got bored with small talk and took off like lightning, but I continued to rattle on. Telling hubby, I decided he should never shoot a deer in front of me because it would break my heart to see such a beautiful animal deader than a door nail...... "Be quiet Pat! You're scaring off every deer in a 20-mile radius. I should've never brought you but I'm such a big dummy I thought you'd like it. We might as well leave. No deer will show up around here for days now that you talked to one. Why did you come to mess up my sport? So, help me it's my own damn fault."

Now I felt bad about the practical joke I'd played. He was such a good sport. I shouldn't have asked to go hunting with him in the first place. I apologized and told him the truth. From then on it was our thing. Eyes are the window to the soul, so we read each other's eyes and it was ok. "You're not feeling good are you, Pat? No, I'm wrong, you're just tired. Go take a nap."

"Uh oh look out. She's hungry and tired. I better go get some take out fast."

"Uh oh, she's mad about something. Get out of the way before she gets her broom. Never marry a woman born at Halloween." Like I said he was a good sport.

THE DEER HEAD

That thing was a whole other story. Wouldn't you know the guys landed two big bucks, a ten pointer and an eight pointer. Maybe they weren't that big, but they were the ones doing the counting. It's a guy thing you know. So, my husband took his deer to the butcher. What else can you do with a dead deer? He came home with a ton of venison. Promising when I cooked it, it was going to be scrumptious, because his buddies said so. I tried cooking that deer every which way except bring it back to life, but every recipe was worse than the last. Even hubby admitted   it wasn't good, and that man ate anything I cooked and never complained. I tried his buddy's recipes, and it was worse than ever. We finally agreed we simply didn't like venison and gave a freezer full of it to his buddies. I figured that was the end of the deer. But no. That was not the end of that deer. There was still the head. One afternoon the phone rang. "Please tell your husband his deer head is ready to be picked up at the taxidermist."

"What were you planning to do with a deer head Walt?" I asked my charming husband. "I was planning to surprise you because you think deer are beautiful, but that dummy has gone and spoiled my surprise." Well, I thought my long-lost prince had fallen off a horse and cracked his head. "I do think they're beautiful...when they're alive, not stuffed and dead!"

"I was planning to hang it on the wall and wait for you to notice Pat." My husband said in all sincerity continuing to look pleased with himself. "Good grief, I would've had a heart attack seeing an unexpected animal on the wall! You must've had a couple beers with the boys when you thought that one up."

"Well, I'm going to get mister buck right now and I'll be back soon, so pick a spot for him to hang because he's got to hang somewhere." Soon he was back with the biggest deer head I could ever imagine. "Isn't he beautiful?" There it was again, that guy thing. "Holy smack Walt! How did you think this monster could hang in our house? We're not living in the Moose Lodge!" At times, this man could be so stubborn. This was one of those times.

"I think he should hang in the living room with my gun rack next to him."

"Now, you think you're a decorator. Well, I've thought about it too and we should make the room off the garage into a man's den for all your hunting and fishing stuff."

"I want him in the living room Pat and that's where I'm putting him."

"Oh no you're not! You're not putting a dead animal in here. We live in the city, not a north woods cabin. That deer head doesn't fit here. Make yourself a man cave and put him there." That evening I went to the grocery store leaving him to watch the kids. When I got back there was the deer head, hanging on the wall above the blue and green sofa. The gun rack hung next to it complete with rifles and shotguns. His red and black plaid hunting jacket, and a pair of orange hunting pants hung from a railroad spike he'd pounded in the brick fireplace. His green hunting boots stood proudly on the hearth alongside stacks of hunting magazines. I couldn't believe my color coordinated eyes! My husband had been busy as a beaver staking out his territory and all my decorating efforts were to no avail. The living room looked like his favorite TV show, Sanford and Son's Salvage, as he proudly pointed out his latest accomplishment. "Fred Sanford gave me the idea Pat. Doesn't it look great? This is my new lodge."

"It looks to me like you're planning to sleep at the lodge Walt." Stubbornly he slept on the couch at his lodge for some time. Then one night he climbed into bed. "It's cold at the lodge can I come in here with you?"

"Ok cutie as long as you don't bring that deer head." Since we still disagreed about Mister Buck we were forced to compromise. Dirty boots and hunting clothes went to the 'would be' man's cave with the fishing paraphernalia. The railroad spikes came down, but the magazines stayed on the hearth. No problem. But when it came to the gun rack and deer head all my pleas fell on stubborn ears. It stayed there watching us for several years. When friends visited, women were startled at the unexpected sight. Men joked that Walt got away with putting a deer head trophy in the living room, and everyone laughed.

Several times a year I threatened to sell it in one of my garage sales. I asked everybody if they would be interested in a monster size deer head. My husband had to know that someday, somebody was going to want it. It's not like he wasn't warned. I wasn't a heartless witch who would separate a boy from his toys. It was a man thing, I got that. But warnings don't go on forever. And this woman wasn't going to live with a dead animal staring at us forever. "You better never sell Mr. Buck." my hubby warned. "Then you'd better put him where he belongs in the men's room." Well, you guessed it. Mister

Buck never went to the men's room. One fine day a gentleman showed up at one of my sales. He inspected the cobwebs covering the antlers, threatening to cover it completely, and he bought that deer head cobwebs and all.

"I bet you'd put me in one of your garage sales and sell me too, wouldn't you?"

"Why would I do that? You're cute. The dead deer wasn't."

"How much did the guy pay for it?"

"Fifty Bucks"

"Fifty Bucks! I paid $200 bucks to the taxidermist alone. I don't throw money away like that."

"I know Mr. Cheapskate."

"Mr. Cheapskate takes you out for hamburgers, doesn't he?"

"Great idea Walt. The kids will love it. Let's go to Daly's for burgers tonight. My treat."

I thought that was finally the end of the deer. But no. It still wasn't the end of that deer. My husband went on and on and on and on and on and on and on and on. He told everyone we knew, and those we didn't, about that dreaded thing. "She sold my deer head and she'll sell me too for a dollar." Well, everyone knows when you keep talking about the same thing what happens. It goes out into the universe and comes back to bite you on the butt. Another fine day a nice lady came to one of my sales and he told her the same old story. Not surprising to me, she took him up on his offer. "That sounds like a pretty good deal, I'll take you for a dollar mister." Poor hubby got all flustered and red faced and didn't know what to say so I went for it. "Sold!"

"Give her back her dollar Pat, I have to be worth more than that."

"Hey mister I don't see any other buyers for you at this sale." She quipped. Boy that gal was a real firecracker, I liked her. But poor hubby already looked forlorn. "You know what lady, maybe I'll change my mind. There's still more work to do on this house, so I better keep him. Thanks for your offer but here's your dollar back. Maybe you'll get lucky at the sale next door. That guys a big stuffed shirt. His wife might let him go for 50 cents."

"Ok I'll try over there but this is the most fun I ever had at a sale, bar none."

The deer head was finally put to rest. Hubby and his buddies were going pheasant hunting now. Pheasant is much better tasting than venison anyhow – after you get all the buckshot dug out. The kids thought it was a small chicken and we never let on different.

THE $15,000 HORSE

In the meantime, our nights out together turned into going to the race track every weekend. Dinner in the clubhouse watching the thoroughbreds. I've always loved watching them race and still do, they're beautiful. Yet I never liked parting with my mad money, still don't, unless I'm getting something tangible in return. What started out innocently as a fun night out would become the beginning of the end. When thoroughbred season was over, we went to the harness races. Walt loved the horses. Or gambling. I've never figured out which came first. It was the mysterious chicken and the egg thing again- as to which came first. We followed the horses to every track, from Northville Downs to Hazel Park, to Windsor. Then came the night he hit the Trifecta and won $15,000. That was it. My husband was hooked.

Unfortunately, the change wasn't transparent. I started to wake up after we stopped going in the clubhouse. It began to dawn on me that he wanted more to bet with. Inside the grandstand was no longer dinner and conversation. He was placing higher bets. I was with a different man. This man was acting like he was a big shot. What happened to my husband? This man was studying the race form with something in his eyes I'd never seen before. Feverishly checking how many times the horse ran recently, what was their finish time, did the horse run best on a fast track, or a wet track, or was it a mud horse? On and on it went until he said he had a 'system.' The very word created a sick feeling in my stomach. "We can't afford to lose anymore Walt, so we shouldn't bet to begin with. Let's just go home."

All the way home we fought about how much he'd lost, him insisting he was using the tracks money. The problem with that logic was he'd already lost all that. Over the years those horses had eaten up that 15 grand. Grade school math proved the point; our checkbook hadn't balanced in years. Then came the night he placed a bet on the favorite, his system said it was a 'sure thing.' Excited race fans jumped to their feet, horses coming around the bend, the announcer blaring; "they're entering the stretch and here comes Fire and Lightning [fake name to protect an innocent horse] on the outside! He's taking the lead! My God He's Down! We have a horse laying on the track! Ladies and gentlemen hold all tickets!"

"That poor horse. I can't stand it. He's not moving. Is he alive? Let's go Walt. Please!"

"I can't leave Pat; I have five hundred dollars on that horse." I nearly flipped my short black wig. Who bets like that? People with real dough, not average family's like us. "I'll get it back on the next race for sure." He said in absolute belief. I was stunned. What more of a sign did he need? There's no such thing as a sure thing. The announcer came back on. "Saddest day in race history this fine horse has suffered a fatal heart attack." I cried on the spot, and we left.

The next weekend my husband was ready to go back. I refused to accompany him. He said he was just going to watch. He wouldn't bet. I wanted to believe him, but I worried. Here we are living on the edge scarcely making our bills, and no doubt he's betting his last dollar right now.

Back I went to the library looking for books on addiction. After all my reading it all boiled down to addiction can happen to anybody. It's a disease. Interesting word. Dis-ease. What do we do when we are not at ease? What's inside eating away at our ease? Far be it from me to try to explain addiction. I didn't understand it when I dealt with my husband's gambling forty years ago, and doubt I fully comprehend now. Maybe dis-ease is at the root of all therapy.

I pleaded with my husband to stop going to the track, but he couldn't admit it caused a problem. He didn't have a problem. He could quit going anytime he wanted. Still weeklong earnings disappeared. He made excuses. Supposedly it was spent on new transmissions for the same truck. Supposedly customers didn't pay when jobs were finished. He was so convincing he believed it himself. Finally, I heard about Gamblers Anonymous, and started going to their support group meetings for the families of gamblers; called Gam a Non. It was there that I first understood that gambling is the quiet disease. It's not like alcohol, drugs, or eating disorders where you can see the effects it has on a person. It sneaks up like a thief in the night to take its toll on a family. Only they know that something is destroying their home. In time the burning question for me became, 'should I stand by the person I love who's addicted to gambling?' It was a question that would haunt the rest of my life. I didn't want to give up. For years I fought to keep us together, remembering what Pop had told me about forgiving over and over. I tried everything to make my husband stop gambling. That's what I did. I was a fixer. A controller driving people nuts, trying to fix 'their' problem. "Let's move to the country and get some horses to ride Walt." Reverse psychology worked on our kids sometimes, maybe it would work on him. He loved horses, so give him something tangible. That's better than pie in the sky.

SOUTH LYON

We sold the big ranch in Plymouth and bought a two-story colonial in South Lyon on four acres. The horse auctions were fun for all. We acquired three beautiful horses and for a while I thought the horse idea was a good one. Everyone rode except me. I figured an animal that size on skinny ankles had enough to carry, why should I add to the equation. We made some good horse deals, or so we thought. Until one turned out to be feisty and threw Michelle off it's back. Another time it jumped the fence and gouged its leg. The vet had to come out to treat it. "You'll have to continue the injections, Pat. we can't afford to bring the vet out here every day. She needs this shot daily at the same time, be careful to get the needle in like he showed us." At the indicated hour I got in the stall. "Hello girl, I've got something to make you feel better. It's just a little needle, it won't hurt." She blinked her big black eyes and I assumed all was fine and flung the needle into her rump. Before I could say splat, she backed me into the corner of the stall with the needle stuck in her backside. Kicking the stall and barely missing me by a horse's hair. There I was, trapped behind a horse's rear. Please God, don't let me go this way. "Whoa there, Beauty, you wouldn't hurt a lady trying to help you would you girl?" That horse knew what she was doing. She swished her tail in my face and waited. "Ok girl, just let me go and I'll get the needle out and bring some sugar cubes." Sure enough she moved over to let me go.

"Did you give Sheronda her shot today, Pat?" my darling asked.

"Sheronda! No wonder she tried to kick me, I called her the wrong name. You better come up with Plan B for her shots because I'm never getting in her stall again!"

LIFE FLASHES BEFORE YOUR EYES

Not long after that fiasco, more dramas came for me down on the farm. I was upstairs getting ready for an appointment one morning; the girls had already left for school and little Mike was still in his room. I approached the stairs in a rush and my high heel shoe twisted in the long shag carpet. Suddenly I was airborne flying down the stairwell, pictures of my life flashing before my eyes in lightning speed. I called on the name of "GOD" and a moment later I was on the floor with my weight on my right arm, and the wind knocked out of me. Mike rushed from his room at hearing his mother taking a short cut down the stairs. "Get up Mom!" he cried out. In a fog of pain, I could see him but couldn't answer. Searing pain was shooting through my arm so severe I couldn't move. "Please get up Mom!" he cried again.

207

"I'm ok Mikey, really I am, just need a minute to catch my breath." I managed to get up, but the pain was excruciating, so Mike ran to get a neighbor to take me to the hospital. They set my arm in a cast, but it didn't heal right, the x-ray showed loose bone fragments, surgery was needed. I was told they broke the arm again and removed the fragments. Then it was set in another cast, and I had to wear it all over again. A small price to pay for my life being spared. Life flashing before your eyes is a true phenomenon, not just a cliché.

In the meantime, my husband started stopping at Northville Downs on his way home from work. "The racetrack caused traffic back up for miles, so I went in for one race," he claimed. Those horses ate every bit of green stuff in his pockets. Then one very late night, I was up again juggling the bills, borrowing from Peter to pay Paul. The telephone shrilled causing me to jump at the sound. What kind of bill collector is calling at two in the morning?

"Tell Walter he'd better have my cash by next week or that horse of his will be shot, and the next time I won't miss. It won't jump the fence."

As soon as the office opened, I was putting the house up for sale on the multi-list, adding a bonus for the selling agent. It sold within days.

FARMINGTON HILLS

The small three-bedroom ranch was in a nice neighborhood of winding streets and large treed lots. The neighbors said there were lots of kids. It was perfect. Nervously I called the selling agent, who had a reputation for being high-powered, and told him I had an offer to present. The next morning, I dressed carefully, then added a small hat, hoping it made me look more confident than I felt. In my most professional manner, I explained to the seller I was soon to be a single mother, and presently could not qualify for a mortgage on my own. Therefore, I wanted to purchase his house on a short term, five-year land contract, with a balloon payment at the end, which could possibly be paid off sooner. He seemed pleasantly interested, until mister strong arm flatly said, "Don't accept this offer." For a minute it seemed all was lost. It appeared mister high powered wasn't going to let him make his own decision. So, I told the seller, that his house was perfect for us, it was close to my kid's schools, and my office. And if he didn't need all his cash now, he'd earn a lot more interest than if it were just sitting in the bank. Plus, if I were to default, he'd recoup the house and still have my down payment. He thought for a minute then said; "everyone starts over at some time, and I'd like to take your offer. I don't need all my equity now, and the added interest is a nice bonus. Where do I sign?" Then he shook my hand happily and his poker-faced agent followed me to the door, where he spewed under his breath, "Who the hell do you think you are, trying to upsell me?" Well, I was totally flabbergasted. There were no words. I quietly reached up and tipped my little hat and left. Lesson number one from Betty Jo; "rise above it."

The divorce of Pat and Walt was on its way. And yet the enabler would not give up. Last resort took me back to Gam-A- Non where a sponsor told me, "There's nothing you can do. Your husband has to do it himself." His statement was devastating. I did not want to accept it. There had to be another resolution. 'It's not too late Pat. Don't let go. My son deserves a strong woman like you.' Oh, why did you have to go so soon Pop?

The hardest lesson I've ever learned in life; is to let the people I love fix their own problems. And this time was no different. We'd made it before, so why not now? "I still love you Walt, but I need you to get help, as long as you do, we'll work it out. If you don't, I'm going to follow through with the divorce and take the kids. We've been fighting about gambling for years, and they shouldn't be hearing this." He went to Gamblers Anonymous. For a few hours I had hope until he came home. "Why did you push me into going to that meeting Pat? Those people have a problem."

"When you continue to go, you'll recognize them in yourself Walt the way I did."

"That doesn't make sense Pat. You never bet more than ten bucks the whole night. Why do you go to those meetings?"

"I'm trying to understand what happened to us, and why you continue to do it Walt."

"I don't need those meetings Pat. I don't have a problem. I can quit whenever I want." So, I held off again.

When do you say I give up? Are you ever supposed to give up on the person you thought was meant for you? Almost 20 years had passed since that summer of '59, when a young girl fell hard for this guy. Where did that crazy girl go? The one who loved so much she thought her heart would stop if she didn't marry the prince. In the beginning he was my rock, but he had changed after his father died. He always looked to Pop for guidance. Pop was our champion. Because of him we came from the brink of divorce. Our love was renewed, and we were blessed with a son. If only we hadn't started going to the track. If only I'd recognized the day, he took the blinders off a winning horse and put them on himself. If only he hadn't won that Trifecta. If only I'd known those horses would race through our home and destroy it. If only always comes too late.

GOING OUT WEST WHERE HE BELONGS

The call from my brother was to the point. "You going to be home Pat, I need to see you."

"Sure, Bob come on over." He arrived within the hour, and I knew right away something was wrong. "Got something to tell you Pat, I'll tell the rest of the family later, right now it's best they don't know, I don't want Mom to worry. I was out making the rounds with a buddy a couple nights ago and got into a fight at the bar with a guy. He said he heard I was a has been boxer and he wanted to fight me. So, I told him come on over to the gym and I'll fight you. But he kept running his mouth and wanted to fight right there. I told him to cool it and got up and moved away. He came over being a bad ass shoving me around, so I lit into him. It was a terrible fight. Now the word on the street is the guy has always been bad news and he's out gunning for me."

"Jesus, Mary and Joseph! What are we going to do Bob?"

"You're not doing nothing Pat, I came to say goodbye, I'm leaving town soon as I walk out your door. I'm not messing with anybody crazy enough to come with a gun. You can wake up and find yourself dead. I started thinking about what you told me when I got in that accident with Jim Bob, and the Lord opened my eyes. I'm going out west to make a new life, I think that's where I belong. I'm going after an engineering career in Aerospace, it's always interested me. I'll let you know where I am later. It's better if no one knows anything until all this blows over. How much cash can you spare Pat? I'll send it back to you double."

As always, he kept his word, he paid it back double and then some. Long afterwards, my brother sent more, because he knew I was supporting three kids on my own. It was manna from heaven when you don't know which bill to pay first to avoid a shutdown of water or electric.

THE RECESSION

Meanwhile, I was 'trying' to sell some real estate. The local real estate market was drying up, alongside Detroit's lagging automobile industry. What's going on now? Oh goodie, a big fat recession with a capital R. Who has time to listen to the news every day? I have all I can do to keep us afloat. One very cold day I was doing floor time at the office, and a man walked in wearing a shabby overcoat. He shook off the cold offering a near frozen hand, and my first thought was he looks more desperate than I am. No gloves on a below zero day like this? Maybe he just came in here because that old car out there is giving him trouble. My heart went out to him. I offered him a cup of hot coffee which he readily accepted and sat down at my desk to drink it. Under the shadow of his unshaven face, I could see he was quite young. Unruly dark hair fell over his forehead covering his collar. His coat fell back revealing his tattered clothing beneath.

By all appearance it didn't seem he had the means to buy a house. But something my mother had told me came to mind: "Never judge a book by its cover.'

The gentleman told me he was looking for a large home, and paying cash, then presented a statement of qualification from his bank. As it turned out the somewhat eccentric young man was a multi-millionaire. Why he happened to walk into our office that day, I'll never know. After closing this big sale, I was able to cover the bills again, but it was with a heavy heart. My husband hadn't even tried to change a thing. Every evening I resorted to searching his truck, only to find the days race forms with his handwritten picks. When I asked why he didn't put his check in the bank he gave the same excuses. Customers didn't pay. The truck needed a new transmission. How many transmissions can you blow in a month? Addiction lies. Addiction convinces a person of their own lies. Addiction is hell. And hell wants to keep a person trapped. There was no decision to make anymore. Whether I loved him wasn't the issue. I couldn't continue to support the monkey on his back. I had to leave to save myself and my kids.

Then came the so-called cat of yesteryears. I happened to run into her in a restaurant of all places. Still cute and svelte she seemed all grown up. I figured time had made a difference. Maybe we should talk a little, like grown up big people. Afterwards she asked in her whiney cat tone; "What happened to you and Walt?" she purred, feigning nicety. Then I recognized her. What were the odds of running into this cat again? She'd heard it through the grapevine and could not contain the cutting remark from within her innards. Then she got up and walked out. Just like that. Without a goodbye, kiss my grits, or finishing her milk, she flounced out like the cat she was. Sheesh. What did I ever do to that cat? Beats me. Guess it's just my time to learn once and for all, how cats operate. Glad I didn't tell her what it's like to come up last behind a horse's ass. Lucky me, I never saw that cat again.

When you're walking alone with three kids, you learn fast who your real friends are. It can be a hard lonely road and resentment is a cold bedfellow. Your ex-husband and your dad should open a zoo for the monkeys on their back. They can keep their untrained monkeys but you're never going to live in anybody's zoo. The most important thing in your life is your kids. They think you're mean and sometimes you are. You can be a witch when you need to reign them in. You won't let them make the mistakes you did. They're the only thing that keeps you going. Yet when all was said and done and the divorce over, I had to know my children's father was okay. So, the kids and I went over to decorate his new apartment. Perhaps it's human nature to try and make amends when things get messed up. Besides, we had three kids at stake. Other than that, we were a pair of good stubborn stock, who'd never give up on each other entirely.

THE COLD FEET PEOPLE

Thanksgiving Day I was pulling the turkey out of the oven when the phone rang. The buyer was calling to say they weren't coming to the closing in the morning. For no other reason than they had cold feet. Yes, that's what they had the nerve to say, we have cold feet. Couldn't believe my ears. How nice of them to call on turkey day. What could I do about it then? Certainly, wasn't going to call the seller and ruin their holiday too. It could wait till morning. Let them have their turkey coma. Unfortunately, this closing was for the nice seller whose garage door I plowed through on black ice. Slick as a whistle and I was inside the garage with the door hanging askew over our heads. There I was behind the steering wheel with the potential buyers in the back seat, startled at how efficiently their new realtor managed to accomplish this little ditty. Of course, the seller heard all the commotion and came to the garage to see what the h was going on. "Oh, it's just you Pat. Thank God. I thought lighting hit the house. Come on in. Don't worry about the small stuff. Tell your buyers we'll get them a new garage door. just sell the house Pat." She said cool as a cucumber. After showing the house we got back in my car. Still shaking from the garage door hanging precariously above, we proceeded to head back to my office. Upon reaching the parking lot I inched along slow as a snail. With a marshmallow toe I maneuvered ever so slow, hoping to slide into the one empty spot and be done with this day. And you guessed it; another patch of black ice was waiting to get me. The big heavy old Chrysler kept going straight as an arrow. Plow! Like a Mack truck we smashed into the side of a fellow Realtors car. He happened to be standing in the office window with another agent, proudly pointing out the brand-new iron baby, he just picked up at the dealership. They witnessed the whole shebang. There I was in another mess. What else could happen? I got out of the car and told the buyers, I thought I'd never see again, to have a nice day. What else could I say? Then I struggled to get across the icy parking lot, slipping and sliding. What else could I do? I had to go inside to call a nice cop and report the accident. By this time, the whole office was watching from the window, so it was imperative I stay upright. Eventually my battered spirit entered the building in a disheveled heap. In a daze I tried to apologize to the agent for smashing his brand-new Cadillac, but something else happened that was beyond my control. His angry red tightlipped face caused me to burst out laughing. Mother of God help me, I could not stop laughing. The entire staff watched me losing my marbles until my kindhearted broker dragged me in his office, shut the door, and pulled the blinds. "Cry it out Pat, you'll be ok." I proceeded to flood Al's office with tears while he called my best friend. "You better move to Florida before these winters kill you." They joked when Walt arrived.

A couple days later the roads were fine. And believe it or not the back seat buyers came in and made an offer on the house. The office staff were all happy my luck was changing. Except the poor sport who owned the Cadillac. He refused to speak to me again. Guess he never met a hysterical woman before. Lucky him. Just so you got it right, these are the same buyers who decided not to show up for the closing. Even though all the ice had melted, and the sun was shining on the newly installed garage door, they evidently decided I was jinxed. Now they didn't want anything to do with the house, after waiting all month for a closing. Seems to me they should've decided that on the day from hell.

On the other side of this merry transaction, the seller was already working at his new job in Florida. He had flown in for the closing and was planning to drive back with his wife. The movers were booked for later in the day. Just look at all the trouble I created in a garage. Now what'll I do? "I'm going to sell your house for you again Chuck and Bridget."

"We're starting to think you can do almost anything Pat." How in the world do you keep from loving people who say something like that after all the mess you made? Now I was on a mission to accomplish the near impossible in the worst market I'd ever seen. Being a realtor during that recession required a strong constitution believe you me. Many realtors had left the business, taking whatever jobs they could get. The Federal Reserve was waging a war with inflation. Nobody was buying with inflation run rampant and interest rates at 18 % Who would want a mortgage with the highest rate in modern history? There I was, caught in the middle of a recession, broke with three kids, ex-husband in addiction, and trying to sell homes in a dead market. That was a fun time.

It got to the point where I didn't know how I'd feed my kids. That's the day little Smokie Wieners were born in the grocery store. When you've got five dollars for groceries for the week you have to be creative. I strolled through the aisles, thoughtfully dividing three kids and myself into seven days of meals. Let' s see, a couple packs of those makes two per person, times four people. Count them again. Sheesh you need to be a mathematical genius to make meals these days. Wait that's enough for three smokies per person, hot diggity dog! Add some boxes of macaroni and cheese at ten cents each and some cornbread mix. Yuk swore I'd never eat that stuff again. Oh well a spoon full of sugar makes the medicine go down and turns cornbread into Johnnycake. A gallon of milk and Cheerios and we're ready to eat kids. My adorable little munchkins loved it all. Mom made their favorites again. A good salesperson knows that it's all in the presentation. We ate little Smokies for a week straight. To this day I can't eat those things and run past them in the grocery store.

215

Every time I wondered how we'd make it I remembered the old man's words, 'she ain't nare gonna amount to nothin.' I'll show him, and he'll have to eat those words. By scrimping and saving, I was able to get the mortgage loan and paid off the short-term land contract sooner than I expected. Then after sales became even slower, I went to the Board of Realtors and got most of the equity out of the house. The president of the board handed me the check and walked me out himself. "Spend it wisely Pat, make good decisions and God bless you." From his mouth to God's ears. Taking the equity in faith proved to be a blessing I never dreamed. It kept us afloat plus I took a business course in advertising, in preparation for other job opportunities. At the same time, I continued to hold open houses several times a week at odd hours. When the course was finished, I still couldn't find another job. Other people were lined up for jobs and employers wanted experience in that field. It was the chicken and the egg thing again. How do you get the experience without doing the job? Help me God. I'm desperate, I don't know how I can continue doing this alone! My ex-husband still works his butt off every day and still takes what he earns to the racetrack. I can't understand it. Why does he still do this? What happened to the prince that I once knew? You're the one with all the answers God. I need a job that pays. Being a part time bartender for my old boss isn't enough. I need one good job to take care of my kids God. You know what I need so help me get it. Please.

One weekday I was sitting in a lonely open house that I'd listed in Southfield. The door opened and a young couple walked in. They fell in love with the house. It was exactly what they wanted. They had cash and wanted to move in now. I took the seller of the house in Southfield to the house in Farmington Hills, despite that it was a colonial and they wanted ultra-modern. They bought the house because they recognized it was a very good investment. Between these sales I earned three sides of the commissions, nothing short of a miracle in this dead market. The seller of the house in Farmington was so happy he offered me a job in Florida. Despite that it was 1,200 miles away, I had to take his offer seriously.

216

Opening salary was enough to take care of my kids. But there was a lot more to consider. Walt had to agree to let them leave the state. And how would I take them to a city I'd never been, with no place to land? There weren't any computers at your fingertips in those days. Nevertheless, every iota was figured out within weeks. It all came together like clockwork. After I paid all the bills there was enough left to drive to Florida. It was now or never. Walt was moving back into the house to take care of the kids. They would come down later. Michelle could go to community college in either state. Holly had another year of high school, her and Mike would come down after she graduated. The plan gave me time to find a rental house. Then the old Chrysler died and was going to cost more than it was worth to fix, besides, I didn't have that much. Now what? The next day a sporty two-seater appeared out of the blue. My broker was selling his wife's car. "Send the payments in the mail Pat," he said and handed me the keys. What a guy. Thank you, Al, your kind and trusting act was never forgotten.

THROUGH THE REAR-VIEW MIRROR

The morning arrived when time to leave. Clothes packed in my new/old 280- Z car, I hugged and kissed my kid's goodbye, then 9-year-old Mike stopped me in my tracks. "Don't go Mom," my little buddy started to cry. That was it. I couldn't go. "It'll be ok Mike, you'll see her again soon," his father assured. "Get in the car Pat before you change your mind and lose the only job opportunity you have," he directed and I got in the car, knowing if I didn't leave now I never would. It was the hardest thing I ever had to do. Through the rear-view mirror my kids were standing next to him crying and waving. It took every bit of anger I had towards their father to keep going. How can I live without seeing my kids every day? I'm so freaking mad at you Walt that it had to come to this. I want to give up too, but I won't. There're baloney sandwiches in the cooler and I'll make it to Florida, but I'll never believe another man's baloney again.

Betty Jo's words from the day before came back to me. "You can do this honey, pull yourself up by your bootstraps. Don't listen to your critics, they're not paying your bills. Rise above it. Someday Walt may get it together and surprise you. He's such a nice man and I know you still love him. If it doesn't work out there, you can always come back with a few extra dollars in your pocket. After you see how things are going, I'll sell the house for you up here. Don't worry. Walt will take care of his kids, I'm sure of it. And Holly is a fine young lady, she'll be a good little mother to Mike until they can come down too. Michelle will be driving down soon, she's not afraid of anything that girl. You won't be alone for long; she'll be there for you. Florida will be good for all of you. Sunshine every day and you won't have to drive on ice and snow anymore. So hang in there honey and drive safe, I love you."

That's the kind of friends I've had all my life; I must have been born under a star named Stella.

THE GREAT AMERICAN MELTING POT

Approximately 22 hours later I arrived at my benefactor's home, bleary eyed and car crazy from driving straight through. I had a few dollars left to last until the first paycheck. Nobody had credit cards back then. Stores like Sears and Roebucks and Montgomery Wards offered credit, that's about it. Two weeks later I received my first paycheck and tried to pay Chuck and Bridget room and board, but they flatly refused to take it. I couldn't accept their charity, so I bought a magnolia tree for their yard, said thank you very much and found a room to rent elsewhere. It still makes me cringe, to think I didn't know the difference between accepting a gift and being a freeloader. Chuck and Bridget taught me what it means to pay it forward. I now understand that people come into our lives for a season or a reason. Paths cross to fulfill destinies. There's are no coincidences. There's reason for everything that happens on our journey.

There were no computers in Florida either. Maybe a few existed in some businesses, but I dare say there were no home computers.

Today's young generation would find it hard to contemplate a world without them. Or cell phones. Back then when a person was looking for a house for sale or rent, they checked the want ads in the local newspaper. Or drove through neighborhoods looking for signs. Or knocked on doors. Word of mouth knew who was doing what. Neighbors talked to each other, and business got done. Cell phones didn't even exist in the dark ages, as my grandson Ryan refers to my day. Communication was eyeball to eyeball. There was no texting, tweeting, e-mail, you tube, or any of that fluff. You had Western Union to send a telegram, which was delivered the next day. Imagine that. Grama's seen a lot of cool changes in my time. Now there's a word that never changes. 'Cool.' Love that word.

For the first time in my life, I was alone, many miles from my family. It may as well have been the other side of the world for how I felt. After growing up in a house with 10 people, then living with Barb's family, then Walt's family, then our own family, I had finally found true loneliness. In an unfamiliar state, an isolated job crunching numbers, sweaty hot weather, and laid-back attitude. Florida was the great American melting pot. People came from all over the world for sandy beaches and uncountable temporary living spaces. At first my new landlady seemed like a nice grandmotherly type but turned out to have a screw loose. After a couple weeks with her, I was literally afraid to stay there. So I rented a furnished apartment from another seemingly nice lady. Funny when you're vulnerable you seem to become victim to nutcases. The new landlady took the liberty of letting herself in when she felt like it. How'd you like to wake up to someone rattling around in your closet, saying she needed something in 'her' closet. Guess she never heard of peaceful domain.

THE GREEN MONSTER

Then someone at work told me about a huge house for rent at $200 a month, and of course, I rushed over there. That was a great deal even back then. As with any good deal there's often a catch. It was very dirty, so Mrs. Clean got busy, scrub-a-dub-dub. When the time came for Holly's graduation I flew up for the ceremony. One of her girlfriends wanted to come down and stay with us. Sure, why not, the house is big enough for everybody. We each had our own room, plus, there was a big room on the back with two more beds. Now I had four kids, the dog, and all their new friends coming around. The kids promptly named the house 'the Green Monster.' The exterior was gaudy green, with red Plexiglass windows on the garage door. When the lights were on the Green Monster greeted all. Winter arrived and Walt came down to look for work, since business was still slow up north. Of course, I told him he could stay with us until he got settled. Loving a person with an addiction, you end up enabling them without realizing you're doing it. You remain their enabler which allows them to continue their addiction. It's a vicious circle. Race forms from the track, soon piled up inside his truck, but he couldn't afford to get his own place. Instead of kicking him out, the enabler made it easy for him to be with our kids. My new friend Diane lived a few miles away and I rented a room in her condo.

DIANE

Diane's humor was spontaneous, she went from serious conversation to infectious laughter in a heartbeat. She was focused on getting her fiancé to the altar. Don was in hot pursuit of getting her to live on his sailboat, which wasn't going over too well. What woman wants to rock and roll on a sailboat continuously, I asked him, then the three of us got into conversations on the mystifying differences between men and women, all while I ached to be with my kids in the green monster house. Yet there I was in a high-rise condo overlooking the intercoastal, with a lovely view but once you've seen it you've seen it. I love the earth beneath my feet. It was evident who was going to win the loving tug of war between Diane and Don, but I never expected what happened because of enabling my ex-husband. Diane won the battle of the sexes, and I attended the wedding at the Chapel by the Sea.

Meanwhile the landlord appeared at green monster's door asking who are you? Where's the lady I rented to? Someone said I moved out, don't know who, but what difference. He called and told me to get my family out of his house, so Walt went back to Michigan. Michelle and Holly rented a small house, I got an apartment for me and Mike.

THE CLEARWATER SUN

In no time at all it became clear that my new job would drive me crazy. Crunching numbers in the mortgage banking business was not for me. When we have the courage to try something new, and it doesn't suit us, faith steps in to take us to the next level. Out of the blue, someone happened to mention the Clearwater Sun Newspaper was hiring and I overheard. The courses I'd taken up north might pay off this time. The interview with the retail advertising manager was going well. I liked this jovial person the minute he started to speak in his thick Italian accent. "A Realtah huh? I like ya Patty, ya got chutzpah. I think we can use ya on dis job."

"What's chutzpah mean Dominick?"

"Ask Jane she knows. Ya nevah gonna wanna leave dis bizness Patty. Once ya get ink on ya hands it gets in ya blood." Dominick was right. Everything about the newspaper business interested me. From the layout room strewn with ads, to the print room with huge reams of paper, to the flurry of the newsroom, I loved the newspaper business. The Clearwater Sun was a small local paper with a daily circulation of 60, 000 at the time. Their logo was, "Any day the sun doesn't shine the paper is free.'

JANE

Jane was unlike anyone I'd ever met. Neither before or afterwards have I met anyone who could talk faster or longer than her. She was my partner in the phone room selling advertising. This lovely lady was immediately and engaging, and she loved men. All in all, she had about five husbands, but who's counting. To each their own. We were the best of friends over 35 years, husband or no, until Alzheimer's or Dementia, I don't remember. Anyhow the day came when she no longer remembered who I was. We remained loyal friends whether she knew or not.

JACK

Jack initially sold advertising at the Sun too, then he was promoted to the Editorial Cartoonist. A brilliant talent creating life like animation captivated me, as did he. I found him to be the funniest man alive other than Robin Williams. Over time I lost contact with my friend Jack the artist, the comedian, and the good soul that he is. Years passed and by odd coincidence we reconnected. Happy to say he's still funny man Jack and the best artist I ever met. Despite that I never met any other, he's still the best. Nowadays Jack and his lovely wife Dudley, (her father wanted a boy and named her that) ... live a couple hours away and are still my friends.

During our workday, Jane and I liked to go to Frenchy's on Clearwater beach for lunch. Back then there was an old causeway connecting the barrier island to the downtown area. We were often detained when the drawbridge opened to allow boat passage, then our short lunch trip became a scenic mini vacation.

After working at the Sun for a couple years, on the day before Christmas eve Jane and I were told they were closing our department, don't come back after Christmas. Just like that. No Merry Christmas. No thanks for the good job. Nothing. Zilch. Nada. "Who do they think they're messing with? I asked a silent Jane who for once was speechless. Then I marched upstairs to the big boss to give him a piece of my mind. Telling him he had to know this was coming. Why didn't he have the decency to give us a little advance notice. He had nothing to say, but it felt better getting it off my chest. Bet he won't do that again. Then I marched back downstairs where Jane and I announced they were closing our department and walked out arm in arm, women workers, no more working 9 to 5. At least now the other employees would figure it out before the other shoe fell.

A lot of things have changed since then besides my attitude. I've mellowed somewhat. The old causeway and drawbridge are gone. It's been replaced with a streamlined version. The entire area has been revamped since early 1980's when I worked downtown. The Clearwater Sun building, previously located on Myrtle Street, east of town is gone too. Downtown Clearwater has changed dramatically. The Church of Scientology has a huge presence now. The Sun closed their doors after being the local newspaper since 1914. A sad day for many, an era was over. Never again to hear the call of newspaper boys shouting, "read all about it." Merely an insignificant story on a home computer today.

TOUGH TIMES AND HIGHLIGHTS

Just because you get a divorce to get away from a problem, doesn't mean life will be better. The most important persons in your life must be shared for their sake. Divorce means not being able to see your child daily. Added to that, being out of state means longer separation periods. Empty nest syndrome hits each time your child leaves. You have time to think. Did I do the right thing? What harm did I cause my children by divorcing their father? Regret. Guilt. Useless draining emotions, yet inevitable. If we have no regrets, we haven't lived.

I swore my kids would have it better than I did as a kid. When times were tough, I came up with ideas to make things seem brighter. One idea was happy hour. I didn't invent it, just took advantage of it. Happy hour was everywhere. Free hors d'oeuvres with drink purchase. Nothing was said in fine print that it had to be booze. Two cokes were fine with our fun meals. Mike and I had the best of times in worst finances. On Tuesdays, we went to Luigi's for his all you can eat, two dollars special. Bless Luigi, his parmesan chicken saved us. Other days we found every special in town. Fridays we went to Whiskey Joe's on the Courtney Campbell Causeway for the hors d'oeuvres and the crab races. We picked out a crab and gave it a name. Put our little he/she on the starting line with the rest of the crabs waiting for the bell. Clang! They were off. "Go Speedy Go! You're going the wrong way! Turn around Speedy!" Being a kid with my kids were the highlights in life. Tough times make you appreciate things more when things get better. I took an in-between job to keep us going. Until you get your dream job, you do what you must do. On Mike's birthday I wanted to take him somewhere special. We went to the 94th Aero Squadron, which at the time was located next to Clearwater - St. Petersburg Airport. The ambiance at this restaurant was something else; seeming like a bunker with sandbags stuffed in the walls, with assimilated flight take off at cockpit- like dining tables. Mike was impressed, frankly so was his mother. It beat Chuckie Cheese for an 11-year-olds birthday. All the waitress's loved Mikey, they made this celebration a happy experience.

A VISIT FROM BOB

On his first visit to Florida my brother got off the plane from LA, sporting a silk shirt. There he was, in sweltering humidity wearing silk, and full of news. He was doing good out there in California, where he belonged. He'd worked his way up from the bottom, becoming recertified at each level, going for quality control inspector. In between each happy line of news, he again complained about the weather, comparing it to California. Go figure.

"You're not in Los Angeles now Buddy. You're in tank top cotton, let it all hang out Florida."

"Sheeeee-it" He stretched the word out as only Bob could do. "This is terrible, we're gonna have to go to Air Condition!" So I took him to the theatre to see Fiddler on the Roof, since he said he'd never seen a professional play in his life. Thinking at least he'd be comfortable in one of the many silk shirts he'd brought. He loved it. He was first to his feet giving a standing ovation.

THE TAMPA TRIBUNE

Another chapter was about to start. The closing of the Sun that eliminated our jobs, and the dead-end job I took afterwards, left me feeling desperately insecure. Sometimes all you need is someone who believes for a boost of confidence. Commiserating with friends Diane and Don, they pointed out my previous success as a realtor and newspaper lady and told me to go to the Tampa Tribune. "A major newspaper! That's crazy. How would I do that?"

Instead of thinking about it I acted and walked into the Tampa Tribune the next morning. A young lady at the front desk said they weren't hiring. I took the Advertising Manager's name and left. At lunchtime I went back, and a different girl was at the desk. With nothing to lose, I humorously asked to see 'Mister Mike.' And like magic her matching humor got me across from him in ten minutes. I told him the name Mike, always brought me good luck, that's why I gave it to my son. And wadda ya know. After hearing I was the advertising gal on the phone at the Sun, he said they'd been planning to open an advertising phone sales division. Would I be interested in starting it up? Holy smoking phones, would I? Talk about timing. The following Monday I was driving across the Courtney Campbell into the sunrise. How lucky was I? Thank you, lifetime girlfriend in a Panama hat, married to handsome white-haired Michael now. Here's to infectious laughter and continuous inspiration.

The Tribune building was five times the size of the Sun, bustling with creativity. On occasion, I took the elevator to the fifth floor to take another peek at the newsroom, wondering how do they got all the stories? It never occurred to me to break the mold. I was a salesperson. Always had been. I wasn't a writer. Today the paper is called the Tampa Bay Times. It was purchased by the St. Petersburg Times some years later, and the name changed. Though that era of working for a newspaper has long been over, may times I thought of going back. Wonder whatever happened to special people like the retail advertising managers, Mike P and Mike O, and classified manager Jeanie P, and Larry P in the art department.

The job at the Tampa Tribune changed everything for Mike and me. Before I got it, we were forced to move four times in three years. Now I had a solid plan. Soon we'd have a down payment for our own place. While he was up north with his dad, a small one bedroom, condo came on the market. It had been upgraded, there was nothing to do but move in. Though Mike would have to sleep on the sofa for the school year, it was a place to start. Then we could sell it and have a bigger down payment for a house. After moving in, I opened the door one morning and the cat from next door walked right in. Miss Fini proceeded to walk through each room checking it out, then sat down in the living room refusing to leave. Clearly deciding to adopt us, liking her new digs better.

By this time, I'd been divorced five ears and wasn't looking to change the status quo. One day an employee I'd never seen before showed up in the workplace. We later became acquainted at an office meeting. A couple weeks later he passed my desk and surprisingly dropped a note. 'Dinner Friday?' Hmm. that's a novel invitation. Maybe I'll just take him up on it. At the restaurant he asked what I was looking for. I took the question literally and told him I was looking for a small house. Then like anyone with real estate experience would do, I started blabbing about the market. "It's a good market here. I bought a condo last year, but my son and I need more space. He's visiting his father up north right now and I hope to surprise him when he gets back." Old realtors never die. Never ask anyone who was ever a realtor what they're looking for. They're going to talk shop. Of course, I figured he was referring to the market. What else would he mean? It never occurred to me that he was asking what I wanted in a man. Why would I think that? I wasn't looking for a man. I was there to eat. But like a man, he assumed he could fix my problem. Hmm all this gal wants is a 'small' house. No problem little lady, I can handle that. In less than six months we were walking hand in hand down the garden path, a justice of the peace waiting by a gazebo. Something was telling me not to do it, but I walked on and did it anyway. Go figure. The woman who needed daddy in a husband, married a man ten years younger. We sold the condo and bought a modest three-bedroom home in Tampa. After tiling all the floors, and adding a Florida room addition with French doors, we sold it two years later, then moved St. Petersburg.

A FATHER NAMED BERNARD

For years I had put it off. There was never time to follow a path into the unknown. My children had always been top priority. Whenever I thought about finding my real father I vacillated. On one hand there was the fear of rejection. On the other my father could be wondering what happened to his little girl. This father would be understanding and kind, the cure all, the father who would make all the bad things that happened when I was a kid go away. Finally, one day I just grabbed the white pages and started searching his last known whereabouts. Back then it was all a person had to work with. There was no Facebook, Google, or Tweeting. Since his name wasn't in the book, I dialed 411 information every day asking operators to search another city. One day I got an operator who went beyond the call of duty. "This is not a common name; I should be able to find it somewhere in the metropolitan area. If I were looking for my father, I'd want someone to help me." After a while she found a match. I held onto the number for months, concerned that showing up out of the past might hurt someone. Finally I decided to stay the course to whatever end there was. A man answered the phone. I told him I was looking for a man named Bernard who lived in Detroit in 1943, and his parents lived on such and such street. "That would be my father, he replied. "I'm Bernard junior. Why are you looking for him?"

"My mother's name is Stella. She told me he was my father. I've wanted to meet him a very long time." Heart pounding, I waited, hoping he wouldn't just hang up.

"A long time ago my mother told us that before they got married our father had a baby girl named Patricia. This means you're my sister." A wave of happiness washed over me. The thing that concerned me most was no problem.

"Patricia I'm sorry to tell you this.... our father died." Elation crashed to overwhelming sadness from those three little words. 'Our father died.' All the years I'd gone back and forth procrastinating, it never occurred to me that I could be too late. Why did I wait to find something that was so important to me? Why did I think the world would wait for me?

"We have a brother and a sister Patricia." He said interrupting my thoughts. "Our brother lives nearby, our sister lives in Arizona. You and I could meet at a coffee shop if you'd like."

My brother wasn't like anyone I'd ever met, he seemed a curious intellectual, and somewhat resembled a young Albert Einstein with his wild black hair. There was a seemingly untouchable side to him. He spoke animatedly about his various inventions. Currently he was having some teddy bears manufactured in China and there was a problem with the blinking eyes. After a while he began to speak of our father, saying he was a good man, who went to church every Sunday. The priest was his friend and often came to their house for dinner. He played the guitar in his band and made a record with a couple whose name was immediately recognizable. Then he gave me a small gift that once belonged to our father, and said he wanted me to have it since I didn't get to meet him. I was touched by his thoughtful gesture. He said the metal disc was used in making 45 rpm records back in the day. It's something I've kept. The remnant of a lost dream. In parting my brother gave me our siblings phone numbers. A short time later I sent each of them a plaque with a poem about music, to honor our father. Soon after I received a phone call from my other brother, inviting me to his home. All these years I hadn't known I had two brothers living within 30 miles.

A BROTHER BY ANOTHER MOTHER

The door opened wide and there was an immediate familial connection. "My sister!" He exclaimed giving me a big hug. My brother by another mother was a handsome guy with black hair. There was an immediate familiarity, it was like I already knew him.

His manner was forthright and down to earth. We sat at the kitchen table talking about Florida, and how he wanted to move there with his wife and daughter someday. At last, he asked what Bernard had said about our father, so I told him. "Our brother doesn't see reality Patricia. His lives in his inventions to escape remembering what happened to us. I'll tell you the truth about our father if you really want to know."

"I've waited all my life to hear the truth, whatever it is I need to know." I said never in wildest dreams expecting what he would say. "Our father was not the good man that Bernard said he was Patricia, he never went to church and the priest never came to our house. The only thing Bernard said that was true is our father played the guitar in his band. To my knowledge he never made a record. The truth is he sexually abused all of us. We were very young when our mother left him so there was no one to stop him. The band practiced in our basement most nights shouting and drinking and we went to school the next day without sleep. We are all deeply scarred. I've been in therapy most of my adult life. If I hadn't met my wife, I don't know what would've happened to me. She saved my life." Visibly shaken he stopped talking, choking back raw emotion showing in his face.

I sat frozen in my chair, stunned by what happened to those little kids. I wanted to run but felt captive to his brokenness. My presence was obligated to his spirit. I tried desperately to think of something to say to console him, but words would not come. They were beyond my capability. It was unthinkable that a father could do this to his own children. I sat across from him quietly at the kitchen table until he broke the misery of our silence. "You were the lucky one!" His voice rose in anguish. "If your mother would have married our father it would have happened to you too! Be grateful she didn't." His tortured voice seared my soul. "All these years my kid sister is still traumatized. She can't get over it."

God help us all. To this day I regret lacking the maturity needed that afternoon. I have no idea what if anything, I said to him. All I felt was the need to get away from this awful information. As soon as what seemed decently acceptable, I left in a fog. Him telling me our sister wanted me to call, giving me a slip of paper with her number. Me backing out of the driveway in turmoil. Him waving goodbye as I pulled away from his home. "The truth will set you free," the spirit inside me spoke and the tears came. A block away I saw the clearing under a huge shade tree and pulled in, unable to drive further. Clear understanding came. I was free from longing for a father that I was better off not knowing. God had saved me from the things that happened to my siblings. I thought about what my mother used to say when we were kids and times were bad; "it could always be worse." If only she knew how true those words were. My biological father was worse than my adopted dad. Why was my mother so unlucky when it came to men? Out of all the good men in the world, why did she end up with abusive ones? Overwhelmed in my own darkness, I stayed under the shelter of the huge tree watching daylight drift into darkness, cursing those men to hell. Damn them! Let them burn forever! Nothing else is acceptable! It was my darkest hour.

"The only good thing about hitting bottom is you have no place to go but up," the spirit within spoke again, refusing to let me stay in darkness. "Forgive me God, it's not for me to judge them but I can't help myself. You are the only one who can help me now. You are my only father. Show me how to forgive, I don't think I have it in me." After a while a measure of peace came, it was just enough to drive home. I still had a long way to go.

A SISTER IN ARIZONA

As soon as I heard her voice on the phone, I felt the same familial connection I'd had with my brother. She was close yet thousands of miles. It was a voice I knew but had never heard before.

"I wonder if we look like sisters?"

"What do you look like?"

"I'm on the chubby side, long dark hair, blue eyes."

"You sound cuter than me but that's ok. I always wanted a sister."

"Hey, I'll share mine with you, I have six of them."

"You're so lucky to have that many sisters. I always wished for just one."

It made me feel bad that she never knew the bond that cuts through everything and binds forever. I was blessed with so many sisters, yet I adopted strays. You can never have too many sisters. A sister lifts you up when you need it. And this one sounded like she really needed a sister.

"My husband and son have also suffered because of what happened to me in my childhood. I never got over it. Be glad your mother didn't marry him. He ruined all our lives. No one even missed him when he died."

"How did he die?"

"He fell down a flight of stairs in a drunken stupor and broke his neck." There it was. That thing called karma. Sooner or later, it comes around.

As the conversation ended, we said we'd meet someday. It wasn't to be. Timing is everything. Meeting siblings that I didn't know I had, came at the lowest point in my life. I couldn't be the kind of sister they needed. I was running from my own pain. I had thought that finding my biological father was going to help. Instead, it made it worse. Through many troubled years, running back and forth across the country, my phone number changed, and I lost theirs. Later attempts to reach them failed. Did they all move? What was Joanne's last name? I never really got to know them, and I'm sorry for that loss. If I could see them today, I'd tell them what I've learned from survival; "You are not what 'happened' to you. You are who you 'decide' to become."

BECOMING A CITIZEN

President John F. Kennedy's words, "Ask not what your country can do for you, ask what you can do for your country," have always inspired me. Since the '60s when my girls were little, those words rang true to me. They fueled a desire to be active in my children's school. To be active in the Jerry Lewis Muscular Dystrophy Telethon. To be active in feeding the homeless. To be active in helping abused women and children. To be active in grass roots politics, and to also be a poll worker at elections for years. I wanted to become a citizen ever since the secret came out. Having a green card made me a permanent resident, but I could not vote.

"I'm going to apply for citizenship Mom, so I'll be getting the documents together. If you want to do it too, I'll get your papers for you."

"For goodness' sake Pat, why would I give up being a citizen where I was born and raised? I have my green card and can live by my kids and visit Canada whenever I want. I can see now how you must have felt, finding out you weren't born here. This won't be easy to do you know."

"Yes Mom, I know. Nothing good comes easy. This is something I want to do for myself."

The naturalization process was lengthy, requiring much documentation and background checks. Knowledge of our country's history and government was required to pass the civics test. There was also a test to determine proficiency in reading and writing English. When the day arrived to be sworn in, the atmosphere in the huge auditorium was charged with excitement. Over two thousand people stood to take the oath of allegiance. I felt the emotion run through that room and my heart swelled with pride. This is my country, the only place I've ever lived. Yet a piece of my heart will always be in Canada for my birthplace and my mother's. In my mind's eye I could see her, a beautiful young woman waiting to cross the Ambassador Bridge with the new life she held in her arms. Did it really cost a nickel to go across the Ambassador Bridge back then, and was it really her last buffalo nickel? I'll have to remember to ask her that question. Then I raised my right hand to give allegiance to the country that had always been my home.

THE LAST AFTERNOON VISIT

All the psychoanalytic books in the world couldn't teach what I needed to do most. Forgive. Try though I might, it escaped me. I began to say a simple prayer daily from the heart. "Help me God, show me how to forgive Dad and let it all go."

One afternoon I was making new draperies on my trusty old Singer sewing machine. Sunlight streamed in warming the wood floors of my charming home in St. Petersburg. It was so quiet I could hear pins dropping on the floor. The machine hummed to the sound of the clock ticking, as the fabric glided under the pressure foot binding perfect stitches. I felt content and happy in my work. From out of nowhere dad's face appeared, softly serene, in my mind's eye. The image of Jesus hanging on the cross followed and I heard the words; "Father forgive them, for they know not what they do." Clarity washed over my entire being. Who am I if I cannot forgive? I am lost forever if I don't. In the middle of an afternoon of sewing, the Lord was speaking to my hear. I dropped my work on the floor and began to pray. "Lord I know you're here and you want me to forgive Dad. I forgive him for everything, all of it. Please forgive me for hating him. Bless him and free us both." A quiet peace came over me, and the knowing that I had just been visited.

Sometime after that phenomenon I got a phone call from sis Sharon. She said some of our family, were driving down from Michigan to see Dad in Kentucky, as he was failing. Did I want to see him too? If so, I could drive up to Kentucky and meet them somewhere. That way we'd all be together if we got lost. Nobody wants to get lost alone, she laughed. So, we all met and journeyed together through backwoods, on a foggy mountain road I would never have found alone. His new wife greeted us warmly with southern hospitality. Ironically, he had become 'Dad' to seven other kids. Funny how life is. He sat on the sofa in light blue pajamas, with an oxygen tank nearby. He seemed much smaller than I remembered. Somehow he'd always seemed more imposing in the past. Now he was just a nice, soft spoken, little old man. For one reason or the other I found myself alone with him while the others chatted with his wife in the kitchen. A way had been opened for us to communicate. "Come sit by me Patsy." He patted the seat beside him. So, I got up and sat next to the mild-mannered stranger who looked like my dad of long ago.

"Ah wanna tell ya sumpin Patsy." He sucked in oxygen finding words to express himself. "Thangs went bad too meny yars up thar. Ah nare shood a went sech a sorry way. Ah dun fergive ya all." For a moment it struck me that he said he forgave us. The next moment I recalled his backward way of expressing himself. After all these years he still spoke in the same manner, and still called me Patsy. I understood what he meant. It came from his heart.

"I forgave you too Dad." "Thank u Patsy, u wuz alwys a kid," he said and wrapped an arm across my shoulders, to which I responded likewise. "Smile!" My brother's voice called as the Polaroid snapped. A momentous moment caught on camera, me in a favorite purple outfit, dad in his rumpled pjs. That picture could not have been taken if I hadn't already forgiven him; I wouldn't have made the trip. Funny how the Lord worked on the day I finally left my dad's house in peace. Then once again siblings found their way through backwoods mountains. This time with very little to say. It was a time for processing. On seeing my brother's contemplation, I realized that each person had their own take away on that last afternoon visit.

In 1998, sis Sharon called to say some of the family, were going to dad's funeral. Did I want to meet them in Kentucky again and go together? I didn't go. The moment had already been provided, and that's the way I would leave it. Afterwards my sisters reported back that his second family had told them he'd been a wonderful, loving dad. Although that bit of information was truly a surprise to hear, I was glad he had found peace in his mountains. And though I didn't feel any love loss, there was no longer any hate. In its place was a quiet assurance that everything was right between us. Perhaps one day he and I would once again put an arm over each other's shoulder. It did not escape me that my mother had prayed fervently for many years for his redemption. Although it could be said, she didn't get any gratitude from him, karma had indeed come around. Oh yes it did honey child, it sho nuff did. Stella Bee was blessed many times over. We all were. That's the power of prayer.

The fact of the matter is that Dad died a year and four months after Mom (which is not sequential in this writing) but it's how it came back to me. The light in the darkness of the soul comes when the heart is open to receive it.

MEMOIRS OF DAD

Perhaps the best memoir of dad was the talking hat. He always wore a Fedora when he went out. There was a Frank Sinatra thing that went with the wearing of the hat. It didn't just get plopped on his head. There was a certain ritual that took place every time he put it on. The hat was placed carefully to the right side with attitude, the brim bent to perfect angle, then that hat was ready to talk. It acknowledged folks on sidewalks of Detroit and Wyandotte with its own lingo. If dad passed another man, he gave a nod and touched the hat's brim. If he passed someone in uniform, there was quick straightening of posture, then a two-finger salute to the hats brim. If he passed a lady with children there was a respectful nod, then slight lift of the hat. But if he passed a pretty lady walking alone, that hat came off his head and bowed with him. Yes sirree, that brown fedora hat with a wide burgundy band, was Frank Sinatra cool.

As a little kid I liked to watch dad shave. He held a brush made of horsehair in one hand, a bar of soap in the other, lathering his face till he looked like a snowman with green eyes, then the straight edge razor slid through the snow. "Ya like wartchin Daddy shave Patsy?" "Yes Daddy, why do you do that every day?" "So, Ah doan look like a bear." "But Mommy doesn't shave." "Go tell yer muther ta shave er legs." "Ha ha ha ha ha ha ha, that's funny Daddy."

Every now and then dad would look around at all his girls and exclaim,' "Ah got me th purdiest bunch a girls n all Dee-Troit. Yes sirree, thas what evar buddy sez bout all theez purdy girls."

One day he came home with an old Victrola Phonograph. After fiddling around installing a diamond needle, it was ready to play a big, 78 rpm record. "Sit down kiddies, n lissen ta this ole boy, this ere's mister Hank Williams." The guitar twanged and struck a chord in my heart, as we listened to the end of the very last, tear-jerking song. "The moon just went, behind a cloud, and I'm so lonesome, I could die." Dad took his handkerchief from his pocket and wiped his eyes. "Yes sirree, that ole hillbilly boy sho kin sang. Sho nuf. It doan git no better n Hank."

The unforgettable lesson was literally shouted at us. Dad had a habit of sitting in front of the radio to listen, as he didn't hear well. One day he turned from it suddenly to question; "Who's th greatest president ever wuz Patsy?"

"The 'greatest' one? Gosh Dad, I don't know." "What they teach ya at tht spensive school enyway? Abraham Lincoln was th greatest cuz he freed the slaves! Lincoln declared evar man hadda toil 'is own crops by th sweat 'is own brow, an all them slaves hadda be let go," he shouted. "What does that mean Dad? What slaves?"

"Well Ah be damn. Yer muther best git sum histry books n here, stead thm fairy tale shenanigans ya keep readin. Lissen up here, Ahm gun tell ya'all what it means. Ever colored man wuz freed n set on thar own to go eny whar they wanna go. Lincoln made it th law. No white man could own a colored man no mo. Thar wuz no mo slaves count of him. Thas what Abraham Lincoln dun! Thas why he's the greatest president ever wuz! Terrble thang what sum white men dun. Went ta nuther country n took people from their own kin. Packed em on ships like theys cattle. Took em off n sold em n made em slaves! Worked em all thar lives. Lil kids like ya'all, workin n fields apickin cotton. Whooped em cuz they's a diffrnt color. Thought they wuz bettern em cuz they's white. Terrble thang what they dun ta colored people! U kids best nare think yer better n eny buddy cuz u ain't! White ain't no differnt n black. We eat n shit th same. Ah best nare hear u dun a bad turn ta sum buddy cuz they look diffrnt. Ah'd hafta skin ya alive fer sho! Ya hear what ah dun tolt cha?"

"Stop yelling Leonard and calm down, that's all over with now."

"It haint over Stell! Whar u ben? Ain'tcha lisnen ta th radio here? Ah dun seen it wif my own eyes on th telly."

"We don't have a television Leonard, where've 'you' been?"

"Ah wuz walkin downtown n seen it n the store winder. People stoppin n thar tracks watchin on th telly, an cryin n the street frum seein such a sorry thang hapnen n ths country. Damned shame what it is! Got me so riled up, hadda git me a cuppel shots a Johnny Red."

"Go outside and play kids till your dad calms down."

"They hain't goin no whars Stell! Gonna set rite cheer till ah'm dun tellin 'em all they needa know. U kids heer what ah ben sayin?"

"Yes Dad, we heard you, Mom already told us that."

"Oh, she did, did she? What'd yer muther hafta say about it?"

"Mom said God made us different colors but were all the same because we all have the same feelings. God says to love everybody and that's all there is to it."

"Yer muther tolt ya good but it ain't good nuff. Ah'm gunna tell ya what it takes to survive n this world. Its dog eat dog out thar. Ever whar ya go yer gun fine sum peeple hatin other peeple cuz they look diffrnt. Ah'm tellin ya thas dead wrong! Ya bess steer clear them haters. Be ready fer em cuz they sneak up own ya. Pay tention to what they's sayin or yer gun be one sorry ass fool. Member what I tolt ya. Ya'all hear what Ah dun sed?"

"Yes Dad, we heard everything you said."

"N don't forgit it cuz me n yer muther ain't gun b roun keepin ya ferevar. U'll b makin yer own way n this sorry ass world."

Crude as it was told dads lesson made an indelible impact. I'm glad I was there to get it. Though I was too young to fully comprehend, his words held such powerful belief, they were never forgotten. He shocked me out of my little white girl world. Today the irony does not escape me, that this was the same man who treated his family so badly. Being much older now, I can see there was another side to him. There's good and bad in all of us. Sometimes we must look deeper to find it. I believe dad wanted to be a better person, as he proved in later years. It's better late than never.

Dad once told me he never went to school. Another time he said maybe a year in all. My mother usually signed his name when his signature was required, but he knew what made the world go round, that's for sure. Though lacking in formal education, he was by no means ignorant. A self-educated person, he read two newspapers daily and kept up with current events and politics. Dad favored the Democratic party, claiming they were for the blue-collar man like him. Although he did jump ship one time. Dwight Eisenhower was debating Adlai Stevenson on the radio, when dad jumped up and exclaimed; "Ah sho do like that ole boy, sho nuf. Yes sirree, ahm gunna jump ship n vote fer Ike!"

One day I overheard Dad telling Mom; "Them two r old nuff now ta make ths trip n send thar granpaw off. We gotta git sumbuddy else n here ta watch theez otha kids whilst we gone." On a hot sunny afternoon, Bobby and I climbed Grandpaw's mountain with a few others, all sweating bullets. We threw a handful of dirt into the hole where he was supposed to be, then walked back down. Afterwards we drove through the mountains, and they were all that dad had always said they were. "I'm glad Bobby and I got to make this trip Dad; the mountains are beautiful. I love them." "I love them too," my brother responded. "Green is my favorite color you know." No vocal response came from behind the steering wheel. Dad just straightened a bit and puffed out his chest, then wiped his eyes with the back of his hand, cleared his throat and lit up another Lucky Strike. And we kept on riding through beautiful, blue-green mountains.

The above memoirs are the best I have for the man I knew as Dad. In the past I've thought of forgiveness as akin to a double-edged sword. On one side I forgave him but on the other when your cut deep it takes longer to heal. Goody two shoes say when you forgive someone, you let it go. Well, I am not and have never been, a goody two shoes. That's not the way it worked for me. Today I realize I was still holding onto many things. A great weight has been lifted.

MEMORIES OF LIVING IN ST. PETERSBURG

One of many things I loved about this city is the streets go north and south, and the avenues go east and west, making it easy to get around. During the decade I lived there with my second husband many things came to light. It was in this house that I first asked God to show me his purpose for my life. "When one turns to the Lord, the veil is removed." Corinthians 3:16

In the 80's, I went back to real estate school and got my Florida license. Business was good for me in St Pete. But every mother's heart is truly saddened when her child leaves home. Though Mike wasn't yet grown, he decided he wanted to return to Michigan to live with his dad. Letting him go was a decision I regretted.

In 1988 my brother called from LA, to tell me he went to the bullfights in Mexico and met a beautiful woman. "Boy I can't wait to hear this story. It could only happen to you Bob. How does a person meet a woman at a bullfight of all places?" "The Lord sent her to me Pat. She's from Costa Rica. She came to visit her sister in LA, and they went to Mexico on vacation. I ran into her while the bulls were charging. The rest is history. Her name is Raquel, and she looks Sophia Loren. She's the love of my life. We're getting married in Costa Rica, where she lives. You coming to the wedding Pat?" "I wouldn't miss it for nothing Bob. I'll be there with bells on."

And what a spectacular wedding it was. Mom, Carole, and Sharon flew there from Michigan. Plus, Nancy and her fiancé George. They had been planning to get married, so it turned into a double wedding. If you've never seen a double wedding, you've missed out. Two beautiful bride and grooms at the front of a church on a tropical island was an extraordinary sight to behold. Afterwards at the reception, Carole caught both bridal bouquets. Days later we all went to the rainforest which was spectacular too.

Sometime in the '90s we had a huge garage sale. I made bright flashy signs and posted them everywhere. A woman from the next block claimed she couldn't help herself. Something made her come to meet the person who made those signs. We struck up an immediate friendship and the next thing I knew we were going to a meeting together. She was the founder of 'Infinity', the league to aid abused women and children. The organization put on fundraisers to assist families of abuse. I was compelled to get involved. Pain in the eyes of the women and children was recognizable. Abuse can be forgiven, but it's never forgotten. It becomes part of your psyche. Someone stole your innocence when you were a small child, on one level you know who did, but on the other you tell yourself it was someone else. Somewhere in the communion of helping others your subconscious begins to find what was taken from you. Getting involved with something bigger than myself was good therapy. When we set out to help others, something happens. Karma comes back to the giver. What goes around comes around. After a while everything started to move itself. Someone wanted to buy our house on the spot, despite that it wasn't for sale. Coincidently my husband had been considering a new career. He'd become dissatisfied at not being promoted up the corporate ladder after earning his master's degree. We decided to move to Orlando for another opportunity for him, since my real estate license was good throughout the state. Another big plus was Michelle and Bill were living there, plus Holly too. The entire move was completed within a month.

SECRETS COME OUT

Orlando was short lived. Though the house was in a beautiful area, and both my daughters and son-in-law lived nearby, we were living a charade, only appearing to be a loving couple. The gnawing feeling that things weren't right had been there for years. The move to Orlando brought clarity. Within months we arrived at the same crossroads we'd been at many times before and it all came out.

Angry and distracted, I couldn't perform the functions of work. Being a realtor requires a happy face. I couldn't find mine. I couldn't stay under the same roof, so I drove 1,200 miles and stayed with sis Carole a couple months, then with sis Rose a few more, considering divorce.

While up there, sis Nancy called one day. Right away I knew something was up when she asked, "What are you doing right now?" It's always a dead giveaway when someone asks that question. "Mom and I have something to tell you Pat. She's been keeping a secret many years. She had a baby in Canada before she met dad and put the baby for adoption. Our sister lives there and she found mom through Aunt Leah. I arranged a meeting and they met days ago." My thoughts were popping like popcorn. Pop, pop, pipity pop pop pop. We have an older sister! I'm not the first born! Yay! I'm not the oldest anymore! Nancy interrupted my popping spree. "Mom is very happy that Mary Anne found her, but now she's worried about telling the family and what they're going to think. I'm really concerned because she's getting more and more nervous. She said we should tell you first."

Sheesh, here we go again; but this time mom's heart is bad. The doctor said she shouldn't worry about anything. I know why she wanted Nancy to tell me first. It'll be easier for me to break this news because I was mom's first secret. That fiasco was 30 years ago. We're not going through all that again. This secret is simple. We'll just cut to the heart of the matter. There's nothing complicated about it. We have an old baby sister, and that's the story. Period. We're going to welcome her and bring mom to peace with her past at the same time. We're going to celebrate. Our crazy bunch is always ready for another party. "What are you thinking Pat?" Sis Nancy interrupted my busyness. "Are you wondering what the family will say?"

"No kid, it's all good. You know they'll rise to this happy occasion. We have another sister! Tell mom not to worry about a thing. We're having a party to celebrate this baby girl. Just take those old records off the shelf and let's have some good old rock and roll with Bob Segar!"

"You're so crazy Pat. That's why we love you," sis Nancy said laughing out loud. "We're all crazy, Nanna Banana. That's why we love each other."

Calling the rest of the crazy eight took a lot of time on the phone. Nobody had multiple call lines back then. Every call had to be made individually. Press button numbers were the big rage. Most phones still had rotary dials. "Guess what? We have exciting news in our family! We have another sister!"

"What's that you say? Your kids are getting another sister? Aren't you in your fifties now Pat? How can you be pregnant?"

"Good Grief, I'm not pregnant! I'm trying to tell you that mom had a baby before she met dad. She gave the baby for adoption and now she's found us!" As sure as the sky is blue, the crazy kept going. It was always the same. No one listened to anything anyone said. It was just the way we were. We grew up in a house with seven girls, plus mom. What else would it be like? Everyone talked and laughed at the same time. It was too hard to talk one at a time, you'd never get a turn if you waited that long. So, we all jumped in talking and hearing at the same time keeping up with all of it. If someone broke chain of concentration that's when it got crazy. Everyone would burst out laughing and someone would pee their pants from laughing so hard. Today wasn't as bad as all that; it was one-on-one conversation, 'normal' questions were asked. "Someone else is pregnant?" "Who's pregnant this time?" "How did that happen?" "When was this going on?" "How come no one told me?" "Where is this baby?" "How old is it?" "Does mom know someone's having a baby again?"

Ye Gads. No wonder I didn't want to be the oldest anymore. Poor unsuspecting Mary Anne was about to meet the crazy eight. Someone should warn her she's in for the ride of her life. While all this looniness was going on, Mom was rushed to the hospital with another heart attack. All silliness came to a screeching halt. Time was of the essence. "Listen up sisters. We need to get this settled before anything else happens. Mom wants us to meet Mary Anne, so start a phone tag and decide where to meet, and I'll call Bob."

Calling my brother was no problem. He listened. But if all the girls were present it was every man for himself. As for our sisters, they were all charged up about meeting a new sister. And sure, as God made little green apples, I heard about it. "We can't go there; I'll never find that." "Where's that?" "Is that in Michigan?" "Whose house is that?" "Does anyone live there?" "Let's pick another place to meet, I don't want to get lost."

That was it. Big sister had enough. "All righty then. We're meeting at the hospital. It'll be easier for Mary Anne coming from Canada. Then we'll all go to mom's room and rattle all the nurses."

Our bunch of loonies arrived bright and early and sat down to wait for the new baby. Sisters chattering excitedly, as multitudes of people passed by. Before long, our brother spoke up with some too late logic. "Why'd you pick this busy place to meet her Pat? How are we gonna know who to hug?"

"Nancy already met her Bob, but if you wanna hug somebody, go right ahead. It's a hospital, somebody's gonna need one. Hey, I just spotted her!"

"How can you spot her when you never met her?"

"Look over there in the middle of the lobby Bob. See those two women looking around? The one in the white shirt 'has' to be her!"

"Oh my God!" jubilant Linda cried out. "It's Mom!" All eyes widened in shocked surprise at the women walking toward us. One of them looked so much like our mother it was like the clock turned back 20 years! Sis Nancy didn't need to introduce this classy lady, we would of known her anywhere. We surrounded our 56-year-old sister crying in unison, "Hello MaryAnne!" Every eye filled with tears as we embraced this younger version of our mother. "I'm so happy to meet you, Mary Anne. I'm not the oldest anymore!" I told her and she laughed out loud and hugged me tight around the neck. I loved her immediately. Some sweet soul in the lobby heard our happy reunion and took our picture, then we went up to see our mother.

After the room cleared out, Mary Anne and I were the last ones there. She sat down on the side of mom's bed and took her hand in hers. "Mom, I'd really like to know about my father, will you tell me about him now?" Instead of answering her, mom withdrew and turned and looked straight at me, then changed the subject. It threw me for a loop! What was that about? Why look at me? What do I have to do with it this time? Good grief. Here we go again. My mother and I and her deep, dark, shameful past she won't talk about. Why can't she spill these old beans and be done with it? Mary Annes face was crestfallen. I felt her pain. It seemed unreasonable of mom to hold back now. She'd told me about my father so why not tell Mary Anne about hers? I decided when she got home from the hospital I'd go over and beg her to be reasonable. Once and for all, all the secrets had to come out.

THE LAST PLEA

Not long afterwards I arrived at my mother's home with that goal in mind. "Mom I have to tell you something. Even though I just met her, I understand how Mary Anne feels about finding her father. I went through it and that was very hard on me. She needs to know this for her own wellbeing. You told me about my father, so why won't you talk to Mary Anne about hers?"

"Never mind Pat." She answered stubbornly and turned away, giving me the cold shoulder. Well, I could be as stubborn as her. I came there for a specific reason and wasn't going to be brushed off that easy. I sat and waited. After a while I began to plead with her. "Please Mom, just talk to Mary Anne about this. The rest of us don't have to know anything if that's what's bothering you. Just tell her." Mom got that determined look on her face, the one I knew well. A look that showed her true character, a woman of survival. She'd overcome great challenges with that determination, and she was sticking to it now. I had no choice but to wait her out, knowing that she knew me well too. A daughter who would wait as long as it

244

took. Finally, she turned back to me. A deep dark shadow passed over her face. It was only momentary, but I saw it, the same way I saw everything in my mother's face. Her soft blue eyes grew dark and disturbed and she looked at me in dismay. She opened her mouth to speak but nothing would come out. It set me all the way back. Nothing was so important that I'd put my dear aging mother in more distress. Quickly I crossed the space between us and wrapped my arms around her as a tear rolled down her cheek. "It's ok mom, it's ok. You don't ever have to talk about it if you can't." "It doesn't matter now." She said sadly.

I left my mother's home that day perplexed. Yet knew in my heart I'd done right by her. Sometimes a secret had to remain a secret, for whatever reason she had.

DECISION TIME

At this point my second husband and I had been separated six months. It was time to go back to Florida and face the music. Before leaving I had to see my mother again. We'd gotten together with Mary Anne several times, and Mom was truly happy to be reunited with the daughter she hadn't seen since birth. Moms' health seemed to be improving so we were all expecting the best.

"I'm leaving to go back to Florida in a couple days Mom and wanted to spend this time with you before that."

"You've been away from him a long time Pat, are you going back with him?"

"I'm not happy in this marriage Mom. I'm ready to give up on marriage for good." For a long moment she didn't respond then she went on a long reminisce. "You have to have hope to be happy Pat. You still haven't learned that have you? Look how I got through all that I did, because I never gave up hope. Now I have all my kids and grandkids to keep me happy. Look at all the fun we've had because I didn't give up hope. Remember when you took me to Los Angeles to see Bob when he started working in Aerospace. We dropped him off at work to use his car to go sightseeing. He told us not to make the wrong turn or we'd get lost forever on the spaghetti bender. Then we went and did it and all those roads really did look like spaghetti. We were laughing so hard about that we couldn't see where to get off and ended up in Hollywood. And you said we might as well sightsee there. We were lost all day but we had so much fun. We saw the Hollywood sign on the hill, just like in the movies. And all those fancy stores and handsome men and pretty women. I couldn't believe I was seeing all that. We were lucky that day because we didn't give up hope.

The next day Bob took us to Las Vegas, and we stayed in that fancy hotel remember? We left the car to walk someplace Bob wanted to go and got lost again. We had him so confused he got mad and told us we couldn't find our way out of a paper bag. Then he saw that other nice place and said let's go there instead. He told the maître d' we were big shooters, and he gave us his best table! Then we got on the dance floor and Bob was showing us how to do the Boogaloo. We were laughing so much we didn't see Mister T dancing right next to us with all his gold. He stopped dancing and talked to us. He was so nice, wasn't he? We had so much fun in there and we didn't even know where we were. Bob said he spent a lot for those few drinks, but it was worth it because we got to meet Mister T. You see what I'm saying Pat? We went in there hoping for the best and we got it!

The next day Bob took us to the airport and waited with us. He told me to pick four numbers to bet on, and I won almost seven hundred dollars. I got to carry all that money on the plane. Boy I sure was a big shot that day. I always wanted to go on a nice trip like that and didn't give up hope and look what happened. All I'm saying is never give up hope Pat."

"Remember how we all used to get together when you were married to Walt? Everybody sang and danced. You and Linda sang the loudest. You two would start laughing and couldn't finish a song. You and that Linda. Everything's funny with that girl. She's like your aunt Loma. You used to smile all the time Pat. I hate to say it but maybe you shouldn't have left Walt. You didn't ask me, or I would of told you. I don't like to say things to my grown kids because they want to do things their way. Especially you, you bullhead girl. Why did you give up singing Pat? You used to like to sing. Sing and be happy!"

"Nobody liked my singing Mom, except Bob."

"What does that matter? It doesn't have to be good as long it makes you happy. Don't give up what you like because someone else doesn't like it. Maybe your voice will improve."

"Boy that's some funny baloney Mom."

"Well, it made you laugh didn't it. All I'm saying is good things will happen if you don't give up hope."

"Ok Stella Bee, I'll start buzzing around again."

"Don't call me that Pat, reminds me of what I want to forget. Why don't you ask everybody to use your real name? I named you Pa-tree-sha, the way it's pronounced in French, it's such a pretty name."

"Everybody started calling me Pat before I was a teenager Mom, they can't switch now."

"It's not easy to break a habit but if you're patient with them they will. You need to learn to be patient Pa-tree-sha. You're even hard on yourself. Why are you like that?"

"I don't know Mom; I don't even know who I am or what I want anymore."

"God will help you Pat. Pray more, you'll see. Let's call the others now and get together before you go, so we can sing and dance some more." That was the last long conversation I had with my mother.

RETURN TO ORLANDO

I returned to Orlando and told my husband what I'd decided. We took our own handwritten settlement to an attorney. He laughed and said he'd go out of business if all his clients were as amicable as us. Funny man. Splitting up is never funny, no matter how civil people are being. Nevertheless, another marriage was over. After 30 years in the institution of marriage, I still hadn't got it right. I better stay out of institutions. Concentrate on making myself happy. Quit expecting someone else to do it. There we were, packing and almost ready to move on when the phone rang. Amidst our splitting up sale amicably selling our marriage bed to strangers, my brother's voice came over the line. "Hello Pat, hope you're doing ok with all that's going on down there. I know you're coming back to the Detroit area to start over, but I've got something to tell you. This is not good news either, so I'll tell you like it is. Mom's not doing good. If you want to see her again, you better get on the road now."

"What did her doctor say Bob?"

"He's a doctor, Pat. He's not God; neither am I. But I know she's not going to make it this time."

"I trust your instinct Bob. I'll be there as soon as possible." My brother and I had always listened to our instinct. Time and again it had served us. This was not the time to start doubting. He was there, seeing what was going on, if he thought it was our mother's time, it most likely was. I quickly began readying for the long drive, then my soon to be ex, gallantly insisted on driving me there and he'd fly back. On arriving, he asked if I was sure about the divorce. "Go back to Florida and make a new life. Thank you for taking care of what you promised me, and for trying to be a good stepdad to Mike." Then he went his way, and I went mine. Straight to my mother's bedside on that cold November day. I sat with her and prayed she wouldn't suffer anymore. At the end of the day, I went to a sister's home to sleep, then back to the hospital the next day to wait. At some point it was as if a great wind had swept into the room. I glanced around to see if there was a window open but not, then turned back. And there at the head of my mother's bed, on each side, were two huge shadowy forms. I was rendered mute by this vision that disappeared as fast as it came. The nurse came into the room to check on her and quietly remarked. "She's gone." Of course, Stella was gone, two angels had come and escorted her to the heaven that she knew was waiting for her. She was already

248

singing and dancing with her funny sister Loma, and all the rest of her dear departed family and friends.

MEMOIRS OF MOM

I'd have to write another book to recount all the remembrances of my mother. First and foremost, Stella was a beacon of hope. She gave us volumes of children's books to read when we were kids. Stories of 'dreams come true' and 'forever after' that made us believe not to settle for less. In the end there was one last thing I had to do for the simple farm girl who never paid twenty dollars for a dress in her life. I never forgot what she told me when I was a kid in Y and Dot, trying to get her to buy a nice dress like the classy lady next door had. "What a person puts on their back doesn't mean they have class Patsy. Just because someone wears expensive clothes, and drives an expensive car, and lives in a big house doesn't mean they have class. It only means they have money. Having class is when you treat people the way you want to be treated. Class is when you say and do the right thing at the right time." Burying Mom in the dress I wore for my last wedding may have been a case for Sigmund Freud. Yet somehow, I knew that Stella the classy lady understood.

HELLO ME

My mother's death brought me to my authentic self. I vividly recall the moment I asked myself for the last time; who am I? Divorced again, what name should I carry the rest of my life? It was changed through adoption when I was a child. Patsy grew into Pat. Then Pat married a prince and took his name. They got divorced and she kept his name because of their children. Then Pat married someone else and took his name. Once again identified as someone's wife. But who is this person now? She'll always be her children's mother; nothing can ever change that. But who is the woman who grew into herself through the decades? Come to yourself Pat. Come on, you can do it. You're almost here. Well, what do you know? It's me! Hello Me. It's nice to finally meet me after all these years. Where've I been hiding myself? This is absolutely superb! Who would think it would take so long? Well better late than never. I am Pa-tree-sha La-bear - as pronounced in French. I am my mother's daughter. I take back the name I was born with. I stand for my mother and the baby who was labeled illegitimate.

IT ALL CATCHES UP

Thanksgiving Day my children's father showed up to pay his respect. "Thanks for coming Walt." "Of course, Pat. You had to know I'd be here. We were together over 20 years and all that time your mother and I never had a bad word between us. She was the most grateful person I ever met. I loved your mother. She was a good woman."

"She loved you too Walt. She always talked about how hard you worked. She respected you because she was a work a bee. That's how she got the name Stella Bee."

"Yeah, I know Pat, the old man called her that. I was there when he ran off and saw how all you kids stepped up for her. I want to be here for you now. She was proud of you kids. It's Thanksgiving, remember? I remember that great stuffing your mother used to make. She used everything in the turkey, even the balls."

"That wasn't the turkey's balls, it was the giblets and the liver and stuff like that."

"What do you think stuff like that is Pat?" Of course, I couldn't keep from laughing out loud. "It's been a long time since I heard that laugh. It's a good sign when I can still make you laugh. Let me take you and the kids for dinner today. If you can stand me around long enough." That man had a way about him, he could make me die laughing over the inanest things. It was the something I'd always loved about him. "You're going to be ok Pat; you'll get through all this, and I'll be here when you need me." There I was, my second marriage just ended, my mother just died, and who returns being supportive 17 years after our divorce, but my number one ex-husband.

A year afterwards, I was living in the condo on Grand River and working at Century 21, when it all caught up. Everything crowded in together, mom's death 16 months earlier, two failed marriages, a dysfunctional childhood with an abusive adopted dad, finding out my biological father was a pedophile, now dad was gone. And I hadn't dealt with any of it. Just kept running, running, running. Run faster so it can't catch you. Maybe some people handle things better than others. Maybe we all grieve differently and find ourselves in our own time. Maybe some people need to be alone, and others need to run. As for me, I stayed in the spin zone for years running to escape the pain. I didn't want to see it or admit it. Why cry when you can laugh, which was why I joined the C-21office in the first place; to laugh. After closing a sale with a top selling agent, that I highly respected, Mark invited me to join his office, saying everyone had a great time there. In desperate need of a happy work environment, it sounded like the right fit. So, there I was, working with fun people, taking a trip with them on convention in New Jersey, walking the boardwalk.

MELISSA

She turned heads everywhere she went. And fun-nee, oh my gosh this beautiful gal was hilarious. We became fast friends. Just what the doctor ordered in a friend, gregariously outspoken, generously bringing me into the family. And what a salesperson she was. She could sell ice to Eskimos. When Melissa married Peter, theirs was the first Greek wedding I attended. After Nicholas was born, I was Aunt Patricia. Every time I came back into town, they'd added onto their home, then added daughters Alena, and Laurel.

EVE

She was another salesperson in the office with whom I hit it off with from the start. Although we became good friends over the next few years our friendship dissolved. Motor mouth me, offended her and my apology wasn't accepted. So, wherever you are Eve, I am truly sorry for hurting such a good person. I wish you the best and may all your dreams come true.

SALLY

She and I adopted each other one day when she heard me telling someone in the office my mother's name was Stella. "That's my mother's name!" She exclaimed. "That means we're sisters!" Just like that we were big sister and little sister, going round and round the lake on a pontoon boat with her dog Cash, and mutual friend Genie, drinking champagne, laughing outrageously, loving life. My first experience of feeding the homeless was with Sally cooking at a church in downtown Detroit. Her boundless energy collected furniture and all kinds of things, donating it all to help Veterans in need. Some of the greatest times of my life were had with this wonderful friend.

TAKE A LOOK AT YOURSELF KID

In fact, I had such good times while at this real estate office, I forgot I was supposed to be there to work. The manager asked me to leave, he said I wasn't producing enough. Imagine that. What a killjoy. One can only run for so long, then it's time to change oneself. Stop and look at yourself kid. Look at the other side. It's not all about you. What was good about your ex-husbands? Look at them one at a time. Stop piling everything together. Your second husband tried to be a good stepfather. It wasn't like he had any experience. He went to the airport one day to pick up little Mike, and a 200-pound baby boy walked off the plane. Mike will always feel loyalty to him for being there in his teen years. Be grateful he had that. Why are you questioning the love you had with these husbands? Just because it didn't last, doesn't mean it wasn't real. Everybody doesn't make it to a golden anniversary. The doubt you have is in yourself. You looked for yourself in them and you weren't there, were you? Look inside now. Where's the anger coming from? You forgave Dad, so what is it? Just because you forgave doesn't mean you forgot. You can't do anything about what happened in the past. Childhood is long gone. It's over. Kaput. This is your life so get on with it. Make yourself happy. Seek yourself first, then you can love someone else. This is your come to Jesus, meeting. See your part in why you got divorced twice. Remember the good in your ex's or you'll become a bitter old bag. You want to be a happy little old lady someday. Not an old crab no one wants to be around. You had a lot of good years with your husbands. Don't trade memories for a closed mind. You had as many faults as they did. Stop blaming them. You tried to make them pay for the sins of your dad. Face it. You know it's true. Nobody will ever be able to love you enough to make up for not loving yourself. You're permanently damaged unless you fix yourself. Nobody can do that for you. Happiness is your God given right. No one can take your happiness away from you, unless you let them. Take time to grieve these deaths. It's okay to grieve. Go ahead. Do it. Death is inevitable. That's the way the big guy planned it when he made this crazy test planet. Life is just a test. That's all it is. Pass this test planet and you'll party forever in eternity. The good talks with myself were great. No one disagreed. How Refreshing.

Yet for the life of me, I couldn't feel a real connection with God. It was so simple, but of course I made it difficult. I couldn't see that he was already living inside me. He wasn't out in space somewhere, or in a particular building. He was in my heart. All I had to do was open the door and listen. Instead, I kept driving back to Michigan, then back to Florida. Every time I got back, I just missed myself. Sheesh, I must have passed myself on I-75. Better go back and see if I'm still there. I'd pack up my hot wheels and be off to the races again, flying with the Eagles; put me on a highway and take it to the limit, one more time. Driving alone through the mountains all night in my 280Z car. Me and frog singing at the top of our lungs with Bob Segar, Ray Charles, Elvis, Aretha, Tina Turner, Roy Orbison, Joe Cocker, Wynona, and others. The frogs favorite; Mister Louis Armstrong. What a wonderful world.. oh yeah. You gotta love Satchmo and his wild jazzy trumpet.

Whenever I got a wild hair or didn't like what was going on, it was as simple as living out a one-year lease, and another moving sale. Time and again I sold practically everything. The only thing owning gypsy was freedom. I was going alone and doing fine, thank you very much, selling real estate in two states, or working in furniture stores. What more could you want besides the love of family and friends? One great thing about having so many sisters is there's always one or the other to run around with. In the spring it was garage sales with sis Sharon, looking for birdhouses and garden décor. Sharon's always mellow and easy going, never takes offense when big sister spews before brain engages. I aspire to be more like her. In the summer it was a great time with sis Linda at her cottage on the lake, baking in the sun till brown and toasted on both sides. Another summer day, sis Carole and I decided to revisit St. Joseph school. Although the outside was strikingly the same, the inside was much different. Entering the building, there used to be a chapel on the right side, but the pews and alter were gone, and the space was converted into an auditorium. Yet I recognized where I'd prayed every morning as a child with my classmates, gazing at stained-glass windows, that were still there, and still etched in memory. Nowadays when I return to Michigan, Sally and I like to revisit the city I knew as Y and Dot. We'll drive 50 miles if we feel the necessity of a hot fudge cream puff sundae. At times we have lunch at Portofino's on the river first, then roam through shops on Biddle Avenue a couple hours before going to Sanders. If you're ever in Wyandotte don't be surprised if you see a couple mother bears running out with tubs of fudge.

PRUDENTIAL

The late '90s I was in Michigan. Hanging out with friends Charlene, Leslie, Helane, Susan, Richard, Raymond, Barbie, Peggy, Jerry, Marlene, Diane, at single's dances and the best the area had to offer. Charlene was a born social planner, organizing events for dozens of our friends. On her recommendation, I went to work at her office for Prudential, where I made another dear friend in Ellie, who later moved to the Carolina's, she's still missed to this day.

Prudential's logo was 'own a piece of the rock.' It so happens I owned a big blue rock, acquired one day while waiting for the mechanic working on my car to finish. A big chunk of blue caught my eye, laying on the ground covered in mud amongst the mechanical clutter on his lot. "I bet this rock would clean up beautifully Andy." "Take it Pat it's yours. It fell out of the sky." He said and I had no reason to doubt him.

Blue glass rock is the one earthly possession of which I'd never part. No matter how many times I moved it was going with me. It was my piece of the heavens, my earth, my sky, my ocean. Prudential was a great company to work for. Life was filled with satisfying work, great friends, great times. I had my own office and blue glass rock was centered on my desk. Life was good.

SUZANNE AND STEVE

They were some of the nicest people that came from Prudential's referral network. I was lucky enough to sell them a house in the Plymouth area. Afterwards she and I became lasting friends. She came to my old house with her own Purdy paintbrush, ready to paint the upstairs rooms. We had the best of times painting the day away. A few years later when I bought a house in Florida, she came to visit and brought her own paint brush again. Funny fence painting lady is a class act through and through. She's a kind, thoughtful person, a true humanitarian, and wise beyond years. To this day I look to her as a mentor. Despite that we live over 2,000 miles apart, she's as close as a phone call. Somewhere around the time I started writing this book she started sending me subscriptions to the 'Daily Word,' published by Unity. Now I can't live without it. It's my daily go-to for inspiration. The ironic thing about the daily verse, is that it applied to what I was writing about on the same day. That's when I started adding scripture to my story feeling it was meant to be.

CHARLENE

The great organizer, arranged a singles night out again; to 'Fash Bash.' Sis Rose was recently divorced from her second husband Roger, so I invited her to join us. Fash Bash being the yearly fashion show at the Fox Theatre downtown, was 'the' place to go. The pre-show itself was something to see. Detroiters arrived in their most outrageous outfits; this being the place for the alter ego in whatever mask chosen. Excitement in the air, the red carpet was traveled, until the theatre slowly filled. It was my one big night of glamour, dressed in a black tuxedo suit, black silk bra beneath. An idea taken from the cover of Halston magazine; sexy and feminine without exposure. Nobody knew my dream of being an actress was being played out on the red carpet; not even my beautiful red head sister dressed in grey silk. It was a secret academy award accepted, for a classy Meryl Streep like- performance, and it was enough. Loud throbbing music signaled the real show was beginning, and within seconds gorgeous models were strutting down the runway. Lights flashing dramatically over striking colors and styles of top designer fashions. A neon blaze of fabric and eccentricity, melding together in crowning music and ego glory. After the show was over, there was dancing into the wee hours. Rose and I danced till the soles literally fell off my shoes. We walked to the car, big sister barefoot, after a night of incomparable Motown music, two tired sisters with soul.

THIS OLD HOUSE

One day at the office while sorting through some listings for a client, an old barn style house fell out of sync. Built in 1880 it appeared to need some work and seemed priced accordingly. A fixer upper. My blood started racing, and I was bound to go look. Soon as I stepped inside something said, 'this is home.' It spoke of a beloved poem, the house by the side of the road. I called Mike to come and look it over. He had the best eye for home structure of anyone I knew besides Walt. To my surprise he brought his dad with him. "Why is this a dream house to you Mom? I think it's a nightmare. There's so much work to do and I'm too far away to be here to help you regularly. This is too much for you to take on."

"Don't try to talk her out of it, Son. I can see that she's got her heart set on it. For some reason she needs this place. It's a sound house. It has good bones." Turned out there was another offer coming in, so I gave full price bringing joy all around. Sometimes you need to spread a little green around, it has its own cheery way. Later I learned the house was listed on the historical registry. It was originally built as the maid's quarters for the big house across the street. Rumor said it was part of the underground railroad back in the day. The old house and its history made me want to do it justice.

Still later, Mike and I made plans to visit his home in Loch Erin. The night before I dreamed that Walt was so sick, his dog was trying to drag him out of the house. I awoke with a start. When my son arrived, I told him we had to go see his dad. "Let's visit him later Mom, I planned to take you somewhere special for lunch today."

"We have to go now Mike; I had a bad dream last night." He immediately turned the car around. Like everyone else in our family he knew when any of us had a foretelling dream, something's amiss. Michelle once saved Holly because of a dream warning. They were living together when it happened. She jumped out of bed at one in the morning and ran outside yelling someone was after Holly. On hearing her scream her friend woke up and ran outside. Two sets of headlights were coming up the street. Holly in the lead car, frantically trying to get away from the car behind. A man had been following, trying to run her off the road. Michelle's friend jumped on the hood of the car, banging his fists on the windshield, he lost his balance and fell off, and the creep sped away into the night. Yes, our family pays attention to dreams and intuitions. They can save your silly life.

Now back to the story about Walt and his dog. When we arrived at his house, we found him in serious trouble. Sitting on the side of the bed in a diabetic daze, Andy next to him covered in mud from running in and out of the house. Just a muddy dog and his dazed master in a muddy bed, being obstinate about going to the hospital. As he grew older, Walt had become more stubborn with each passing year. Like an old mule he righteously earned the name Jackass. On this day he was a royal pain in the ass. Mike stepped outside to lighten the mood while I tried to talk with Jack. I took his hand and Andy moved her muddy body closer watching expectantly.

"I had a bad dream last night Walt; Andy was trying to tell me you're very sick. Please come with us to the hospital. Our kids need you, and I still need you too."

"Ok Pat I'll go, just don't call the siren paddy wagon. Mike can take us."

The next day I went back to the hospital. A doctor stopped me before I reached his room. "I need to talk to you madam. Your husband's diabetes is the worst case I've ever seen. We have to amputate his legs but he's being very uncooperative."

The doctor announced that little tidbit without any trace of empathy whatsoever. "What did Walt say about this doctor?"

"He told me to go to hell, he wasn't going along with it, and if I didn't give him his pants, he was leaving here naked."

"That sounds like him doctor but Walt will die if you cut off his le.. Doctor Gruff interrupted in a big hurry to get on with his importance. "He won't die from this procedure I assure you madam. I hoped you would convince him it will save his life," he snapped like I didn't have a brain in my head.

"I understand doctor but what I was trying to tell you is how Walt thinks. If you cut off both his legs he'll die because he will decide to. He's climbed ladders every day of his working life, and still does some construction and roofing. If he told you he won't do this, he won't. Please try something else first or transfer him to another hospital who will. For the record we are divorced, but we are committed for our children's sake. My family needs you to make a miracle happen."

"What did that doctor say to you Pat? That shit for brains has an attitude problem and tried to say I had one. He wants to cut off my legs! I wanted to punch him in the nose, but they got me so drugged I can't move. They took my pants so I can't leave. I'm naked under here. Look!"

"No thanks Walt I'll pass."

"He thinks he's got me trapped here Pat. Go get my pants and let's leave before he comes back or I'll throw something at him. What did you say to that quack anyway?"

"First of all, you need to calm down. He's not too happy with you either and probably has good reason not to be. Whatever you said didn't sit too well with him. He's not a quack but he does need some polishing on his bedside manner. I told him in a little nicer way that if you said you weren't going to do it, then you wouldn't. And they need to try and make a miracle happen or transfer you somewhere else. What'd you think I'd tell him you stubborn old codger?"

"Atta girl Pat. I knew there's a reason why I keep you around. You don't waste time speaking up. Stick around kid and you can watch my dog. If they can fix me up like new here I'll stay."

"If you promise not to shake the sheets and flash me, I'll stick around Walt."

Many days I sat outside the hospital in his old truck taking a break from hospital smells. Uncertain at times whether my presence was needed, but if I expected a miracle I had to stay and help keep his spirits up. The weather was so bleak and gray I wondered why I came back to frostbite Michigan in the first place. 'Here I am sliding all over the place on icy streets, driving in conditions that are hazardous to me. It's cold and dreary and I'm chugging along in this old truck with a half-baked heater that might not make the next mile then what'll I do? Why am I doing this when he's not even my husband?' I asked out loud and the answer came immediately; 'sometimes we're called to do what looks like the impossible.' There it was as plain as the frost on my reindeer nose. I heard you

God. Walt would be there for me if I needed him. He doesn't have two nickels to rub together anymore, but he would come running in the middle of the night if I needed help. That's the kind of friend you sent back to me, so no matter how much he ticks me off, I'll be there for him.

Walt apologized to the doctor and he grandly reciprocated. Jackson hospital was wonderful, they did everything we didn't dream could be done. After two months of sitz bath treatments on his legs, applications of medicinal creams, rewrapping his legs in gauze, and everything else the dedicated doctors and nurses did, the new skin finally appeared. They saved his legs. If you'd seen them beforehand, you'd say it was a miracle too. They even allowed Andy to visit. The dog was so smart she trained with a snap of a finger to sit by my side. Walt wasn't impressed. "What have you done to my girl Pat? She's not interested in me anymore."

"For Pete's sake, what dog likes medicine smells? She likes me because I smell better that's all."

 Andy was so beautiful that everywhere we went, men stopped me to ask about my dog. There's a tip for the gals who're still looking for Mister Right. Take a Weimaraner for a walk. Borrow one if you have to. As for me, I wasn't interested in finding one, one sick guy was enough. The hospital said he needed home care and the next thing I knew; he was coming home with me. Good grief. Am I up to this? Taking care of the treatments he still needs on his legs? I'm not a nurse. Everybody knows that.

"Let's get this straight Walt, you know I'm no nurse. Everybody knows to call nurse Nancy if they need a nurse, but she's living in Georgia now, so we're in big trouble."

"It'll be fine Pat, don't worry about it."

Easy for him to say. Good old Walt was just happy to be reunited with his dog and someone to cook for him. The only thing he cooked was loose hamburger, mixed with a can of mushroom soup, that he poured over toast. Ugh. Weeks later, I woke to the sound of the house falling apart and flew down the stairs. There he was all wired up from a whole pot of coffee swinging a sledgehammer with all his might. "What the Sam Hill are you doing down here? You scared the he be gee bees out of me!"

"What does it look like Pat? I already knocked out a wall and going for round two. It's after eight already. You stay up too late and can't get up with us roosters. I'm working to earn my keep. You can't afford that highway robber's estimate. That dummy doesn't know what he's talking about anyway. He said these walls are load bearing. He was just trying to jack up the price. I didn't say anything because I thought he was a friend of yours. I was waiting till I felt better to do the work. Go get your work clothes on and let's get to it. We've done this a dozen times together, there's no reason to stop now."

"Oh yes there is! You need to see your doctor before doing this. What if your legs conk out?"

"I'm sick of doctors Pat. I want to do something besides sit, I'm having a good time so let me at it. You want me to make that steep stairwell come down too?"

"Just leave the stairs alone Walt, let's see if you make tomorrow first."

"Don't worry about me kid. I feel like a million bucks."

And so, we worked. Pulling up carpets, knocking down plaster walls, like days of yore when we started out owning rental properties in Norwayne. We worked ourselves to a frazzle on every house we ever owned. But this house was the kick butt. I never worked so hard in my life. Exhaustion caused old pent-up anger to come out which somehow converted into energy.

"Take that you ingrate. The nerve you had telling me to fix my attitude. Fix yourself then you can talk about mine."

"Who was that for Pat? On second thought never mind, I'm better off not knowing."

"This new anger management thing is really working Walt."

"Take that you rat!"

"Look out Andy she's coming for us."

"That wasn't for you Walt, it was for the old man."

"Uh oh, she's still working on her old man. Thought she was over that but doesn't sound like it. We'd better work outside Andy before she gets to me."

"That was for a different old man you never met Walt; my real father was a real live dirty rat. I finished the bit about you last week when you were on the back porch."

"Glad I missed that. You haven't got to your second husband yet, but there's still lots more work to do here."

Then out went the old plaster, the old flooring, the appliances, the kitchen counters, the kitchen sink. With each day of laborious struggle, the old anger dissipated. The charming old kitchen cabinets remained to be re-painted. The claw foot iron tub was a hard decision, to stay or not to stay. Fighting a shower curtain in a tight space every morning outweighed nostalgia. It went to the curb and was immediately grabbed. Trash barrels lined the living room like trophies. Week after week we filled them and dragged them to the curb. Then one day the demolition stopped. "Here it is Pat, the open floor plan you wanted. Well, what do you think?"

"I think it's too late not to like it. It looks brighter in here. I love it."

The work was far from over. New plaster was added in places and had to blend into the old. New wood floors went down over damaged old floors. Period tiles were used for kitchen and bath. After the kitchen sink and bathtub went in, it was time to choose paint. A soft warm color called Barnyard Rose from Home Depot, picked up the rose hues in the wood floors in living room and dining room. A goldenrod yellow complemented the black and white tile in kitchen and bath. Then deep white cornice was installed, enhancing the high ceilings and baseboards. Through it all, we fell asleep most nights exhausted in our chairs. I woke up long enough to climb the steep stairs to bed. Walt stayed in his comfy chair with his faithful dog. The next day, we worked again, stopping only for fast food on the porch surrounded by June bugs.

For some reason it was the best season ever for them, never saw so many ladybugs in my life before or after that month. One afternoon, driving back from Burger King, we found an old fireplace mantle alongside the road, waiting for us. As luck would have it, it matched the simple baseboards perfectly. Walt cut a hole in the wall backing into the big bathroom closet, lined the space with some fireproof material, added an iron tray to hold candles and we were done.

Now the real fun started, going to garage and estate sales in Birmingham, Bloomfield, Troy, Southfield, and Farmington Hills for furnishings. At long last the cozy home I'd visualized was finished. Walt and Andy got the first-floor bedroom. Since it didn't have a closet, I found a small armoire, painted it army green, and trimmed it with gold. The upstairs was my domain; two small bedrooms and a sitting room with French doors, led onto a small flat section on the roof.

"I hear you out there on that deck at night Pat. You better not take one step too many or you'll pitch off in the dark without your broom. Andy will find an old bag of bones in the morning. She loves bones you know. Just saying."

"Ok funny man. I hear you too, telling Andy she can get on the new comforter on your bed. You're spoiling her so rotten she won't even listen to me anymore."

"She just likes me better Pat. So be it."

One spring night I had a dream. A baby boy was holding his arms out to me, as real as life.

"It sounds to me like somebody's having a baby Pat. Who do you think it is? It's not Holly, she's not married. That leaves Michael or Michelle. So, which is it?"

"How do I know? I'm not clairvoyant you know. I just have dreams. Michael said he's not thinking of having kids. Michelle said her and Bill gave up, so what's your guess?"

"That's your department Pat, but somebody's going to be calling with news soon."

Shortly afterwards the call came from Florida. "Guess what Mom? You're finally getting your wish. You're going to be a grandmother!"

Needless to say- I was ecstatic. The highly anticipated day finally arrived. My exuberant son-in-law Bill, called one morning while I was working. "He's here Pat! He's here! Ryan's finally here! It's UNBELIEVEABLE!" Bill thundered with more than his normal gusto. Everyone in the workplace heard his voice all the way from Florida. Suddenly it was impossible to concentrate on work. I was missing the first days of my only grandchild's life. "Boss, I have a situation. My one and only favorite grandchild was just born! I need to get on the next plane out of here! Do you have a problem with that?"

"No problem, Pat. Congratulations. We'll see you when you get back." What a guy. I flew down alone to meet baby Ryan since Walt was suddenly acting chicken, afraid to fly. I was a bit miffed at him about that. A couple months later, we drove down together. It was a long, long trip. Did I say long? This trip took forever. In days gone by I'd driven alone all night without a second thought. But this time we were plain ole pooped out from working so hard on the house. By the time we arrived we were half dead with exhaustion and there was only one bed. Neither wanted to sleep on the couch so what were we supposed to do, draw straws? "Oh, the heck with it, Walt, let's just go to bed. I've seen your underwear a million times."

"Ok you talked me into it. But stay on your own side of the bed and don't be trying to wake me up in the middle of the night."

"Stop dreaming Walt, you're not asleep yet." So, we climbed into bed and no sooner did we settle in than the absurdity of it had us laughing out loud. There we were, two exhausted folks in bed with our ex, surprised at finding ourselves there. "How goofy is this?" we asked each other, then could not stop laughing. The mere thought of this ridiculous state kept tickling our funny bone and it was impossible to stop laughing. Meanwhile in the next bedroom Michelle and Bill were not prepared for all this action. It appeared their seemingly free-spirited parents had crawled into bed after midnight and the old folks were keeping them awake with all their gaiety. "What's going on in there?" They asked each other in the dark. The next morning their bewildered expressions said we were from Mars. "Gosh Mom, doesn't it seem a little strange to you and Dad to be sleeping in the same bed? It does to us. You're divorced! It doesn't look right. I figured one of you would sleep on the couch. What were you two laughing about so long?"

Well, that puritanical attitude was so funny it set us off on another binge of uncontrollable laughter. We'd catch a breath to explain, but the look of perplexity on their face set us off on another fit of laughter. Even funnier that some kind, of reasonable explanation was expected. How do you explain the crazy things that happen? It was too simple to explain. Two overly tired worn-out old folks wanted to sleep in a comfy bed. So, we did. Then don't you know, later that day we got a phone call from Holly and Mike both. "What's going on down there, Mom? Are you and Dad getting back together!?" Funny all over again. What was all the fuss about? We'd stayed under the same roof many times after our divorce. Sure, we had different rooms but what's the difference? Did we need to recite a code of honor that we'd always been good kids? Didn't they ever wonder about us before? They had to know we weren't the usual divorced couple, for whatever reasons we had. We weren't sure what they were ourselves. We had kids so we had to remain friends. Other than that, we were comfortable with each other. Like an old shoe. You don't throw out your most comfortable shoes, even when they start looking bad. Simple as that. Yet we could make each other madder than hornets. There was no one on earth who could make me madder than him. And vice versa. At times he'd slam out the swinging back door and head for Irish Hills to rent a room. Just so you know the geography, Irish Hills is out by our old cottage at Devils Lake. Sometimes I wonder who makes up the names of cities, like the one named Hell in Michigan. Think I'll take a pass on that city. Who wants to live in Hell? I bet residents of

Hell take a lot of roasting. Can't wait to get back to Hell. No pun intended. Anyhow, we started back home from the trip of laughter. And soon as we reached Michigan's potholes, they caused a big argument. "You piss me off so bad I'm not coming back this time!" Walt complained. "Fine with me!" I retorted and he left with his dog in tow.

Time passed without having him around. Sometime later he had a heart attack. There I was again. Going back to cheer up my old friend. Couldn't seem to stop myself. When he was ready to leave the hospital, once again he was coming back to this old house. A couple months later I woke up to loud pounding on the roof. Sheesh, it must be those crazy woodpeckers again. Nope. It was just a crazy old man. "What in the world are you doing up there?

"What does it look like kid? I need to get this roof replaced before winter sets in, or all the work we did inside will get ruined. Shingles are going to be flying down so get out of the way. You can start picking them up and throw them in the dumpster. Look out below!"

"You have to get off that roof! You had a heart attack! What if you have another one up there?"

"Guess I'd just fall off the roof then Pat."

"Stop being a blockhead Charlie Brown and get off the roof!"

"I'm not coming down till I finish it Pat. Go in the house, you're slowing me down."

"Hello Michael, it's your mother. I'm calling to tell you that your dads on the roof and won't come down. He says he's not coming down till it's done. He must have lost his noggin getting up there after a heart attack! Now I'm going to have to call the cops to get a grown man off my roof. I don't know what to do with this man anymore. He doesn't listen to anyth...

"Mom. Listen Mom. Listen To Me Mom. Be quiet and LISTEN MOM! STOP TALKING! Geez Mom. I'm sorry I had to yell at you, but you know how dad is. He's going to do it no matter what because he wants to do this for you. Help him out like he said. Just do what you can, and I'll drive over this weekend to help. Dad is strong like a bull. He knows he's okay or he wouldn't be doing this, so stop worrying. He's going to take a little of the roof off at a time and cover it up in between. He knows what he's doing. He's worked like this all his life. Tell him that I'll be there this weekend and we'll get it finished."

The next day we went to the wholesale roofing factory to pick out shingles. We chose a slate gray to complement the black shutters, white siding and red door. As it turned out, before they could be installed, four and five layers of shingles had to be removed from sections of the roof. Over the years repairs were piled on top of other repairs. When he got to the roof boards many were rotted and had to be replaced. It turned into a much bigger job than anyone had thought. Before the first snow arrived, it was finished. And what a beautiful roof it was. It so happens that the roof is the first thing I notice on a house. A good roof equals a dry house. Simple as that.

The first blizzard brought eleven-month-old Ryan to visit Grama and Grampa for Christmas. Along with mascots Aspen and Angel, two Great Pyrenees weighing over a hundred pounds per pup. They drove over 1,200 miles for Ryan and the pups to see snow the first time. Michelle commented dryly about the fun trip she had in a truck with two huge dogs slobbering on her shoulder all the way. Hey, there's an idea. Dog bibs. Wonder why that hasn't caught on. Slobber bibs for big sloppy kissing dogs. They all arrived, including Holly and her fluffy dog Cody, in time to see the aftereffects of a blizzard that left four feet of snow in a hundred feet of my driveway. Somehow, I'd overlooked that minor detail when purchasing this old house. Which had made it necessary to trade a perfectly fine Infiniti, for a four-wheel drive to get to my door. So, picture this - a winter world of white, two huge white dogs, our colorful family, and a small furry fluff who looked like Toto from the Wizard of Oz. His feisty personality loved his master Holly but disliked everyone else. Michelle quickly renamed him, furry little #*%^*! Seems Toto wasn't as sweet as he looked. All in all, it was a dream come true of an old-fashioned Christmas in my homey old house, with my family, a beautifully browned turkey and three dogs. What more could I ask for? Lucky me.

Things were about to change again. The day my family left for home I was already missing the little boy who was going so far away. I wouldn't see him grow by leaps and bounds. One day I'd go visit and he'd be towering over me like Mike did now. Today he was a baby, and I could read him stories. Tomorrow he wouldn't know Grama if I didn't seize the day. It was a painful decision to sell the house after all the work and love we'd put into it. This old house had seen so much. Many children had grown up here and if the house could talk, I'd hear their laughter. Nothing is sweeter than the sound of a child's laughter. If I were to miss my only grandchild's laughter, that would really be a sad mistake. Somehow the house and its history no longer seemed as meaningful. The memories would remain of the vacation I took to Italy with Diane, when Walt watched the house and saw the vision for it too. And the great time had by all at the family picnic in the backyard. And the all-night, girl's only party, with my sisters. And the holiday get-togethers. And the time Nancy, Chelsea, and Sawyer stayed with me after relocating back to Michigan from Georgia. This old house had done a lot for Walt and me, too. It turned resentment into a labor of love, healed broken hearts, sealed a lifelong friendship, heard hours of talk about our children, and gave renewed health. Yes, the house had served its purpose for us. Perhaps it was time for someone else to own it. Walt didn't want to move to Florida, insisting that Michigan was his home. Home for me was wherever the heart leads. So I went back to humid, sunny Florida, to search for seashells on the beach, with a happy little boy.

"For where your treasure is, there your heart will be also." Luke 12:34

ARIZONA

After several years of being grama, my son-in-law Bill transferred with his job to Arizona. Visiting them there was an adventure. I loved Scottsdale's diversity. Sedona's chapel in the hills, appropriately named, Church in the Rocks. Flagstaff's snow and ice-skating pond was the last thing I could ever expect to see in Arizona. The lakes were stunning bright blue against red canyon rock. There are no overhead utility lines, they're all buried underground, providing an uncluttered view that makes a significant difference. It's quite beautiful there actually. We celebrated New Year's Eve at a rustic resort on Canyon Lake. Just getting there was an adventure. Traveling a one-lane narrow red dirt road all the way up the canyon. "What happens if another vehicle is coming down Bill?" I asked somewhat disconcerted, as on my left was a steep drop to No-where-Ville. "Guess we'd have to back up then," Billy Blast Off, replied laughing.

LAURA

Another friend from our real estate days in Florida, Laura had moved back to Arizona, so I spent a couple days with her. She was a newly licensed masseuse now. Still gregarious and full of news as always. We drove all over Scottsdale and surrounding areas, her telling stories of growing up there. The view from Cave Creek was spectacular. Harold's cowboy saloon was cool. The rustic store across from it, had metal, adobe, wrought iron, and huge wood furnishings, reflecting Pueblo, Indian, Spanish, and Southwestern vibes of the area. I loved it all, including the beautifully designed homes.

Suzanne and Steve had sold the house in Michigan and moved to Arizona, so I stayed a couple days with them too. She took me to Frank Lloyd Wright's architectural compound in the desert, designed by the master himself, where he trained his apprentices. It was all very interesting to a realtor from the upper Midwest.

Suzanne and Steve built a contemporary home, with colors taken from the desert. An expansive patio embraces cactus covered desert and scenic mountain background. Exceptional sunsets merge into orange, purple, pink and fiery red skies. Followed by a zillion stars so close you can almost touch them. More recent, she won a new family member at the Arizona Humane Society charity luncheon where she had the winning raffle ticket. Nowadays, puppy like, adorable Bella, texts me often.

After five years in Arizona, Michelle and Bill moved back to Florida, where Ryan's baseball life would soon consume us all, with his dream of playing in the major leagues. Whether he plays baseball or sells widgets, he's a one in a million kid.

WALT MOVES TO FLORIDA

Time went on and Walt was sick again, so back I went to Michigan to interfere in his life, couldn't seem to stop myself. "You keep talking about going up north, to live in the woods in your cabin. You're not the fabled woods dweller Jeremiah Johnson, catching fish with his bare hands. Do you think you're still going to stalk deer when you can barely walk anymore? Maybe it's time to make life a little easier. Mike's been helping you for years and he deserves a break."

"Yeah, I know Pat, he's such a good kid. I made my own damn mess and he got stuck with it. Now we're both stuck."

"Nobody's stuck Walt. You can always change things. Why not come back with me to Florida this time? Michelle and Holly want you to live there. Sooner, or later Mike will come down too. The sun shines every day, and you'll catch fish big as whales with Billy Blast Off on his boat. He loves fishing as much as you do. What do you say old codger?"

"Ok I'll go to Florida with you, old witch but I'm not promising I'll like it."

"You're going to love it, Walt."

"Ok Pat if you say so. When do we leave?"

He lived with Michelle and Bill and Ryan a year, until my friend Mary Ann had the perfect listing for him on the north edge of Tarpon Springs, near the water. Though he couldn't fish anymore, arthritis in his fingers prevented it, he still drove to his favorite fishing spots every morning. A few times I went along to listen to fish talk. "What'd you catch?" "Boy, those are some beauties there." We'd sit out there smelling the salt water, wind in our hair, the sun overhead. Weekends Holly and I went to clean and grocery shop for him, and Michelle took care of all his medicine and doctor appointments. Then we'd go to his favorite seafood buffet in New Port Richey. Often in the evenings we'd talk for an hour on the phone. Every now and then he'd drive to my place for lunch or dinner. In mid-October, a certain day rolled around, I hadn't thought about in years. That morning I opened the door and found a mysterious heart shaped box, wrapped in red foil. Hmm one of the kids must have left this, wonder why, it's not my birthday. "It wasn't me, Mom," they each said when I called. "Maybe it was Dad."

"What do you know about a mysterious box that found its way to my door Walt?"

"It's sweetest day Pat, don't you remember? I wanted to do something nice for you. You're always doing nice things for me."

"Uh... well ok, thanks. Guess who's coming to dinner?"

"Sounds like a good deal for me, a box of chocolates gets me a steak dinner."

"Don't get carried away buster, we're having spaghetti."

"Sounds good to me Pat."

So, we continued that way, me driving to his place for lunch out, him to mine for a homemade dinner. Afterwards we'd watch the egrets in my yard digging up their meal. "Why do you still take care of me Pat? I don't deserve it after what I did."

"I forgave you a long time ago for that because you kept the promise we made in the beginning. We said we would take it, as long as we told each other the truth, remember?"

"I remember Pat. You're the one who forgets everything. I thought you forgot and that's why you were still doing nice things for me."

"I didn't forget, it just gets easier over time to do what God wants, that's all. Besides, you helped me on the old house. That's the way it goes. We keep helping each other."

"Are you still going to that church you took me to Pat? I liked that preacher, he made me think."

"Nobody ever interpreted verse like pastor Lloyd. I don't know why he left that church but when he did, I stopped going there. I've been to so many since then, I've lost count. Most of time I stay home to listen to Joel Osteen. Did I tell you I got baptized and dunked underwater? They give you a robe to wear instead of your clothes, then you walk into this big glass tub in front of the church, and the congregation can see the minister dunk you under the water. Holly brought Ryan to the service. When it was over, he came running up to me all excited and said, "Grama did you meet Jesus under the water? I saw him too!"

"Maybe I'm going to hell for what I did Pat."

"My mother always said if you're sorry ask God to forgive you, and he will, because he loves you."

"Do you still love me Pat... is that why you forgave me?"

"I don't know about love anymore; I forgave you but couldn't forget. We lost something after that and couldn't get it back. I don't love anybody now except my kids. Love is scary to me, maybe I'm still crazy."

"You were never crazy Pat. You were just an overly sensitive kid. You and your brother were most alike. Trying to act tough because of how you were brought up. It's a wonder you kids turned out so good. I remember how hard you tried to make it better than what you saw as a kid. But you sure were hard to get along with. I knew what that old man did to you, so I let you get away with it. I understood you Pat. You might not think so, but I did. I knew you better than you knew yourself. I could look at your eyes and know when something was bothering you and got the hell out of your way. Your eyes always told me everything. You're not crazy and you've been fine for years. Florida was good for you. It made you the good witch of the north. I'm glad that I came here with you. The only thing I worry about is you don't remember shit. You should see a doctor."

"Why, so they can give me drugs and I miss half of what's going on? That's all they're going to do, and you know it. I just need more vitamins and brain food, that's all."

"Thank you for what you and kids do for me Pat, wish I still had something to leave you guys."

"You gave us a lot when we were young, maybe it was better to have it then. Remember what my mother used to say; money isn't everything you know.

"Yeah, I remember your mother's goofy sayings. Bet she knows everything where she is now. Bet she even knows about the seafood buffet. Let's go there again tomorrow for lunch."

"Ok Waldo."

"Karen's the only one who ever called me that. How's she doing these days?"

"She's still the same fearless Karen. Whenever we talk, we pick up where we left off. We don't get in any good trouble anymore because we live too far apart."

"Tell her I miss her and remember when she dressed up like a bubble dancer on Halloween and all the guys wanted to bust her bubbles. You'll probably forget to tell her that won't you?"

"Probably, but it'll come back when we start talking about the old days. She was so funny with all those balloons pinned to her long john underwear. She couldn't sit down all night. Ha, ha, ha, ha. That was one of our best parties, wasn't it?"

"Yeah, old witch, you looked so real it scared me. I couldn't get a hard on for weeks. My wife the green witch. Can't believe I let you dress me up like the Jolly Green Giant. I couldn't get all that green paint off for days. What a pair we made, a green witch and a green giant. Ha, ha, ha, ha, ha. The next year you dressed me as Herman Munster, and you were Lilly. You looked hot in that costume kid. There were some good costumes that year, my buddies really got into it. Wish I could see those guys again, Smitty, Jack, Bob, Rick, Al, and all their wives. We sure had some good times didn't we Pat?" "Yes we did Waldorf."

Sometime afterwards I was in Michigan staying with sis Rose again. While I was out one day, I happened to pass a pleasant ranch for sale on a wooded lot. For one reason or another I made an appointment to see it, despite that I wasn't in the market for a house, especially not in Ice Ville. All the house needed was some minor updating and decorating. The thing that got me was the enclosed sunroom on the back of the house overlooking the woods. I envisioned Walt watching the wildlife in the backyard. He would love this house. Perhaps it was time to bring him back to his beloved Michigan. "Hi Walt, I'm calling you in my car. Remember the time when I was so late getting home in the bat mobile when I was pregnant with Michelle?"

"Whatever made you think of that Pat?"

"Because I told you they should make phones for cars. Now I'm calling you in my car on the phone! Isn't that great?"

"You crazy kid. Is that why you're calling me? To tell me you're calling me?"

"I just wanted to see if you remembered, and to prove that I do remember stuff. The real reason I'm calling is that I looked at a house for sale that would be perfect for us. I'll make an offer on it if you want to come back here. So, what do you say?" It was quiet on the other end for too long. "Walt? Are you still there?"

"Don't make any offer Pat. Just come back and we'll talk."

"Ok Walt, see you soon."

The next day I was still at Rose' condo when my cell phone rang and her little dog Lacey, barked hello. Holly was calling to tell me she'd gone to take her dad out for Father's Day and found him asleep on the sofa. He died sometime in the wee hours of the morning. Never did I want to be with my children more. Yet we were in four different states, thousands of miles from each other, sharing this crushing news. At length we hung up and I doubled over with the realization. The love of my life was gone, and I hadn't known I still loved him. How complex was I? He was gone and I didn't say I love you when he asked. "Dear God help me!" I cried out loud and from the other side of the room, five pounds of fur ran across the back of the sofa. Wonder Dog flew in air and jumped in my arms, licking my tears, snuggling close. Dogs are all heart. Thank God for Lacey that day.

Today I see how Walt's last kind act stopped me from buying that house. He knew I'd rather be in Florida. He also knew he was going someplace better. We decided to have a celebration of life in a park in Michigan. Sis Sharon found the place for our family picnic. The afternoon we arrived, there was an old man with white hair, fishing from a small boat, the sun shining on him. Sis couldn't have found a better site. Walt's favorite area was around Traverse City. The kids and I drove up there and left his ashes in the wind with sleeping bears on Lake Michigan. The father of my children still visits in my dreams; he is forever young and handsome. That's the way it is in heaven. Good night sweet prince.

THE WRITING EXPERIENCE

Writing this book turned out to be the best thing I ever did for myself. It's been my catharsis. I've let go of long overdue closures. Even more wonderful my memory came back from exercising my brain. That squiggly little mass in my head needed exercise too. Why sis Mary Anne thought I could write a book after reading a few e-mails still amazes me, but she was right. There was a story inside that came out bit by bit, pushing hour upon hour in front of a computer. Putting myself in the zone of where I was when that

275

occurred, seeing the surroundings, the colors, hearing the music. Each detail brought back another, then another. For the most part, writing about my childhood and twenties was agonizing. Many times, I was forced to stop for weeks at a time, tortured whether to continue. Friends and family provided the much-needed ear that pushed me on. Cousin Monica prayed so hard over the phone she started talking in tongues and scared me. The writing experience was brutal hard work, akin to knocking down walls in this old house, yet worth every bit of it. Releasing everything, I am a new person with a newfound respect for writers. God bless them all, they must be born wordsmiths. Writing was a long-forgotten childhood dream, never to be taken seriously. I'd put away frivolous fantasies and fairy tales. Writing released the kid in me. Being a kid at heart is believing in dreams come true. If this labor of love helps one person, Sis Mary Anne's words were prophetic.

PEOPLE PURPOSE AND PASSION

Today I happened to hear a frustrated person ask the same question is used to ask; "Why am I here?" The question answered itself. We're here to find what God is. How in the world could I have missed this answer so long? When he was right there in every sunrise, sunset, rainbow, mountain, seashore, lake, and every genuine person who reached out in love. People cross our paths every day, not by coincidence but for purpose. They leave their mark whether we realize it or not. It can be a casual encounter while waiting in line. Or at one of the annual Kentucky Derby parties at BJ's house with Connie, Doris, big Chris, Vicky, and couples Michelle and Chris, Gator and Mike, Jane and John, Mary Ann and David, and others too...where Holly and Aloha Joe always bring Mumsy for fun with their friends. And BJ and Connie always encourage me to sing. So I fly the ocean in a silver plane to see the jungle wet with rain. The song is so old nobody knows it, except oddly enough, one young guy named John, who just so happens to also be writing a book. And we get into a long discussion on the intricacies and difficulties of the book journey. Later as he and his wife are leaving, he says; "I just heard something on U tube –

inspiration comes when least expected to one who needs it. Don't stop working on your dream." And once again I am inspired to continue the work that is becoming my passion.

THE RAINBOW IN A CROWD

Among many treasured memories the rainbow in a crowd was a once in a lifetime experience. Four sisters decided they would make a trip to Niagara Falls. Sharon, Carole, and I drove to Canada to pick up Mary Anne. After visiting with her son Gil, and daughter Michelle, we drove to Strathroy and stayed overnight with her daughter Janice. On reaching our destination the next day, we parked and continued to walk to the falls. Strolling leisurely along velvet green grass on a perfect summer day. The air was filled with fragrance of thousands of flowers, the sun warm on our skin. No need to rush, we were living in the moment. Sis Carole kept stopping to take another picture then struggled to catch up. "Let's wait for Shorty," I called to Mary Anne and Sharon who were getting too far ahead. It was reminiscent of yesteryear when a little girl walked behind to school. Eventually we reached the dam where a crowd had already gathered watching the immense power of spectacular waterfalls. Colorful sprays of mist started to rise into the air above their heads. A murmur arose from the crowd as the mists began to merge, forming a colorful arch only yards from where they stood. A hush of stillness fell over the crowd. They stood transfixed on the loveliness taking place before their eyes, as an invisible hand painted in the sky. Heavy spray showered them, yet no one moved away, held captive in the last few seconds of completion of a magnificent rainbow. The crowd clapped in unison at the wonder of the master's hand. One more snapshot along the way, and four sisters would have missed the entire performance. God's work is perfect timing, it's synchronization at its finest.

THE DREAM 2012 - 2013

My dead mother was in the dream, and she was alive! She was young and beautiful, and I was so happy to see her. Then the dream began to grow dark, and I felt anxious as she kept whispering to my sisters. I couldn't distinguish which sisters, the dream grew more unsettling, the anxiety grew. Why won't mom tell me too?

"He said to them, "Listen to this dream that I dreamed." Genesis 37:6

For some time before the dream occurred, I'd been wondering, 'what is my purpose?' Now I felt the dream held significance in the answer to that question. A couple days before Thanksgiving of 2012, sis Mary Anne told me her husband Jim was diagnosed with bone cancer. Shortly afterwards she was diagnosed with lung cancer. Days later I was diagnosed with bladder cancer. She and I would soon discover we had both kept our diagnosis' secret until the holidays were over. One person in the family with bad news was enough. Thanksgiving was already shadowed by Mom's death. Suddenly it was January 2013, in a new year, knowing I had to tell my adult children the urologist already scheduled my surgery. Then I called Mary Anne to inquire how Jim was doing. We were overwhelmed by the coincidence. Three in the family diagnosed with cancer within a month! What's this God? You've got my attention, I'm listening. In February we each received our prognosis. Jim and Mary Anne's news was not good at all, signaling the inevitable. My news signaled a cure. The cancer was stage one, level one, caught in time and removed. How could I be happy for myself when their prognosis looked so bleak? My spirit stayed in a troubled state of questioning. Why was I the lucky one? Why not me? Why was I shown grace? 'Do you have another plan for me God? I've just been going along being a good grandmother. if you have something else for me to do, show me. And please make it clear this time. You know a lot of things go over my head.'

It's my habit to talk to God like he's my friend, which usually works well. But this time he was quiet, so I figured he wasn't ready to talk. That's the way he is sometimes. Talks when he's good and ready. When he figures out the plan, he lets me know. I'm supposed to sit tight and wait.

'I need your help with something else God. As you know my sister is going through Chemo and she's 1,300 miles away. It's not like I can hop over there anytime I feel like it, but there has to be something I can do to make a difference for her.'

One day I happened to call right after one of her treatments and she was feeling very sick.

'God let me say the right thing to help her get past this hour,' I prayed silently, and the words came tumbling from my heart instead of my head. "I'm going to write to you every day with goofy stuff to make you laugh so you have something funny to look forward to."

"You're going to write to me every day? That'll take a lot of stamps to get that many letters to Canada, and they'll take a while to get here too." Recently retired from Canada Post, she was still thinking like a postman. "I'm not going to send letters in the mail, I'm gonna send e-mails!" She laughed joyfully and for the first time in months I was happy to be on the right track.

Now I'm no stand-up comic mind you; sometimes it took half the night to come up with wacky. Exerting lazy unused endorphins, twisting them to their max was no easy feat for me, but once the cuckoo started, it took off. Cheery letters floated on invisible e-planes through cyber space magic, ziplining 1300 miles to glide down a frozen chimney in Canada.

E- MAIL SAMPLES - NO POSTAGE NEEDED

... it's past midnight ... can't sleep

... lots in my head ... there's a laugh

... been thinking ... what do u still want to do

... make a bucket list ... small stuff ... not gonna wanna do Paris

... so go to a fancy little place in town ... and celebrate your life

... get all dressed up ... like the pretty French lady you are

... wear your favorite color ... favorite jewelry ... sparkle's the word

... tell yourself today is mine ... what happy can I do

279

... go inside beautiful buildings ... just to see the architecture

... visit an art museum ... get lost for hours ... don't worry they'll find ya

... invite friends over ... make reservations... don't all come at once

... tell them to bring their funny face ... it's their job ... you need to laugh ... a lot

... eat pizza for breakfast ... ice cream ...chocolate... whatever the hell you want

... go somewhere you've never gone

... see the male strippers at Danny's ... be daring ... break the old rules

... ok, ok, not my thing either...so go somewhere u always wanted to and didn't

... see only funny movies ... guaranteed to make u laugh ... or get a refund

... take one grandkid at a time ... more hugs that way

... get double dip ice cream cones ... different flavors

... walk in the park ... listen to birds ... watch squirrels play

... sit on a bench, watch people... talk to their dogs

... watch a sailboat float out of sight ... wonder where ships are going

... walk barefoot in the grass ... smell the flowers, fresh cut grass

... send flowers to yourself ... every week

... pick some of the neighbors ... tell em your sister made you do it

... talk to God ... He's your best friend.

PS.

... buy a red dress ... wear it everywhere.

THE LAST REQUEST

Goofy e-mails continued to let this little light shine in the only way I knew. Then one day Sis called from Canada. "What's the weather down there in Florida?"

"It's almost 70 here."

"I can't believe it's April and it's snowing here again. Anyways, I called to thank you for your e-mails, I love them, they cheer me up. Now I want you to write a book."

"Do what!?!"

"Write our story Patricia. Tell how we met after all those years and what our mother went through having us. People want to read a book like this."

"Good grief Mary Anne, I'm not a writer!"

"Yes, you are, you're a writer Patricia, you just don't know it yet. My kids say so too. It's in you. You can do it, I know you can."

"Listen Mary Anne, you don't understand. It takes me half the night to come up with those screwy e-mails. I never wrote anything before in my life."

"There's a first time for everything, and you're the one who has to do it. Write how we never met our fathers. And what it was like for our mother having us. And how you grew up the oldest. Tell the whole story. You can do this I know you can. Do it for me; please Patricia. The book is going to help a lot of people."

Those last ten words changed my life as I knew it. An electric- like tingling started in my gut and went to my heart and there was knowing. "I'm going to do it for you Mary Anne."

"Really? You promise?"

"Yes, I promise, and I'll dedicate it to you too."

A DAY AT CAESARS

The frozen north was a land of ice. Leaving sunshine is a risky thing for a bear with wobbly knees to do. Weebles wobble but don't fall in sunshine. June was perfect. On my arrival at Detroit Metro Airport, dear Sally showed up with an extra car. "Go to Canada and see your sister, I love you," said this person with a heart of gold. Driving through the tunnel to Windsor, I thought about the night before when Mary Anne called at the last minute. "There's been a change of plans Patricia. My friend gave me a gift of an overnight stay at Caesars Casino! Meet me in the lobby tomorrow morning instead of driving to my house. Some of my girlfriends are coming tomorrow night. I'm so happy to go to the casino one more time; and my friends will get to meet my crazy sister from Florida!"

"Can't wait to meet them Sis, since you're not up to gambling we'll have an old hens party in Caesar's high roller suite." She laughed heartily and made me happy too.

Arriving in the casino that early hour of the morning was strangely odd without flashing lights and one arm bandits beckoning. Unusual circumstance had brought us to this nearly vacant establishment creating a feeling of being somewhere in time. Something was saying it wasn't coincidence our plans had been changed. Fate had somehow rearranged things for its own purpose. What is this strange thing going on in my head? Is this de je vu?

The suite was stocked with enough booze to knock us flat. Despite that we drank like mice, and all I needed was to smell the bottle caps, there's got to be a booze selection, for when someone gets down on their luck. After all someone needs to lose some dough. Otherwise, Caesar's not going to be happy. He's not giving away sweet suites for no reason. He's no dummy. We settled in for a day of relaxation and good long talk. That's what sisters do when they get together...they talk, talk, talk. Then they talk some more. It's a sister thing you know. And we had a lifetime to catch up on. She plopped a ton of pillows on the king bed, and I chose the chair by the wall of windows. From downtown Windsor, the mid-morning sun played on Detroit's Renaissance Center, creating a beautiful skyline. Blue green water separated the two countries, diamonds bouncing across the waves, with a stark white sailboat gliding serenely. "What a lovely view!" We exclaimed in unison. A melancholy moment passed realizing we'd lived on opposite sides of this water most our lives, not knowing we had a sister on the other side.

"What was it like for you growing up the oldest of eight kids Patricia?" She asked.

"I can't believe you asked that question! I thought no one ever would. You grew up with one sister Mary Anne. I can't imagine what that would be like. It was always hectic and noisy in our house, I longed for my own space and peace and quiet. What was your life like?"

"It was a good life. I mean we never really wanted for anything; I'd say our life was normal."

Hmm, she said normal. Always wondered about that word. What is normal anyway? How does one know what's normal?

"When did you find out that you were adopted Mary Anne?"

"My sister Theresa and I were told when we were very young. It didn't seem to make any difference; I mean we knew they loved us. But when I got older, I thought about my real parents a lot and wanted to find them. I'm happy I found our mother in time before she died. It was none too soon, wasn't it? I only wish she would've told me about my father. No one knows anything about him. It's such a mystery. Now it looks like I'll never find him, time is running out. Did you ever wonder why mom told you about your father but wouldn't talk about mine? Did she ever say anything to you about him?"

My mind went back to the day I'd gone to see Mom, to ask her to tell Mary Anne what she needed to know, but when Mom had got so upset, I'd let it go. This would be the time to say something about that but there was nothing to tell. Nothing that led to anything anyway. The secret had gone to our mother's grave. Now Mary Anne was waiting for an answer. I looked across the room into her questioning face, so much like our mother's, with her peaches and cream complexion, and wished there were something I could say to acquiesce her longing. But all I had was the truth. "Mom didn't tell me anything about your father Mary Anne." She stared at me with the same blue eyes as our mother's, then eerily spoke the exact same words mom had used. "It doesn't matter now."

Goosebumps popped all over me. It was like our mother was in the room with us! It came to me that Mary Anne thought finding her father would be another happy ending. The way it was when she'd found us; abiding love and 17 years of good times we'd all been blessed to have. And yet I truly understood her great disappointment at not finding her father. I knew firsthand the wondering that never ceases. We were kindred spirits her and I. We'd each searched for something we'd never find. Our biological fathers. The need to know your father is an intensely personal thing. Maybe something in the genes creates the longing to connect with the first speck of your life. A father is the beginning of your existence. You need to connect to feel whole. Something is missing for you. There is a void. A blank spot that can't be filled. I once heard Oprah say, "the hole in your heart is the size of your father."

 Though I'd found out about my real father from my three other siblings, the heartbreak it brought was far worse than not knowing anything about him. Finding out what he'd done to them was an awful thing to live with. My dear sister was dying, I was not going to burden her heart with this information. A few months ago, I'd vowed to send her off laughing and that's exactly what I was going to do.

"What did our mother tell you about your real father Patricia?"

"Mom never had much to say back then Mary Anne. And it wasn't any different when I finally persuaded her to tell me. She said they were in love, and when they realized she was pregnant, they went to see his parents to get their permission to marry. They refused to give it, saying he was too young. He was 20 and Mom was 23 when I was born. By then he had joined the army. Mom said she saw him once afterwards, when he came to see me sometime after I was born."

"So did you ever meet him when you got older Patricia?"

"When I finally got around to finding him, he had already died. I found two brothers and a sister. My brothers lived less than an hour from where I used to live in Michigan. I regret not meeting my sister in person. She was living in Arizona. We spoke once over the phone, and I felt like I already knew her. It was like when I first met you, the same way."

"So, what did your siblings tell you about your father Patricia?" There it was. The thing I buried and wanted to forget and never talk about again. Help me God, I can't burden her with this. Not now or ever. It has nothing to do with her.

"The thing is Mary Anne, if our mother would have married my father, my life would have been much worse than it was. And if she hadn't given you up for adoption you wouldn't have had the nice life that you did. So, the way I see it is, God protected both of us."

She didn't say anything for the longest time, seeming to comprehend it all. "So, when did they tell you that you were adopted Patricia?"

"Actually, they never did. I found it out by accident because my first husband Walt and I went to the racetrack in Canada. On the way back the border patrol held us there for hours. They weren't going to let me cross back into the U.S., but they finally did. Later mom and I had to go to the Immigration Bureau downtown where an official laid it all on the line and told me everything."

Then I told her the whole immigration story while she listened intently. "That must have been hard on you Patricia, learning you had a different father, and you weren't a citizen, and there was a father you never met. That's a lot to hear at one time. Did mom ever tell you what it was like for her when she had us?"

"She only talked about it once, and it wasn't easy to get that out of her either. She said it was very different back then. When I look

285

back at history, I can see why she felt so ashamed. Being unmarried and pregnant in a time of oppression was hard on any woman. It was an even bigger double standard back then. It was ok if men had sex, but women were scorned if they did. When an unmarried woman gave birth, the baby was scorned too. Imagine having to move far away where no one knows you. Or feeling forced to give your baby up for adoption. It must have broken her heart. Everything is so different today. Women have overcome since the stone age. Now they can order a baby in a test tube."

Mary Anne laughed really good at that one. "You always make me laugh Patricia."

"That's why I'm here Sis."

Back in 1996 when Mary Anne set out to find her mother, Stella was married with a different last name, living in another country. Technology wasn't at your fingertips like it is today. Phones on the kitchen wall were the big thing. Young people can't imagine how different it was just that many years ago. Mary Anne had to search the old-fashioned way to find her mother. First, she went to the adoption agency, her adopted mother had told her about. From them she learned her birth mother's maiden name, and that she was living in Windsor at the time of her birth. So, Mary Anne started asking people all over town if they knew this person. And one day fate interceded. Someone knew a man named Joe. It so happens that Joe was our mother's brother. But Joe had died. So, Mary Anne kept asking around until she found Joe's widow. Aunt Leah was more than happy to talk. She was quite the talker that one. Leah made a long-distance call to the US to reach her sister-in-law Stella. According to the two or three versions I heard of the story, it went something like this.... the call came on a bad day so Stella bit Leah's head off. Nancy had just brought her home from the hospital, and she wasn't in the mood for surprises. She'd hardly had any sleep all week after her heart attack, with them fixing her ticker and all. "I don't get you Leah. Why are you bringing up something that happened way over 50 years ago?" Stella snapped at her sister-in-law. Thank goodness Nancy was there and took the phone away from Grumpy. The next thing she knew there was a new baby in the house! Nancy didn't waste no time. She moved everything out of the way for a 56-year-old baby to meet her mother.

Now here we were at Caesars, recounting what happened over the past 17 years since we'd met. "I'll never forget that first meeting with my mother. I was so nervous. Then we looked so much alike that I was shocked. When she told me that I had seven sisters and a brother I could hardly believe it. What a surprise! I couldn't have dreamed something like that!"

"It was quite the surprise for us too. Hearing we had another sister in Canada was a day none of us will ever forget. That was 17 years ago Mary Anne. Funny how time flies, isn't it?"

"I'll never forget that first meeting with all of you. I want everyone to know how much happiness you brought me. Finding a brother and seven sisters was one of the nicest things that ever happened to me. It was always such a good time when we got together. I love the whole crazy bunch. I only wish I could've met all of the aunts and uncles and cousins."

"We love you too Sis and so would they if they'd gotten to meet you. All together we had 20 aunts and uncles including their spouses. Plus 54 first cousins and 75 second cousins, and who knows how many third cousins. Plus, all the nieces and nephews, but who's counting."

The day was ending when Mary Anne's lady friends arrived. It was an honor to meet her closest friends. When it came time for me to go, their presence made it somewhat easier. I told my sister goodbye, thinking I'd never see her again. We said we'd see each other next time in Heaven. Then she told me to get started on the book, you never know how much time you have.

A half hour later I was on Aunt Leah's block looking for her house, and there she was. Standing on the curb in the dark waiting. I had to laugh at the cute little 87-year-old lady with curly white hair, waving me down. We sat in her living room having a great conversation until my head hit my chest. "Wake up Patricia, you still have to

287

climb the stairs to bed, eh?" The next morning, I woke to an empty house. She was out in the driveway washing my friend Sally's car. "Hey Aunt Leah, what're you doing out there? That's not a job for you."

"It was dirty," she chirped. "It's nothing, I wash my car every day. I thought you'd never wake up I've been up since 5:00. Go get ready, I'm taking you to Tim Horton's for breakfast. I'll introduce you to my morning friends." Every person in the place knew her smiling face. She talked with all of them, knew them all by name. She's really something. This vivacious gal is one of a long line of feisty ladies in our family. A generation of aunts and uncles that are all gone now, making her even more special.

A PERIOD OF SUSPENSION

After returning to Florida, thoughts of my sister were constant. Knowing what she wanted me to do weighed heavy on my mind. Weeks passed and still I could not begin. How did I get myself into this? How and where does a person start writing a book? Mary Anne's words were constant in my mind; get started you never know how much time you have. They hung in front of me in despair. I became depressed. Not even my friends could lure me out. I felt miserable. I'd made a promise that I couldn't keep.

Then it was October, my favorite time of year. Mary Anne called, sounding like her cheery, chipper self. "Come and see me again, I want to talk to you. I'm at Hospice now. They have rooms for out-of-town guests, or you can sleep on the sofa in my room. I have my own condo here." So, there I was, flying back to Canada wondering what she could possibly want to talk about. We'd talked ourselves blue on the last visit. By the time I reached her bedside her condition had taken a turn for the worse. "Glad you made it; you're probably wondering why I asked you to come here again."

"Was there something else you wanted to tell me Mary Anne?"

"No not really, we already said it all, just wanted you to be here," she answered and dozed off. As I sat by her side a feeling of gratitude came over me that God had given me more time with her. She opened her eyes and peered around the room. "Patricia, you still here? how long can you stay?"

"As long as it takes Sis."

"Good, glad you can stay, it won't be long now. How's the book coming?" How I hated to tell her the sorry truth; "I haven't started yet."

"When are you going to start? Don't wait till it's too late. Don't put it off. You never know how much time you have, get started now!"

"I promise to do that as soon as I get home. I'm having a hard time figuring out how to start it."

"You can do it, I know you can.... the priest was here a few minutes this morning, I made my peace."

"He'll have to stay a lot longer than that when he comes to hear me out." It was good to hear her laugh.

A couple days later in a semi-conscious state, she appeared to be experiencing something. "Ohh, it's so beautiful ... the light ... it's so beautiful here ... my mother is here... I'm so happy you're here...my other mother is here too...they're all here ... home is beautiful ... I want to stay ... no -I don't want to go back ... I want to stay."

The hair on my arms stood up. My sister was describing the place I'd seen the night I stopped breathing in my sleep. I floated through a long dark tunnel with a bright light at the end. The light grew larger, until it burst into wondrous beautiful light, surrounding me. Consciousness floated in absolute loveliness. Mere words cannot describe the feeling beyond euphoric. An all-encompassing love enfolded me ...as I floated in pure bliss in the palest soft pastel light. Then a sudden feeling of leaving interrupted it. Consciousness knew I was leaving; I did not want to go. "No! I don't want to leave!" On hearing my own voice, I awoke with a start sucking in air, my mouth dry as sand.

Days afterwards the wonderment stayed with me. I didn't want to talk about it with anyone, fearing if I did, it wouldn't be believed.

Now here I was at my sister's bedside, trying to decide if I should I tell her children, Janice, Gil, and Michelle. What should I say to them? That I had a near death experience? And their mother just described it? They'll think I'm totally nuts. Maybe our belief system is different. Mary Anne's nurse was just here and told us when a loved one is passing, they hallucinate, and seem to talk to ghosts, and reach out for what's not there. That's not what I believe, but who am I to disagree?

Since that day I've learned of others who've had near death experiences. I now believe a higher level of consciousness exists before we exit this realm. I no longer question these kinds of experiences. I simply accept them as spiritual. Not everything has a logical answer. The science of medicine is known through intellectual reasoning. Spirit is known through the heart. For some years prior to my sister's death, I'd been asking God to show me his purpose. What was the something in particular - that was mine alone to do? I now believe when Mary Anne, and Jim and I were diagnosed with cancer within days of each other, I was being prepared for what my sister would ask me to do.

There's a time for every purpose unto heaven. God's plan is revealed in synchronized timing. When you see it, you are stunned, for you know that it is God. It is the creator in you. It is the something good inside that makes you want to give all you've got. It's when you awake and can't wait to get to it again. It is taking your broken heart to make art, pouring out all, until you hear the voice in your soul. It is pure joy. It is passion.

DOGS ARE FAMILY TOO

Some are so smart they lead their humans. It's us humans who think we're leading the dog. The day before my sister passed a beloved Doberman was coming to visit. As the car was being packed for the 10- hour drive to Hospice, Oryx grew impatient and bolted down the street. When his master called, he stopped, looked back, then fell from a massive coronary. His family arrived at mim's bedside, doubly heartbroken. The following day I went for a walk, strolling through the crisp fall air, admiring fiery autumn leaves. Until a small King Charles crossed my path, his gait slow and steady. He looked like my sisters four-legged family member. Why would Brady be out here wandering alone? I called out to him, but he didn't acknowledge. Maybe it was just coincidence and wasn't him. Then it hit me. The little dog was a sign that Mary Anne's time was near. I ran all the way back to her room. Minutes later she went home.

"You never know how much time you have," I awoke the next morning hearing her words. I'd spent the night in Canada, slept in my sister's sea foam bed with her daughter Janice. Now I could hear her family in the next room, talking quietly. From the bedroom window I looked out at a spectrum of red and gold covering the back yard. Another glorious fall day in Canada. Anxiety washed over me. I need to get home asap! I have a promise to keep.

As the plane climbed higher into the clouds the tears came. Never again would she tell me, you can do this. Doubt and insecurity started to creep back in a same old familiar pattern. 'How will you ever accomplish this?' the lousy devil taunted. 'Your memory is shaky old girl, you can't remember what you went in a room for, how will you remember enough to write about? This is a monumental task. Take a nice long vacation instead dearie. Go to Paris for a year. You always wanted to go there. Forget about the book. There's millions of them already.'

That stinking devil was trying to trick me like he'd done so many times before, taking advantage in a vulnerable time. But we were 30,518 feet in the air. Heaven was too close for something like him. Before we could fly through another cloud, my sisters' words came to knock him off that plane. 'You can do this Patricia, I know you can, just get home and get started.'

'Ok Sis, I'll write one paragraph at a time. It might take years but how does a person eat an elephant....one bite at a time, right?' I heard her laughter in my heart. That's when I knew it wasn't just about a book. We had told each other; I'll see you next time in heaven.' We'd said the words. And they were written.

291

The day of her funeral I felt her spirit around and started to write. Memories started coming back. Words flowed through my fingertips, hundreds of disjointed paragraphs. I wrote into the night until falling asleep at my desk, thinking about the dogs who'd made a memorable impact. The small King Charles who sent me timely back to her bedside. The big Doberman who left timely to lead her home. Dogs show up in crucial times with unconditional love, and they're always happy when we come home. God is like that too. Hmm, ever spell dog backwards?

LIFES BIGGEST LESSON

The inevitable is going to come whether we like it or not. And we don't get to pick our own poison. Some believe we don't stay here forever because Adam and Eve got us thrown out of paradise. If that's the case, they messed up big time. Affecting us all over a little fruit doesn't seem fair justice. But since they're already paid for, we might as well get our share of apples. Keeping in mind as go our merry way, that we're all in this together. Which brings my mother's favorite psalm to mind.

"I give you a new commandment, that you love one another." John 13:34

When the followers of Christ asked him, which commandment was the greatest, he replied that they love one another. After hearing that one frankly I had to give it some thought. After all, how do you love someone again who's hurt you to the core? Before doing this work, I never dreamed the root of my pain would be revealed. At times I found myself working while the rest of the world slept. In the stillness of night, words came from the something inside that is greater than I am. About 3:00 AM on Thanksgiving 2015, an extraordinary thing happened while typing on my computer. A black blur flashed in front of my eyes and a veil seemed to be pulled aside. In a nanosecond I saw what happened to me as a three-year-old child.

"When the spirit of truth comes, he will guide you into all truth."
John 16:13

I jumped away from the computer and began pacing across the room. Anxiety reaching the point of unbearable, I slid to my knees praying as never before. "Dear God, I don't want to remember this. Take it away. It's more than I can bear. Help me Father God, don't let me live with this another second. I lay it at your feet. Release me from the past and let me live the rest of my life knowing your peace. Amen."

Then I rose and went to bed and fell into a very sound sleep. Hours later I woke with a start, knowing it was late. I had a three-hour drive ahead of me, where my family was preparing the holiday meal. As I traveled on I-4 there was a huge new billboard proclaiming in bold black letters. "And you will know the truth, and the truth will make you free." John 8:32

It was the second time in my life that same scripture rose in front of me. Each time I'd learned the truth about the two men who'd been in my mother's life. It came to me that she had known what happened to me all along. She was bathing me on the old iron sink when I'd told her what he'd done. She approached him and was nearly killed, as well as her unborn baby. Yet she had taken him back. Good God Almighty! Why would she do that!? Why? Then it came to me why. 'Out of the hospital. Broken. Battered. A premature baby in an incubator. Two small children waiting for her. A one-year-old and three- year- old. No resources. Lacking education. A human being. Being human. Trying to survive.'

Wisdom finally arrived in my old age. Stop judging. Stella did what she had to do. Maybe she made mistakes. How many have I made? Countless. No doubt I'll make many more. Pray my children forgive me too. That long drive on a day of Thanksgiving, was long enough to put it all into perspective.

Sometime afterwards I finally got life's biggest lesson. Of all things I was driving down the street again when it happened. I was on my way to Tampa to meet Ann, when I noticed a man walking on the sidewalk ahead. From the back he looked just like dad, same height, balding, same swagger to his gait. I stopped at the light and watched as he reached the corner and turned, then merged in with other pedestrians. A wave of love washed over me for my dad, and I realized fully forgiving is freeing oneself to love. Rest in peace Dad.

FRIENDSHIP

Friends are the flowers you give yourself. Without them, life would have no pizazz. Being blessed with out of state friends means visits on the phone for hours. Funny but a person's voice never changes. As soon as you hear it, they're in the room with you. Barb, Karen, Sally, Suzanne, and Laura are mostly voice visitors these days. As well as Jack who lives three hours away. The heart knows no distance when it comes to friendship.

ANN and I have been friends over 50 years. We met when our daughters Michelle and Julie became friends in the first grade. For several years now Ann and I have been going on the Tampa Garden Tour. After touring neighboring gardens, ladies in flowered dresses gather at the park, enjoying dainty petit fours while being serenaded by a band. Then we go back to Ann's house to walk through her gardens. Both her front and back yards are loaded. A vast variety of vignettes range from humorous, to skeletal pieces coming out of the ground. Candelabras of all shapes have solar lights and are lovely at dusk. Iron rabbits and frogs, peek from under flowering plants, watching us wind through Grandmas Garden. A tall cowboy in a red bandana ignores the cat watching a bird, while a skunk awaits the opportunity to blast them all. Sleeping Pedro and his donkey are unaware of our passing admiration. A high heel shoe hangs over a rusty chair covered in greenery. An old fountain gratefully extinguishes the thirst of a rusty crane. Mirrors on fences give the illusion we can walk to the flowers ahead. Iron benches and colorful chairs welcome a rest. Squirrels scamper possessively at the intruders in their garden. Birds of all colors grab seed before the squirrels get it. Flowers and plants grow out of rubber boots and cowboy boots as the tin man sleeps. An old work boot with its sole hanging soulfully, is home to a happy lizard. A big colorful rooster claims its spot on the back fence, and you wish he'd crow just once. Every time my friend and I walk through her garden she tells me names of plants. She says many are named because they resemble something. That makes sense but somehow, I still can't connect the pots with the dots. I still call the huge stag horn, a reindeer plant. She laughs knowing I'll try to remember but promptly forget. I love visiting Ann's yard. It's like coming home. Over the years we've become family. Her daughter Julie has called me Mama Pat since she was a kid, and her son Jeff is like another son to me. Ann's husband Phil, also known as Mr. Smiley, died on Easter Sunday, 2018, breaking all hearts. Prior to his passing he and Jeff traveled the world. Julie and husband Dan have two grown sons, Sam and Max. Jeff and his life partner Sterling commute back and forth from Washington DC. Who could have known we'd all end up in Florida, lifetime friends, walking through yard gardens?

TRUDY

She is a mutual friend. She and Ann initially met in Friendship Park in Tampa. Later Ann introduced us on her birthday celebration held in her garden. Trudy has an indomitable spirit. Having overcome pancreatic cancer, it returned. She's determined to overcome it again. Recently she gained six pounds and is looking good. Trudy wears baldness with bravado style. What class this gal has, she makes positivity look like a new idea. Honored to be a third wheel in this mutual friendship I can hardly wait until us girls can get together again. Prayers for Trudy are welcome and greatly appreciated.

MARY ANN L

We became friends in our real estate days, when we worked in the same office here in Florida. Her work ethic and sense of humor are admirable. Mare, as I sometimes call her, is homemade Italian meatball Sundays with the family and her dog Tobey, three million dollars in a birthday card, the Dali art museum, the theater, office Christmas parties, dancing with Eagles, dancing with Leo, more dancing and more dinners, a church of generations, more northern family, more lunches and more fun. For all these and more, thanks for so many great times together girlfriend.

CAROL G

Another friend from our real estate days. This lady is straight forward - deluxe. Whenever brain cobwebs need cleaning, she helps me get rid of them. She's always ready for every adventure, whether auction, garage sale, the theater, museum, scavenger hunt, or off to Europe with one of her family. Besides taking care of her 95-year-old father's business, she visits him daily at the nursing home, entertains nine grandkids, sells real estate, and only recently retired from her airlines job. Whew! Always in a good mood, blue eyes twinkling, she listens till all I have to say is out, then says what I need to hear. Carol G. is honesty walking.

CELIA

In one word: she is delightful. Celia is enthusiastic about life, bubbly and a joy to be around. The daughter of a renowned artist, she's creative, artistic and loves crafting. Sometimes I wonder if she realizes how talented she really is. Previously we were next door neighbors and morning walk buddies. After learning I planned to use the buffalo nickel in the title of this book, she quietly set out to find one. Then lo and behold on returning from Tacoma Washington, presented me with an authentic, old buffalo nickel. And just like that this thoughtful person, went from friendly neighbor to treasured friend.

JUDY

She and I met through garage and estate sale ventures. She's a big collector with very good taste. Thankfully, we've been able to share our common interest, creating a break in the strain of the pandemic. Behind twinkling aqua blue eyes, is a spirit to be admired and a tinkling laugh to make anyone smile. She is a sweet, kind person, and a great conversationalist. I learn something from her every time we talk.

NICK

He is a former neighbor who became my friend. Nick is funny, honest and direct, and I value his opinion. We ran into each other today while out on our morning walks. "Hey Pa-tree-sha...there you are! Where've you been hiding? Gimme a hug." So, I told him I'd been hiding inside the book and sometimes wondered how it was going to be taken and often felt like chucking it all. "Hey, hey Pa-tree-sha, don't say that! You're going to finish it. It's your perspective and you've got a right to that. Hey, that's a good title for it; My Perspective." Thanks anyway Nick. I liked your idea, but the book named itself, and made you a legend in your own time good buddy.

THE LAST SECRET COMES OUT

I got a call from sis Rose one day. She'd gone to Canada with a couple of our sisters to attend Aunt Leah's funeral. Afterwards a lady came up to them and said she was a friend of Theresa's. (Theresa being the adopted sister Mary Anne grew up with) The lady said Theresa had told her something important before she died. "Mary Anne's father was my father!"

Frankly, this news bowled me over. Why had it never occurred to me before? Because I believed my mother. That's why. I let it go. Because she said so. And she was my mother.

After giving it some thought, it made sense when I did the math. My mother had told me that my father was three years younger than her. Mary Anne was born in 1940, our mother was 20 years old then. So, our father would have only been 17. Understandable why his parents objected to their marriage. I surmise they never stopped seeing each other, as I was born three years later. His parents objected to the marriage all along. 80 years ago, was a whole different standard of morality. A 20-year-old woman in love with a 17-year-old boy was disgraced. So, our mother gave her first baby up for adoption to a good home, then carried the shame of being in love with someone considered to be too young for her. The last secret was out. Furthermore, it came out at our dear talkative, aunt's funeral. Another angel got her wings.

UPDATE ON SISTERS

SIS MARY ANNE and Jim were married 57 years. She died October 9, 2013, Jim followed her, March 30, 2017. Their children are Janice, Michelle, and Gil.

Janice was married to Earl. Their four children are, Mike, Zack, Josh, and Brittany. Mike is married to Brit. They have three children, Burke, Avery, and Roderick. Zack is married to Wendy. They have four children, Finley, Ellie, Halle, and Mac. Josh is married to Mackenzie. They have two children, Peyton and Cameron. Brittany is single.

Michelle was married to Craig. They have one daughter, Candace. Candace is married to Kevin. They have one daughter, Ariadne.

Gil was married to Laura. They have one son, Jack.

My very best memory of my sister Mary Anne is the day we met.

SIS CAROLE was married to Melvin. Their daughters are Rebecca and Dawn. Rebecca has two grown sons, Bryan and Carlos. Bryan has a son. Dawn is married to Ernie. They have two sons, Hunter and Ryan.

Carole married to second husband, Phil. They have one son, Jason. Jason is single

Carole and third husband, Paul were married 30 years, until he died in 2017. She's now enjoying   retirement with a pint-sized Chihuahua and her family who live nearby. Among special memories with this sister is the rainbow in a crowd.

SIS SHARON and Art have been married over 55 years. Their children are Artie and Joey. Artie married Angela who he called 'his angel.' He is her angel now. Joey is single. He has one son, Connor. Among special memories with Sharon is the time she visited me in Florida. The first thing she wanted to do was see a Tigers spring training game. So off we went to Lakeland with Michelle, Holly, and Ryan, it was his first time seeing the Tigers, thanks to his great aunt.

SIS ROSE was married to Mark. Their sons are Mark and Eric. Mark Jr. is single. Eric is married to Leah. They have two sons, Liam and Eli.

Rose and second husband, Roger divorced but remained friends. She now lives with a little black terrier poodle who runs the show. Among special memories with Rose is the time we went to Pontiac with Nancy on Thanksgiving Day, to cook dinner for the homeless. We ran around the soup kitchen working hard, until the spirit of giving suddenly overtook Rose, and she grabbed me up in a big bear hug, squashing the stuffing out of me.

SIS LINDA and John have been married over 46 years. They have one daughter. Jenny is married to Andy, they have two funny dogs who I met on Facebook. Among many special memories with Linda is when she came to Florida making my birthday a surprise, howling at the moon.

SIS NANCY was married to George. They have one daughter and one son. Chelsea is single. Sawyer is single. One of many special memories made with Nancy is when I visited her in California in a cool Spanish adobe on the beach. We walked all over Manhattan beach solving world problems as near naked people roller skated past oblivious of our great efforts. Right at the top is another great memory of vacationing with their family at their home outside of Atlanta in a yellow gingerbread house with a dog named La Bear.

SIS LUCY is single, she has one daughter. Rachel is single. Most special memory with this sister is when five of us had an old hen's party. Someone was trying to take a picture of us and Lucy said something so out of character for her, that it knocked Linda off her feet.

BROTHER BOB married Raquel later in life at 44. They have one daughter, Stephanie. Stephanie is married to David.

So many special times with my brother, it's very hard to pick just a few. The four of us, Bob, Raquel, Stephanie, and I vacationed on Samara Beach in Costa Rica. This lovely resort was quiet and laid back, palm trees swaying, simple sleeping cabins, with occasional riders on horseback. We also vacationed together at La Playa Resort, where the tropical landscaping was incredible. We sat on underwater stools in one of several pools, drinking margaritas in paradise.

On another vacation, Bob and I visited Elvis' home in Graceland. The last room on the tour held an impressive display of his records mounted on the walls, floor to ceiling, with one playing softly in the background. The touching tribute brought us to tears, reading the names of all the records we'd loved. After touring the Meditation Garden and the grounds, we saw the airplane named for Lisa Marie. Then had lunch at the Elvis café, in a pink Cadillac booth, but did not order the peanut butter and banana sandwich on the menu.

On his last visit to Florida, my brother was all about buying a car for Stephanie and shipping it back to Costa Rica. Bob being Bob, thought a car over here was somehow better. I drove him to every car lot from here to Timbuctoo. What a challenge it was to find a perfect car in one week. The last day on his schedule I was bonkers from looking, when my determined to find perfection brother, finally decided on one. The dealer shipped it to Port Manatee, but we still had to drive all the way down there, as Bob wanted to see it off. We made it to the airport in the nick of time to catch his plane back to Costa Rica. After he got home, he continued to call regularly to pester me. "You still working on that book Big Shooter? When you going to buckle down and finish it?" "I'm working Bob I'm working. It's the hardest thing I've ever done. It's like trying to hold a tiger on a leash. I want to let go but afraid to tell all." "What have I always told you Pat? Tell it like it is. Finish the book. I want to read it."

SAINT PATRICK'S DAY - 2017

Our brother passed to eternal life on this day. He was still the mischievous, fun loving, twinkle in his eyes, football loving, poker playing, adventurous Detroit boy from the streets. After Bob reached his career goal in Aerospace of Quality Control Final Inspector, he chose to do contract work. His reason being that it provided time between contracts to travel to Costa Rica to be with his daughter Stephanie. Still best friends with his former wife, whom he called Rocky, he was living near them in the same city. During a meaningful conversation of late, my brother told me that, he knew God. A quote that speaks of the way he fought to protect his mother, his sisters, his daughter, his ex-wife, and his dog, Foxy, to the end. Raquel and Stephanie sent the funeral ceremony via video to us. Then carried out his last wish of cremation and let his ashes go on Samara Beach in Costa Rica. Sis Rose hosted a celebration of life at her home in Michigan that summer, held in the yard to accommodate a crowd from near and far. We planted 'the Bobby Tree,' befitting the man who loved nature. His passion for photography is now in treasured albums. Some words written on the back of one of many photos capturing its splendor; "Nature is always painting us a picture." Peaceful, quiet, words from a man who fought his way through life. Rest peacefully now dear brother. "The Eye of the Tiger" will always be your song.

"But I will see you again and our hearts will rejoice, and our joy no man can taketh." John 16:22

A WEDDING IN 2018

I went back to Costa Rica for Stephanie and David's wedding. It was held in a tropical outdoor grotto in a setting Bob would have loved. His chair was front and center wearing his Costa Rica t-shirt. The reception was also outdoors, amidst tropical magnificence complete with a mountain waterfall, candlelight and stunning floral arrangements. At dinner, Stephanie asked me to speak for Poppy. Unprepared, I hadn't even thought of doing it, since I don't speak Spanish and most of the guests didn't speak English. But Maria, (Stephanie's aunt) interpreted and I managed to come up with a few words to honor mi hermano, and wish his hermosa hija and guapo yerno, amor eterno, which meant I hoped, that my brother would want to wish his beautiful daughter, and handsome son-in-law eternal love. All uncomfortableness vanished, on realizing my lack of proper wording didn't matter. The language of love was spoken at the most beautiful wedding ceremony I'd ever attended.

CELEBRATING ANCESTRY

While in Michigan for Bob's celebration of life, cousins Richard and Pauline invited me to their home in Canada. It was just what I needed. Time in the country visiting with cousins; Eileen and Leo, Georgette and Paul, Lorraine and Phil, Diane and Luke, Ray and Edna, Rosaire and Madeleine had pictures of their 13 children. Arriving at cousin Donah's home, his daughter Joanne was there, compiling work her mother had done before she died. Annette had researched the wedding days of our ancestors on my mother's side of the family, all the way back to 1662. What a wonderful surprise it was to meet 7 generations of my ancestors! In honor of Annette's romantic heart, the following is 'ma Cheri amour' on the La Bear side.

ANNETTE'S RESEARCH

December 2, 1662, in Montreal Quebec- Francois married Jeanne Tetard. She was from de Norte- Dame-de-Pitres, Normandie France.

October 29, 1698, in Montreal, Quebec- Francois the second, married Marie-Anne Magnain. He was Captain of the Militia de la Fourche, a La Praire, in 1729.

October 7, 1730, in La Praire, Quebec- Francois the third, married Marie-Charlotte Lefebvre.

February 18, 1765, in Norte-Dame-de-la-Praire de, la Madeleine, Quebec- Ignace married Marie-Anne Degneau.

August 8, 1826, in Ste-Marguerite de Blairfindie, L Acadie, Quebec- Jean-Baptiste married Angelique Labrecque.

January 16, 1860, in St-Jean, Cte St-Jean, Quebec- Julien married Emilie Simard-Dumais. She was native Indian.

July 6, 1908, in St-Joseph Riviere-aux-Canards, Ontario- Ludger married Rose Meloche. They had 11 children; Stella was love potion number 9.

Receiving this genealogy meant a lot to me; it was some of the roots I'd longed to know about. It says I'm part of the eight generation on my mother's side of the family. I no longer think about where I came from, but rather where I am, and where I have yet to go. The people who are, and who have been in my life, as well as those who will still cross my path are my blessings. I've had a wonderful life, traveled near and far, lived, loved, laughed, and learned with many for whom I am eternally grateful.

2020 AND 2021

It's a new year and here I am, still editing a collection of stories that keep unfolding. I've been trying to finish for over a year, but all that was anticipated in the seemingly magical number of 2020 last year became a pandemic of statistics. An unknown disease started overseas, spreading rapidly to other countries. It was given the name, Covid, or Corona Virus. Common sense should have dictated it would spread here too. After all, people travel from one country to another, and germs travel free. The first cases were reported in the US in January 2020. We were told it would go away. After all we're America. We're above germs. Within months the virus started kicking butt and taking names. In our family they were, Phil, ex-brother-in-law who died in March in Michigan, leaving adult son Jason. Then George, ex-brother-in-law, who died in April in Indiana, leaving adult children, Chelsea and Sawyer, and his former wife and friend, Nancy.

In April, Artie Jr, died from a blood clot to his heart. The stress of losing his job due to Covid shutdown, surely played its role. He left his wife Angela, his parents Sharon and Art, his brother Joey and nephew Connor, and all the rest of our big family, plus uncountable friends. All shocked to lose him, and we can't get together to hold loved ones in our arms to console each other, as the probability of spreading a dreaded disease prevents it. Leaving us wondering how many others will be affected whether directly or indirectly. People all over the world have been profoundly touched by this pandemic. Struggling to keep their homes and feed their families due to economic impact of business's forced to shut their doors. Economies can and will be rebuilt. But lives cannot be replaced.

Scientific research shows there's been a pandemic every- one hundred years. We were due. The Spanish Flu spread worldwide in 1918, killing 500 million people. Never in my time has the phrase, 'one day at a time,' seemed more applicable. This is a time when holding onto hope is imperative to one's mental, and physical health. Inner peace is essential to maintaining mind, body, and soul, on a dailybasis. Surely there will be a new 'normal' after this pandemic is over?

As I draw close to finishing this book journey that helped keep me grounded through Covid, I wonder what God's next purpose is for me. What good can I, as an ordinary citizen contribute? It's a new year, January 6, 2021, to be exact and my country is growing more unrecognizable each day. A horror movie is taking place live on my television right now in Washington, DC. The title of the movie is, "HATE."

This is America? It's not the America that I believed in all my life. This is a far deeper systemic problem with the potential to be far more destructive than a pandemic. Will there be a vaccine coming in time to heal the division that threatens to destroy decency and democracy? Have our politics overcome 'LOVE?' Can we not seek respect and unity, empathy, and compassion for one another anymore? Is that not what Christ and all manner of a holy universe taught?

"If it is possible, so far as it depends on you, live peaceably with all." Romans 12:18

"May God fill you with all joy and peace in believing, so that you may abound in hope by the power of the holy spirit." Romans 15:13

GRATITUDE AND DEVOTION

Family are the stars that light my path. Daughter Michelle, strong courageous woman of sage wisdom. Son-in-law Bill, humorously gregarious, husband of Michelle, and father of Ryan. Daughter Holly, middle child, and heart of our family. Aloha Joe, kind easy going, life partner of Holly. Son Michael, thoughtful cuddly bear, generous heart. Kristin, sweet loving, fiancé of Michael. Grandson Ryan, a loving dedicated young man with a bright future. They have the future, I have the past, we learn from each other. Even the dogs Kuma, Marly, Leia, and cat Mittens, have something to say. Living in gratitude keeps our traveling circus fun and funny.

I cannot end this devoted journey of eight years, without one more short story. Though there's more to tell, they're in the 'wannabe' stage. For now, this is one about devotion to baseball. There once was a three-year-old kid who pitched baseballs to his grama, laughing because he made her run so far after them. This kid became known as the gentle giant, as he was always taller than all the others, and very kind. Suddenly he was graduating high school with a baseball scholarship to college. Grama felt lucky to be attending the event, since a pandemic created a looming threat of no ceremony at all. But a careful structured, well thought out social distance plan had made it possible. Though not the normal pomp and circumstance celebration, Grama was nonetheless proud of six foot six 'Tank,' who took it all in stride as he did everything else. She watched him waiting in a social distance line to receive his diploma and her thoughts went back to yesteryear. She'd taught him to drive in the vacant parking lot of a church a couple years back. He had his learners permit, but his parents wouldn't let him get his license until he could handle a car well. So, he drove Grama's old SUV round and round the building with her instructing on rules of the road. Making him do left turns, and U-turns in tight spots, judging distance and wheel span. Backing the vehicle up, over and over, until it was parked where it was supposed to be. Between the lines. "There you go Ryan, you finally did it!" "Thanks, Grama. I can't wait to get my license so I can drive to my baseball games." She laughed out loud knowing there was nothing he wanted to do more, then asked him a rhetorical question. "Baseballs in your blood Ryan; you really love it don't you?" He responded with his own rhetorical question. "You really love decorating; don't you Grama?" Then he flashed that big wide, million-dollar smile and added; "I've got a serious question for you this time Grama. What's your passion?" And she knew that he knew that she knew, he already had the answer, so they laughed out loud in comradery.

So now I ask you dear reader; "What's 'your' passion?"

"For you shall go out in joy and be led back in peace; the mountains and the hills before you shall burst into song, and all the trees of the field shall clap their hands." Isaiah 55:12

Mom and her kids before MaryAnne found us.

This is a self-publication. If you would like to support the further distribution of this book, please contact the author at; lebertpatricia@gmail.com